Also by Jeanie Miley

Ancient Psalms for Contemporary Pilgrims: A Prayer Book

Becoming Fire: Experience the Presence of Jesus Every Day

ChristHeart: A Way of Knowing Jesus

Dance Lessons: Moving to the Beat of God's Heart

Joining Forces: Balancing Masculine and Feminine

Joint Venture: Practical Spirituality for Everyday Pilgrims

Meeting Jesus Today: For the Cautious, the Curious, and the Committed

Sitting Strong: Wrestling with the Ornery God

The Spiritual Art of Creative Silence: Lessons in Christian Meditation

Smyth & Helwys Publishing, Inc.
6316 Peake Road
Macon, Georgia 31210-3960
1-800-747-3016
©2015 by Jeanie Miley
All rights reserved.

Library of Congress Cataloging-in-Publication Data

Miley, Jeanie, 1945-
Fierce love : radical measures for desperate times / by Jeanie Miley.
    pages cm
    ISBN 978-1-57312-810-0 (pbk. : alk. paper)
    1. Love--Religious aspects--Christianity. I. Title.
    BV4639.M475 2015
    241'.4--dc23

2015008584

Disclaimer of Liability: With respect to statements of opinion or fact available in this work of nonfiction, Smyth & Helwys Publishing Inc. nor any of its employees, makes any warranty, express or implied, or assumes any legal liability or responsibility for the accuracy or completeness of any information disclosed, or represents that its use would not infringe privately-owned rights.

Advance Praise for *Fierce Love*

Anything that helps us, individually and collectively, to love more and love better, is worthwhile. . . . I believe your readers will find his or her love "pearls" among your wealth of experiences, explanations, Scriptures, and inspirations.

—Denton A. Cooley
Founder and President Emeritus, Texas Heart Institute

Imagine immersing yourself in a bath of pure love, and lying in it until your whole being has been saturated, revived, and set free to be God's gift to the world around you. That's what reading this book is like. Fierce love—not an ordinary, anemic kind of love that we so often imagine and try to practice, but a love that is vigorous, unrestrained, and completely overpowering. That's what Jeanie Miley presents in this extraordinary book. I won't ever be the same after reading it—and neither will you!

—John Killinger
Author of The Ministry Life *and*
The Caregiver's Bible

Putting the words fierce and love together is only the first surprise of many in this guide to a healthy heart by Jeanie Miley. In her characteristic way, she takes you deeper than you thought you wanted to go only to find that when you do, fear gives way to love again and again.

—George A. Mason
Senior Pastor, Wilshire Baptist Church
Dallas, Texas

Books on God's love never go out of fashion. No doubt it is because most of us struggle to believe that beneath all the suffering, failure, and conflict we see around and within ourselves, what remains is a God who loves. Jeanie Miley—an admitted learner on the subject of God's love—adds her voice to the chorus of saints who have staked their hope on nothing less. Jeanie is a good friend to have on this journey. Take and read.

—Steven Purcell
Executive Director, Laity Lodge
Kerrville, Texas

Above the accusatory jangle of a world grinding its gears, Jeanie Miley's *Fierce Love* is a descant so clear and true, it makes me want to weep and pump my fist at the same time.

—*Julie Pennington-Russell*

There can be—and are—some truly wise books about love. There are, however, very few books about love that are practical. The unique thing about *Fierce Love* is that it manages to be both wise and practical. It is also, by the way, gentle, rich, personable and, in places, downright beguiling.

—*Phyllis Tickle*
Author, The Great Emergence

FIERCE LOVE

Radical Measures
for Desperate Times

Jeanie Miley

Dedicated with love and gratitude
to Dr. Dwain Dodson,

pediatrician and friend of God
who embodies the faithful and *fierce love* of God
for his family and friends,
for his patients and for his church,
for the natural world,
and for Lake City, Colorado.

Thank you for showing us what it means to love one another.

Contents

Preface		ix
1	Love: It Changes Everything	1
2	Love as a Way of Being in the World	17
3	Becoming the Beloved	29
4	God's Fierce Love: Theory or Reality?	45
5	The Great Romance	59
6	The Beloved in Search of the Beloved	71
7	Love in the Hard Times (or Love on the Rocks)	81
8	Song Sung Blue	97
9	Life's Big Secret	111
10	Jesus' Mandate: Love YourSelf	121
11	Out of the Shadows, Into the Light	135
12	Love as Blessing	149
13	Can You Drink this Cup?	161
14	Street-smart Love	175
15	A Higher Love	189
16	Trust and Trustworthiness	201
17	How We Love	211
Lessons for Group Discussion and Personal Reflection		223

Preface

In an interview after the dramatic repair of the heart of a baby girl who was born with two-thirds of her heart outside her body, Dr. Charles Fraser, a congenital heart surgeon at Texas Children's Hospital in Houston, Texas, said, "When it comes to infants' and children's hearts, you can't be too accurate or too careful." His words have echoed in my memory as I have written this book.

When I listen to Chuck talk about repairing the hearts of newborns, I tremble. He speaks matter-of-factly and quietly about what he does every day, but his composure belies the impact of his unusual skills and the gravity of his work.

I shake my head in wonder when he talks about working on a baby whose heart is so damaged that touching the heart is like touching wet tissue paper. When he describes surgery on a heart the size of a strawberry, I get weak in the knees.

Dealing with matters of the heart—loving and being loved—is not a matter of life or death like it is for Dr. Fraser and his team of experts in the surgical suite.

Or is it?

It is common knowledge that infants who are deprived of human touch and love will not thrive and may, in fact, die.

I'm pretty sure that adults never fully outgrow that need to love and be loved.

You may have heard of someone dying of a broken heart. People talk about heartache, and we all seem to know what that means. We speak of hard-hearted and cold-hearted people, and sometimes we describe someone as having closed his heart.

Loneliness can be a full-body experience, consuming us with its pervasive pain, and yet we speak of the Lonely Hearts Club.

On the other hand, there is nothing so engaging as a person with a warm or open heart. Some people are described as tender-hearted, and we even speak of someone stealing our hearts. Jeff Bridges won an Oscar for his part in the movie *Crazy Heart,* and every time I go to San Francisco, I leave another part of my heart there in that city by the sea.

If I give my heart to you, the crooner sings, and we all know that it isn't the actual pump in the chest that is offered.

"Mommy, is it the baby in your tummy and Jesus in your heart, or the other way around?" my daughter asked me when she was three.

Biology and theology do get confused sometimes, especially when we are learning to speak in figurative language.

We understand that those expressions about hearts are figurative language, and yet we also know that having what we describe as a closed heart, a hard heart, or a dark heart can lead to actual physical conditions.

Love and work, according to Sigmund Freud, are the cornerstones of our humanness and seemingly necessary to our happiness.

Tolstoy, in a letter to Valerya Aresenyev wrote, "One can live magnificently in this world if one knows how to work and how to love."

Magnificently?

That's a pretty big word and a big calling, a beckoning into vast places—filled with both desert and garden, peak and valley, flood and drought, danger and possibility.

Love evokes all kinds of images and language, doesn't it? I tremble, joining the throngs of people who attempt to write or talk about this amazing potentiality placed within mere humans.

Indeed, we hold this treasure, this powerful force called love, in earthen vessels.

Jesus sets the bar high for us with his teachings about love, and great thinkers and writers, scientists, song writers and poets, physicians of the body and the soul, and teachers take it as a given that love—loving and being loved—is highly valued and even necessary for human beings to flourish.

I know that the topic of love is mystery and as indefinable as God. I want to be careful in handling matters of the heart, as my friend Chuck Fraser is careful with tiny hearts, but any attempt to be accurate looms as an impossibility.

This one thing I know for sure: this mystery we call love cannot be pinned down, boxed in, or defined. We may talk about it and write about it, but ultimately no human can have the last word on love. Love is the diamond of life, and its facets are infinite.

I used to think that if it was work, it wasn't love, but there came a time when I had to give up that adolescent fantasy or neurotic yearning and recognize that whatever is of any worth is going to be hard and costly.

All forms of authentic love exact costs we never imagined. Love, if it's real, will cost you time and money, but that's the easy part. Love makes demands on us that we may not have the strength to give, but in the straining toward the goal, we draw closer to fulfillment than we could ever have imagined.

Authentic love is a refining fire, and it probably takes a lifetime of failures and mistakes to learn the difference between fleeting attraction and actual love, a love I'm choosing to call *fierce love*.

When I chose the topic *Fierce Love: Radical Measures for Desperate Times* for a yearlong Bible study for the women who gather with me on Thursday mornings, I put my head in my hands.

Was I praying, or was I staggered by the enormity and the importance of the topic that had come to me in the middle of the night?

The answer is yes to both, and I knew that if I launched into that ocean for a yearlong study, I would be changed. I put myself in love's tutelage, I would be tested, perhaps beyond what I thought I could bear. I was convinced that whatever I chose to study and pursue responsibly for these women I have come to love deeply over twenty-two years would require me to learn whatever I was trying to teach. It's the pattern.

It turned out that I learned more than I ever imagined in that yearlong study, and now, having completed this book, I am still a beginner in understanding the mysteries and the ways of loving and being loved.

I learned long ago that we teachers often teach what we want to learn. I learned that if I took the role of facilitator in my classes, instead of lecturer or dispenser of truth, I would be learning from the women whom some would call students. I knew, as well, that I would be changed in ways I could not imagine, learning from life about love in new, deeper ways, and the thought both thrilled me and scared me.

It should have.

Indeed, I willfully chose to walk where angels fear to tread, and I'm glad I did—now that I've recovered a bit from the intensity of the year's teaching.

Fortunately, that year brought many gifts. My efforts to understand love and my efforts to love more deeply changed my understanding, my perspective, my approach to life and love, and all the distortions we have come to call love.

I am changed because I have been brought to my knees in a sense of awe and humility before the enormity of Jesus' challenge to us to "love one another." I am changed because I know that I am on a lifelong pilgrimage of discovering layer upon layer of this power we so casually call "love."

I am changed because now I know the power of love, and in all of that, I now know aspects of God I did not know before, and I know more fully and confidently the one statement about God that is big enough to define God: God is love.

We dare not interpret those three words lightly.

We take God's nature and his commandments to love for granted at our own peril.

Finding someone to love is not the point of this book.

Whether or not you see yourself as a lover in this world in general and of people, pastimes, pursuits, and God is the point.

How you love is the point, much more than if you love or if others love you. How you love is more the point of this book than what you love or whom.

This book isn't about whether you have been disappointed in love or not. The truth is that if you are past twenty-one, you probably have been disappointed by God, jilted by someone, or betrayed by someone in whom you put your trust.

This book is about learning to see yourself and know yourself as a conduit of love, operating from a full heart instead of trying to find someone to whom you can hook up your emotional hose and fill up your empty heart.

This book isn't about the quest for love. It is about waking up to the love that is at your essence. This book is based on these ideas:

(1) You are made for love—to love and be loved. It is in your DNA.
(2) Better yet, love is the spark of divinity within you. It is also the sparkle of divinity.
(3) Because you are made in God's image and since God is love, it seems to follow that your very essence is the expression and embodiment of love. You reflect God, and God is love. Therefore, you are made to reflect God's love in the world.

Possibly, you may have a resistance or a reaction to these words so far. Perhaps some voice in you has been educated in a theology that starts with the premise that you are inherently flawed, conceived in sin, born into sin, and governed by the original sin and dark stain that is within you.

If my words have activated that voice, I ask you to stay with me.

I'd like for you to answer Dr. Phil's bottom-line question about that theology and your position: *How is that working for you?*

I am asking you to stay with me while I lay out another point of view, and that is the way, the path, the challenge of God's great love for you.

If, by the end of this book, you still prefer to begin your theology and your position in the world with the doctrine of original sin, go ahead, but at least give the idea of original blessing a chance.

How to Use This Book

Each chapter in this book follows a similar format. I write as I teach, weaving the rich resources from the wisdom and knowledge of my own teachers with the teachings from the Bible and personal experience. Each chapter includes questions for reflection or for discussion with another person or with a group.

In most of the chapters, there is a section titled "Getting Personal" and, at the end, a part called "Growing Edges" in which I explore a place in my own life where I am still growing. Life, for me, is an ongoing learning experience with love as the primary course of study.

At the end of the book, I have included the questions from the *Fierce Love* Bible study, questions that were prepared each week for the members of the class. The questions do not follow the sequence of the chapters in this book, except for an emphasis in the first half of both on the Old Testament, with an emphasis on the New Testament in the last half of both. The questions at the end of the book are in the format of a twenty-one-session Bible study. The chapters of the book and the Bible study sessions are intended to support each other in content, but not in a week-by-week way. The Bible study can be done apart from the reading or study of the book, or the content of the chapters can be woven into the Bible study.

My prayer is that this book will deepen your experience of God's love for you and increase your willingness to love and be loved by other human beings.

Jeanie Miley
April 2015
Houston, Texas

Chapter 1

Love: It Changes Everything

This scientist just might cure cancer.

The headlines for the Sunday Houston *Chronicle* instantly riveted my attention to a front-page article about a maverick researcher at the world-renowned M. D. Anderson Cancer Center in Houston, Texas. I was grabbed first by the headlines and then by the big color picture of the scientist featured in the article.

The claim was so big that I sat down and read with interest the lengthy article about Dr. James Allison, a pioneer in cancer immunotherapy research with a long-time interest in research that has led him to the discovery of a unique treatment that frees the immune system to attack cancer. His approach is to work with the T-cells, necessary for the health and function of the immune system, to build up the patient's immune system so that the body can help cure itself.

"By creating this brilliant approach that treats the immune system rather than the tumor, Jim Allison opened a completely new avenue for treating all cancers," said Dr. Ronald DePinho, president of M. D. Anderson. In a prepared statement, he went on to say, "That's the most exciting and promising area of cancer research today."

A caption under Dr. Allison's picture stated that he had just won the 2014 Breakthrough Prize in Life Sciences. Describing the event when Allison won this award, given in Silicon Valley, the *Chronicle* writer noted, "It [the red carpet and his black tie] was unfamiliar territory for the small-town boy from South Texas who had become a scientist and spent his research career on what many considered a lost cause, the study of the immune system's cancer-fighting potential."

Immediately upon reading this article about Dr. Allison's revolutionary work, my imagination began making the leap from T-cells in the human body to one's spiritual life.

Two thousand years ago a maverick named Jesus burst onto the stage of a religious system that was stuck in a mode of legalism and declared that the system's laws were "breaking the backs" of the people who were trying to find health and meaning in life—and, incidentally, please God.

> *We have three things to do: Trust steadily in God, hope unswervingly, love extravagantly. And the best of the three is love.*
> 1 Corinthians 13:13
> (*The Message*)

"I've come to preach good news to the poor," Jesus declared, reading from the scroll of the prophet Isaiah in the synagogue and announcing his mission statement, adding that he had been sent to set prisoners free and give sight to the blind, to release the oppressed and to proclaim good news (Luke 4:18-19).

Jesus' words so disturbed the status quo that he was run out of the synagogue and the town, but the rabbi with the new and liberating vision of how things were supposed to be between God and people continued to proclaim his message.

"There's one commandment you need, and it is the greatest commandment," Jesus told his followers: "Love the Lord your God with all your heart and with all your soul and with all your mind . . . and love your neighbor as yourself" (Matt 22:37-38).

Please make the leap with me from the building up of the immune system of the physical body to the radical idea that loving and being loved builds up the mind, heart, and soul—the spiritual immune system, if you will—so that when you are faced with heartbreak and despair, tragedy and terror, agony and anxiety, depression, anger, hopelessness, or any other of the hard and sometimes unbearable facts of life and the dark emotions that break and bruise us, you will have the fortitude, courage, and perseverance to bear the unbearable and endure your suffering.

"I hope that you can carry your burdens a little more lightly," my friend, writer and teacher John Killinger, told me and set me on a new path of learning just how to do that. His words, spoken with tenderness and love, gave me a challenge I wanted to meet.

"Carrying my burdens a little more lightly" sounds much like Dr. Allison's work, as well as advice from Jungian analyst Pittman McGehee about *learning to love the parts of our lives that we don't like and, even, shun.*

Excited about the connection I made between the sophisticated and cutting-edge approach to medicine and the simple practices of faith that I teach, I suddenly had an image in my mind that fired me with energy and a focused sense of purpose.

This—teaching people the ways of connecting with the source of the power of love—is why I teach Centering Prayer and lectio divina!

This is why I teach people about walking the labyrinth, studying the Scriptures, and doing all the other spiritual practices! This is why I am a spiritual director and count it as privilege to sit with people as they sort out their life experiences, asking questions about what God has to do with a crisis or a tragedy, what God wants for them and from them, and whether or not there is a God and, if so, if God really is *love*.

Those faith practices build the spiritual immune system!

Truth sometimes shows up in strange places and from unexpected sources. These words of singer Jimi Hendrix resonate deeply in me: "When the power of love is greater than the love of power, then we will know peace."

That is part of the message that Jesus entrusted to those of us who are audacious enough to call ourselves followers of "the prince of peace."

The reason I am so fervent and fierce about the power of love is twofold: First of all, I am horrified by the way human beings continue to kill each other and spread hate, violence, prejudice, and disrespect for each other and, most especially, when those acts are fueled by so-called religious motivations.

More significant, however, is my passion for the power of love and my belief that we have not begun to tap into that power or learn fully the ways and means of loving and being loved. One of the ideas that has shaped my life is this quotation of Pierre Teilhard de Chardin: "Someday, after mastering the winds, the waves, the tides and gravity, we shall harness for God the energies of love, and then, for a second time in the history of the world, man will have discovered fire."

Let me hasten to add that I count myself a learner, and like most teachers, I both teach what I already know and, perhaps more effectively, teach what I want to learn.

> *There is life without love. It is not worth a bent penny.*
> Mary Oliver, "West Wind #2"

As I understand it, the whole point of any spiritual practice is to strengthen our connection to God and to increase our faith so that we can live more freely and closely "the one wild and precious life" Mary Oliver talks about in her poem "The Summer Day."

The word *religion* comes from the word *religare*, and it means "to tie back together." Our religious rituals and practices are our attempt to tie us back to the source, to God.

That maverick Jesus, who walked into the lives of his culture, reveals a picture of God, whose name is love. Attempting to heal and transform individuals, to liberate and empower them, Jesus spoke to his disciples about keeping the commandments: "This is the greatest one," he told them, and that commandment is to love God, love others, and, implicitly, love oneself.

Jesus also told his disciples, right before he was to leave them, that they must love each other *as he had loved them.*

He didn't tell them that they should straighten each other out and chastise each other. He didn't say they were to make more rules, have fancier rituals, follow the laws more carefully, or offer more expensive sacrifices in order to be whole. Neither did he say that they were to establish some hierarchical institution or some new feel-good system that would help us avoid our real suffering with bromides and bumper-sticker theologies.

Instead, Jesus admonished his followers to follow the greatest commandment, to love. He told those followers that by loving God and each other, they would be fulfilling the law.

The word *salvation* comes from the same word as *health and wholeness*, and the process of *becoming whole* is so much more than just saying yes to Jesus so that you can stay out of hell and get into heaven. *Salvation* is about living a healthy, whole, holy life *now*.

Reading the article about Dr. Allison's work in strengthening the immune system, I began to see that a conscious and persistent intention to love God and each other really is the way to abundant life and to wholeness. Perhaps it is the way of salvation.

It is interesting to me that James Allison has been called a maverick.

Where on earth would we be without our mavericks and rebels and revolutionaries who dare to move us forward in human consciousness and discovery?

How is it that love, the most powerful and necessary force in the world, is often so threatening to people?

Recently, I overheard a rose expert tell a man he was training, "If you feed the roses—or any plant—the proper nourishment, that food will help the roses resist the diseases and bugs that afflict roses."

An expert in alternative medicine, Dr. Ben Thurman told me that in Chinese medicine, the approach is to discover which of the systems of the body is out of balance or weak and to work with the body to strengthen it. While it is important to know when to use which modality, the idea of working to strengthen the body makes sense to me.

Babies, deprived of human touch and love, fail to thrive. In my experience, that need for love is in all people, but perhaps that inherent need to receive love grows and matures into a need to give love as well.

It is my conviction that learning how to give and receive love is necessary to our emotional and spiritual well-being, as well as our mental health, and that the decision to deepen and refine the art and ability to love and be loved is one of the primary tasks, challenges, and opportunities of adults at all stages of the life cycle.

> *The only thing that counts is faith expressing itself in love.*
> Galatians 5:6b (NIV)

Learning how to love in order to fulfill Jesus' commandments to us is a sacred challenge. Is there any clearer statement of the importance of our love for each other within the body of Christ than Jesus' words in John 13:35. Take a moment to reflect on these words, but better yet, take them with you throughout your day's activities. Better than that, take them with you when you gather for worship with your community of faith.

Here is what he said: "By this shall all people know that you are my disciples, if you love one another."

When the idea of *fierce love* came to me, I knew that I would be put on a steep learning curve.

From past experience, I knew that if I ventured out in the deep waters of love, I would be changed. I knew that if I put myself in love's tutelage, I would be tested, perhaps beyond what I thought I could bear. I knew that I would learn more than I would teach, and so I wavered, thinking that perhaps we could study something easier and simpler.

The truth is that I did meet challenges unlike any I had met before in that year, but my commitment to lean deeply into love and its power sustained me so that my efforts to understand love and my efforts to love more deeply changed my understanding, my perspective, and my approach to life and to love. I came to understand more deeply the distortions and substitutes we call love.

One night, faced with a challenge I'd never faced before, I stood in a hallway in our house, literally in a liminal space between rooms and figuratively between choices of how to handle the challenge.

"I don't know anything to do but go deeper into God's love," I said to my husband, and that is what I did.

The way I did that was to deepen my Centering Prayer practice and continually reaffirm my intention to *let love prevail.*

Over and over, I was brought to my knees in awe before the enormity of Jesus' challenge to us to "love one another," and I began to see that I am on a lifelong pilgrimage of discovering layer upon layer of yet one more aspect of this power we so casually call "love."

I am changed as well because now I know the power of love more fully and have a deeper reverence for love's power to heal and transform us, empower and liberate us. Now I understand many things about God that I did not know before, and I know even more about how much I don't know.

I know more fully and confidently that this one name for God —this definition for the source of life—is the only one that is big enough for that which we call God: *God is love.*

Those three words are simple enough for a child to memorize but deep and complex enough for theologians and students alike to ponder for a lifetime.

So what is *fierce love?*

How is it different from tough love? And why do I speak of *radical* measures?

Doesn't that seem a bit extreme?

Sometimes I come in the back door to define *fierce love.*

Fierce love is not need-love or codependency. It is not love that masquerades as manipulation, and it isn't the kind of love that can be used to describe our appetites or preferences for such things as ice cream or the new dress a neighbor is wearing. It is not infatuation, and it isn't puppy love. It is not weak, wimpy, or unable to hang in there when things are tough. It isn't indulgence, but it is generous.

It isn't enabling, and sometimes one of the biggest tests in loving another is discerning when you are enabling and when you are loving.

Fierce love is faithful love, fired by bold courage. It has stamina and is robust and strong. *Fierce love* is tenacious and stubborn in the way God is, encouraging the best for the other person. It is passionate, caring, eager, persistent, authentic.

Fierce love delights in the object of love and works for the good of the other. It demands honesty, yet it is tender and compassionate. *Fierce love* encourages the other person toward wholeness and, when necessary, protects the other.

And why would I use the word *radical*?

I chose the word *radical* because it indicates going to the root of things, the origins. My life experience is that the only lasting change that takes place in a person, relationship, or a family, religious, or organizational system is change that goes to the root of the problem or dysfunction and works at the ground level.

> *Love is the answer to everything.*
> Sister Mary Dennison

My belief is that at this time of seismic shifts in the culture, people are feeling tossed about, having been uprooted from a long-time dependence on the social, cultural, and religious institutions and norms that have kept us grounded, certain, steady. As a culture, the old ways are no longer reliable as norms we can count on, but the new ways have not yet been formed. Can anything but radical measures, applied to the root of things, stabilize us in the in-between times?

Is my choice of the word *radical* and the adjective *desperate* to describe the times we are in an overreaction?

If you think so, please do these things:

Read the newspaper, and watch the evening news.

Listen to the stories your friends are telling about their children, their co-workers, their marriages, their siblings, their elderly parents, and ask yourself where the hurt is. Whose heart is aching or broken, and how could that hurt have been prevented if only love had prevailed? Who do you know whose life has been blown up by the carelessness or outright arrogance or violence of another person, often a "loved" one? How can that life be healed now?

Look, too, at our culture.

Can we as members of the human family sharing this fragile globe *really* continue to bear these interminable wars?

How many more people must commit suicide before we address this epidemic symptom of a deep sickness of the soul among us?

Where do you see people treating other people as objects or players in a chess game? Within a week's time, how often do you hear about someone killing another human being? Who has destroyed himself with some substance or another, looking for "love" in all the wrong places? What tragedy has been inflicted on innocent people by crazed individuals? Is there anything but radical love, extended over a long time, that will heal us of our individual and collective horrors and tragedies?

Finally, take a look at yourself. How are your relationships with the people you say matter most to you? Where are the broken places? Is there some relationship you've lost that you wish you could restore? When was the last time you said, "I'm sorry"?

Name your own fears about what's going on in your life. Admit your failures, and then ask yourself how often you depend on your old ways to make new patterns in a relationship.

How's that working for you?

What is the source of all the hate-talk in our culture? Why is it now acceptable to insult people, spread lies about them, and ridicule people in leadership? When did it become okay to treat people disrespectfully? Why are we so blasé about killing other human beings, and what do we use to justify murder, at home and abroad?

When did hate *from people who claim to be religious leaders* become acceptable?

Have you noticed how we throw away people when they are no longer useful or attractive to us, as if people were Styrofoam cups or outdated computers? How long can we get by with treating other human beings as dispensable objects?

How long has it been since you have heard a religious leader quote the Golden Rule, "Do unto others as you would have them do to you"?

Have you noticed how many religious leaders are leading the parades of one group against another? And have you noticed how some groups promote themselves as being "right," implying that others are "wrong"?

What happens to people today who attempt to follow that Golden Rule?

I rest my case.

I don't know about you, but I know that my journey into love's depth is just beginning. I submit to you that the journey into love is nothing short of a hero's journey.

Please take the journey with me.

Getting Personal

Below are questions to prime the pump of your own life experience so that you can, from the beginning, create a dialogue between your experiences and what you are reading. As you move back and forth from the content of the book to the questions about your life, that dialogue may deepen your understanding of your life, especially when it comes to your ideas and experience of loving and being loved.

These questions, then, are highly personal. As you respond, ask God to give you God's point of view about those deep experiences.
1. When was the first time you really felt loved?
2. Is it more important for you to be respected or loved?
3. Do you think more about giving love or being loved?
4. In what ways have you tried to "get" someone to love you? Did it work?
5. What is the difference between people-pleasing and loving?
6. What is the difference between codependency and love?
7. What is the difference between approval and love?
8. Whose approval do you want/need?

9. Which of the following emotions keep you from experiencing the love of other people or the love of God: fear, guilt, shame, anger, jealousy, resentment, hate, bitterness?

10. What are the ways you have tried to overcome your blocks, if any, in loving others? How well has that worked for you?

11. Have you ever withheld love from anyone? What did that do to you?

12. What makes it possible to get through hard times with a loved one?

13. Have you ever been unable to forgive someone you loved?

14. Do you see God as judge and jury or as love?

15. Have you ever thought someone loved you, only to find out you were being used?

16. How do you feel about God giving us the commandment to love each other?

17. Do you feel loved by God—unconditionally?

Growing Edges

Years ago, I began writing a weekly column for a newspaper in San Angelo, Texas, where my husband and our daughters and I lived for eighteen years.

> *One can live magnificently in this world if one knows how to work and how to love.*
>
> Leo Tolstoy

It was a cold winter day when I proposed the idea to the editor of the San Angelo *Standard Times*, but I was full of fire and passion about choosing an incident, a challenge, or a question from everyday life and then meandering around it for the purpose of discovering a bit of truth in it that might liberate the reader to see beyond the moment to a larger picture.

"Those places where life is perplexing or where we don't know what to do, I'm calling *growing edges*," I explained. "The places in life that are unfinished or unresolved are *growing edges*."

That editor signed me up, and for the past thirty-five years, I've had a growing edge of my own to explore as I have attempted to write a spiritual truth in ordinary, practical, and non-religious language.

Apparently my hunch that "the more personal something is, the more universal it is" has proven to be correct. I have gained a lot of friends through that weekly newspaper column.

I have also learned that love, with all of its beauty and complexity, remains my most delicate and tender *growing edge*. Like Michelangelo, I am always learning, especially when it comes to love.

When it comes to loving and being loved, I'm a perpetual beginner, albeit one with a resumé of mistakes and failures as well as joys beyond measure.

This book on love is not the definitive "Book of Love," nor do I present myself as an expert or authority, except when I am speaking about my own life.

I am a learner, and I am deeply curious about the fact that we humans, made in the image of God, are designed and created with the capacity to connect with other humans and with God, to experience intimacy of all kinds with God and with others, and that no matter how disappointed we may have been or how deeply we have hurt others and been hurt by the most significant people in our lives, most of us continue to hold out the hope, and sometimes our fragile hearts, that love really is the answer to the deepest longings of our hearts.

> *If I need to apologize for misrepresenting God's love, I'd rather apologize for overstating His love than for understating it.*
> — Steve McVey

Love is the key; it is what matters most when it comes to being human.

Love wins, and love has the potential of healing us, transforming and liberating us. Love is the ultimate power, and love empowers life like nothing else.

Love is my *growing edge*, now and forever.

It is

>   what-might-have-been
>   that is the sting

    at death.

    It is love left
    incomplete,
    shrink-wrapped,
    unopened,
    returned to
sender
    that leaves
    an aftertaste of
    sorrow.

It is the regrets
for what-we-missed
together
that make
grief so hard

    and the grief over
what was but is no longer

    that is in
    these tears—

It is those
griefs that make
me question what
was
real and what was
not-real.

    It is the open hand
  refused—
        the effort
    spurned—
            the gesture

    ignored—
             the amends
left dangling
between us
in thin, stale
air
      that form heavy
stalactites
and stalagmites of regret.

    And yet—
would love be so
    sweet
without the shadow of
not-love?

    Would beauty
   startle and
   delight

without the ugly and
the plain?

    Doesn't the extraordinary
    need the ordinary, the commonplace

even to be extraordinary?

    Would hope be so
exquisite

    without the specter of
hopelessness?

    Would life be so
beautiful, after all,

without the
drumbeat of death
growing more audible
with time?

    Would the sacred be so
thrilling
without the
profane?

    Would the miraculous be
miraculous

if there were no moments of futility?
    Would embracing be so dear
if letting go
were not hovering so

heavily
    over this fleeting moment?
. . . this brief exchange . . .
this tender
meeting?

Would I take this present moment—this
eternal now—for granted . . . .

if I knew how quickly

life was over?

JM 1/18/13

Chapter 2

Love as a Way of Being in the World

"I want you to spend twenty minutes, twice a day, sitting quietly and simply loving God," my spiritual director said to me.

I knew that Bishop Mike Pfeifer had directed countless people in his lifetime, but I was a bit startled by the assignment he gave me early in our work together. I had asked him to be my spiritual director because at the time, the early 1990s, and where I lived, San Angelo, Texas, I couldn't find someone who was trained to be a spiritual director except the bishop of the Catholic diocese.

Admittedly, this was an interesting challenge for him and for me, given the fact that our religious backgrounds were vastly different, but I wanted the experience of spiritual direction with all my heart. I had first learned about this ancient practice at the Church of the Savior in Washington, DC, and from then on I had sought someone who could discern the movement of the Holy Spirit within me and guide me in the direction I wanted to go.

I was prepared for heavy reading assignments and guidance into the spiritual disciplines, and so it was that I was surprised by the simplicity of sitting for twenty minutes, twice a day, simply directing my love toward God.

Being surprised was an appropriate response. Being humbled by the assignment should have been my next response. Not only was the assignment to be harder than I'd imagined, but the truth was that at first, I didn't have a clue just what to do.

With my personality and background, I was more accustomed to showing God's love to other people!

Maybe I was better at telling people that God loved them than I was at actually loving them.

Thankfully, I have had good teachers and role models when it comes to learning that God is first, fully, and foremost love.

God is not the punitive hall monitor, just waiting for me to make a mistake. God isn't a judge I can never please, placate, or cajole into liking me.

Neither is God a Santa Claus or a cosmic bellhop for whom my wish (or prayer list) is his command.

In fact, any idea I had about God other than that of God as unconditional love has had to go. Any of my projections onto the Almighty had to be challenged.

When I read J. B. Phillips's *Your God Is Too Small* in college, I began a lifelong process of removing my limited and limiting notions about God from my belief system and opening my mind and heart to the infinite mystery I call God.

I've learned that I minimize God at my own peril.

I have learned that I take his commands lightly at my own risk, especially the one about love.

The starting point of my theology, and the starting point of this book, is that *God is love*, but don't think for a moment that I'm talking about some sentimental, greeting-card, bumper-sticker idea. I am talking about the God whose wildness and largeness are too much for me to comprehend and whose love and compassion are greater and mightier than any feeble idea I could capture in all the books ever written.

That one small sentence—*God is love*—is big enough to command my interest, curiosity, and quest for a lifetime.

> *For one human being to love another: that is perhaps the most difficult task of all . . . the work for which all other work is but preparation. It is a high inducement to the individual to ripen . . . a great exacting claim upon us, something that chooses us out and calls us to vast things.*
>
> Rainer Maria Rilke

God is also mystery, and frankly, God and love are often mysterious to me.

I take seriously the belief that we humans are created in the image of God, and in that reality, we have been given the blessing of four aspects of God's nature.

(1) We are created with the capacity to be creative.
(2) We are created with the capacity to communicate with God and with each other.
(3) We have the capacity to love and to be loved, albeit imperfectly and conditionally.
(4) We have been given the freedom to choose.

It is an enormous gift we have been given, this capacity to love. It is both blessing and burden, like so many of God's gifts to us.

Some of us take to relationships more naturally than others, but all of us want to be loved and most of us want to love. Indeed, some people are wounded early in relationships and develop defenses against either giving love or receiving it, but that impairment doesn't mean that the person is incapable of love; it does mean that perhaps the person needs to be healed, or it means that the person may simply need to be taught the ways of loving and being loved.

Some of us get stuck in need-love so that we think we are loving others when, in fact, we are simply trying to get our own needs met by codependent behavior.

Some of us, too, are so deficient in the ways of love that we resort to manipulation, power, and control. Carl Jung said that "where love is lacking, power and control rush in."

Read that again. It is a profound statement, and holding that statement in consciousness can change things around boardroom tables and dinner tables. It certainly couldn't hurt just to grasp the concept, could it?

I have turned Dr. Jung's wise words upside down to say that wherever power and control rule, love dies. (I should tremble, tampering with Dr. Jung.)

However, my belief, forged on the anvils of human relationships, is that a commitment to learning how to love with gift-love and the persistent and patient practice of giving to another has the potential to change the destructive ways of power, manipulation, and control. I believe that we all can learn how to love and receive love.

Professor, philosopher, and author Jacob Needleman says in his small but powerful book *A Little Book on Love* that "whatever the meaning of our lives may be, it has to involve love." He suggests that we have reached a point in our evolutionary process where we can move beyond romantic love (called *eros* in Greek), where we are able to choose love as a way of being in the world.

Take a minute and ponder Needleman's words. When we talk about "being in love," we often sound as if this magic just comes upon us, taking over our minds and hearts and leaving us helpless in the arms of passion. *Choosing love as a way of being in the world*, on the other hand, indicates consciousness; it indicates a person with the maturity to make good choices and thereby create a relationship that is based on wisdom and good, common sense.

One can love passionately, fervently, and with delight—and if love is going to survive, both delight and good sense make for stronger and happier relationships.

"The first love, the love of *eros*, draws us to each other," Needleman says, and then love "lays a bridge down for us . . . and we must cross that bridge, learning sustained love."

That is what I hope to do in this book. I hope to "lay a bridge down" by the exploration of a kind of love that I am calling *fierce love*. I hope to deepen my own commitment, by the writing of this book, and encourage my readers to "choose love *as a way of being in the world*."

To choose love as a way of being in this world implies that one doesn't spend his life trying to find love. Instead, accepting that love is available to you and is, in fact, your natural way of being in this world somehow gives you a place to stand, a position from which to move out into your daily life, a foundation of confidence and courage.

Think it over. *Choosing love as a way of being in the world* might change your life.

My foundation for this idea is based on my growing, evolving, ever-changing understanding of God as love. Love is God's nature, but the love of God warrants an entire library of an infinite number of volumes that are constantly being changed and updated as people open hearts wider to love's possibilities and our minds to deeper and greater understanding of the grandeur of loving each other as part of our God-likeness.

There will be more about God's love in the next chapter, but I don't want you to miss this one important building block of the idea of fierce love: *Love starts with God. God is love, and God's love is faithful, life-giving and . . . fierce. God never gives up on us.*

Two things and more can be true at the same time.

I wouldn't be so passionate about love, giving and receiving it, if I hadn't also experienced not-love. I know what it means and what it feels like to fail at love; it feels horrible, and it is awful. Those relationships where I fell short of loving in ways that another could feel my love and the times in which my love relationships have been broken are deeply painful to me.

On the other hand, I am so passionate about love, being loved, and loving because I have experienced love deeply—both the giving and the receiving of love that enriches, sustains, and nourishes life. I have experienced the joy of family and friends, and in mysterious moments I cannot fully capture in words, I have felt and known the love of God and the love for God in ways that continue to astound me.

> God is love.
> 1 John

Both realities—failing and losing and connecting and cherishing—make up the rich, multihued tapestry of my life. Love is the golden thread that is woven throughout that textured fabric.

I believe that authentic love—*fierce love*—is love that is filled with forgiveness, mercy, and grace enough to take our failures and our faults and somehow make something beautiful out of that which we have broken. Perhaps it is *fierce love* that is that quality or that response to life that is able to wait patiently in the pain of that which is imperfect and unfinished, accepting the flaws and foibles of each other in a way that somehow transforms our suffering in love to joy.

I don't know anything that can hurt like love can hurt, and perhaps the reason people wall themselves off behind defenses, excuses, and rationalizations is that the risk of being hurt is too great. Kahlil Gibran says in his classic book *The Prophet* that "the deeper sorrow carves into our being, the more joy we can contain."

When I held my first grandchild in my arms when she was about four months old, I suddenly shuddered and said, "It almost scares me, I love her so much," and my daughter said, "I know."

We sat in silence with Abby cooing and kicking between us, both captivated by the wonder and mystery of loving and being loved and stunned by the risk of loving deeply.

To love is to open oneself up to great ecstasy and fulfillment. Loving also opens us up to the possibility of great pain and ultimately loss, for at some point, somebody has to leave first, either by walking away or by death.

Frankly, I'm rather weary of sorrow and suffering, but the truth is that they are part of what makes loving and being loved so valuable.

If it isn't hard and if it isn't costly, it probably isn't love.

On an early spring morning, I rode in a bus with a group of pilgrims from the town of Glastonbury, England, to the ancient stones of Stonehenge. Mostly, we were quiet, reflecting on the mists in the distance as the sun gradually began to rise.

The night before, our leader, Judith Tripp, had asked us to write a statement that we would declare from inside those stones. The statement was to be what we would stand for in our lives. It was a sobering assignment.

We were asked to stay on the bus until our guide came to lead us into the circle of stones. Judith had asked us to walk to the stones in silence.

As we walked in a single file across the dewy grass, the gravity of this experience seemed to fill the silence among us with holy expectation. When I stepped inside those huge stones, I was surprised that tears began to flow down my face. I noticed that others were crying too.

Was it the impact of being *inside* Stonehenge that touched something deep, primal, holy within us that elicited the tears?

What was it that moved us so deeply as we moved in and around and through those standing stones, doing what Judith had asked us to do, "getting acquainted" with them?

My mind was running wild with imaginations about others who had gathered in those stones for centuries. I thought about the people who had gotten those stones to that site and placed them in that specific circle and the various imaginings and theories of others who had been captivated by the mystery of them, a mystery held in the mists of an ancient past.

Had the site been intended for religious ceremonies and rituals?

Had some of my ancestors gathered there for a religious event?

What prayers had been offered there? How many tourists had viewed those stones, checking off yet another famous site on the list of things to see in England?

I wondered if anyone else wished those stones could speak. I wished that I could touch the stones and feel the stones with my palms or my forehead, but we had been warned not to touch them.

After a few moments Judith called our group to a circle in the center of the stones with the plaintive sounds of her flute, and we silently moved together, forming a close-knit circle.

Alone in the center of the stones, except for a couple other sightseers and a few birds who had built nests in the crevices of the stones, we stood in silence. Then, one by one, guided by Judith's leadership, we stepped into the circle and declared what it was we were willing to stand for in our daily lives.

It was a holy moment like nothing I had ever experienced. Each of us wept as we made our declaration, and then we prayed aloud for others, loved ones, people for whom we were burdened, for each other.

And then it was silent again, and we could feel the solid earth beneath our feet, earth that had been trampled and trod by pilgrims and sightseers, some on a holy pilgrimage and some on a mere trip to famous spots in the traveler's guide.

One of our fellow travelers, Paige Netherton, left the group, picked up Judith's flute, and began to play "Amazing Grace." It was the perfect benediction to our ceremony under the clear blue sky.

Love expresses itself as grace, doesn't it? And isn't grace wrapped in love?

And isn't it amazing when any one of us can step over ourselves enough to extend grace and love to another human being?

On that day and with those witnesses, I declared that I would stand for love—for giving it and receiving it—and for hope.

I had just spent the year teaching the material in this book to the women in my Thursday morning Bible study at River Oaks Baptist Church in Houston. Many of us had been challenged and changed by going deeper into the study of God's love for us and the call of love among us.

The study of love had sparked the idea of the next year's topic, "Practicing Resurrection: Radical Hope in Everyday Life," so I stood within that ancient circle with both love and hope filling my mind and heart. Love had challenged me for a year, and it seemed that on that spring morning, I was being pushed by love toward hope.

> *Love the Lord your God with all your heart and with all your soul and with all your mind. This is the first and greatest commandment. And the second is like it: Love your neighbor as yourself.*
>
> Matthew 22:27-29

This impulse or inspiration was not new to me, but the call was coming from a deeper place. Love and hope had been calling to me, motivating me, fascinating me for my entire life, and I knew that I had not yet even begun to scratch the surface of the depth of either.

I knew as well that love and hope had grasped me and invited me to go deeper into the love of God and that, in a way, I had no choice but to live out the rest of my life with those great gifts as the themes of my life.

Though at that time I had not read the latter part of the Rilke quote at the beginning of this chapter, I knew on that morning that love had called me, and I intuited that it would lead me to "vast things." I knew, too, that love was and is the hope of life and that to love is to hope and to hope is to love.

I trembled at the call, frankly.

I tremble any time I sense God's nudge into a new vast place of unknowing and the unknown, but I have learned to trust the nudging, and I have learned that the other part of the equation is the faith to step out into the vastness of the call.

Faith. Hope. Love.

They are beautiful words and lofty ideals in Paul's letter to the Corinthians.

Perhaps those words define *fierce love* perfectly.

I have loved these words since I was an idealistic and adolescent dreamer.

I have learned to love those words as a lesson on love, a guide for loving, a standard for assessing the quality of my love for others.

In Stonehenge, I heard those words as a calling, and I trembled, but it was the trembling of joy. It was the trembling of new beginnings.

It was life, stirring in the embers of my losses and sorrow, calling me out into vast places.

There is no more eloquent definition of what *fierce love* is, no better place to begin, and nothing that sets the bar of possibility better than these words of Paul from 1 Corinthians 13:

> If I speak in the tongues of men and of angels, and do have not love, I am only a resounding gong or a clanging cymbal. If I have the gift of prophecy and can fathom all mysteries and all knowledge,

and if I have a faith that can move mountains, but do not have love, I am nothing. If I give all I possess to the poor and give over my body to hardship that I may boast but do not have love, I gain nothing. Love is patient, love is kind. It does not envy, it does not boast, it is not proud. It does not dishonor others, it is not self-seeking, it is not easily angered, it keeps no record of wrongs. Love does not delight in evil but rejoices with the truth. It always protects, always trusts, always hopes, always perseveres. Love never fails. But where there are prophecies, they will cease; where there are tongues, they will be stilled; where there is knowledge, it will pass away. For we know in part and we prophesy in part, but when completeness comes, what is in part disappears. When I was a child, I talked like a child, I thought like a child, I reasoned like a child. When I became a man, I put the ways of childhood behind me. For now we see only a reflection as in a mirror; then we shall see face to face. Now I know in part; then I shall know fully, even as I am fully known. And now these three remain: faith, hope and love. But the greatest of these is love.

I learned long ago that faith is more a verb than a noun. Faith is not so much something we *have* as it is something we *do*. Though it sounds awkward to our ears, we are called to "faith it" in life, to put what we know to be true into action.

We who call ourselves followers of Christ, then, are called to venture forth in life as lovers of God and this world he has made not only for us to care for, but to enjoy. We are called to love God deeply and fully, and that is a challenge of a lifetime.

I suspect that the assignment of our lives as human beings, made in the image of God, is to learn how to love and be loved and that the challenge of our relationships is to face the places where we cannot connect with each other, the places where we are wrong in our loving, and to own up to our mistakes and failures with radical honesty and in partnership with the God-whose-name-is-love, to learn the lessons we need to learn.

Love is the great hope, and once we commit to love as a way of being in the world, it is amazing how many opportunities present themselves to us in daily life to "faith it" through to a cleaner, healthier, more honest way of following Jesus' great commandment.

Getting Personal

(1) How does the idea of "choosing love as a way of being in the world" resonate with you? Does it feel natural or unnatural? How?
(2) Is love a feeling, an act, or a state of being?
(3) When Carl Jung said, "Where love is lacking, power and control rush in," what might he have meant? Does your life experience support Jung's comment?
(4) When have you felt that power and control in a relationship led to the death of love?
(5) Rainer Maria Rilke's quotation about love's being "perhaps the most difficult task of all" is not something one wants to hear in one's adolescence. What is it about love that makes love a difficult task?

Growing Edges

When I was a little girl, I attended a tent revival at an encampment in east Texas with my parents. The preacher for that meeting was a stereotypical fire-and-brimstone kind of preacher, and by the time he was halfway through his sermon, I was sobbing in my mother's lap. I was terrified, whether by his rhetoric or his mannerisms I don't know. For all I could tell, the last judgment was right before us, and I was likely going to be plunged into a fiery furnace.

My mother, herself a preacher's daughter, was a mild-mannered, gentle woman, until she wasn't. At some point, when she had had enough of the situation, she stood up, took me by the hand, and walked out of that meeting.

I'll never forget the purposeful and firm stride in her steps that night as we made our way through the darkness to our car, nor will I forget how tightly she held my hand.

"From the time I was a little girl," she told me, "some preacher has been threatening the end of the world, and it hasn't happened yet. Don't worry about it," she told me, and from that time until this, I haven't.

People who grew up in other religious systems that tried to scare little children out of hell and into heaven with various other manipulative tactics have shared their horror stories with me. Others left such religious systems as soon as they could, never to return.

By the grace of God, I have gravitated always to the message of God's redemptive love.

I've stayed with people who believe in grace and with the religious leaders who really do believe that when we talk about the "wideness" in God's mercy, we are also willing to extend it.

Whatever I believe about God—whatever God-concept I hold in my head—is going to determine much of how I live my life. I'm choosing a God of love from now on.

Chapter 3

Becoming the Beloved

To test Jesus, the Pharisees, experts in the Jewish law, asked him what was the greatest commandment in the law.

Often, when teaching or leading a retreat, I ask the group which one of the commandments Jesus identified as the most important. Most of the time, at least half of the people in the groups where I am speaking or teaching have been in church or Bible studies for most of their lives, yet it is astounding to me how few people can answer that question quickly.

I don't judge that knee-jerk silence. After all, loving one another, being kind and compassionate toward others, and treating others as you want to be treated—all teachings of Jesus—are not being talked about much in the current religious/political climate of the times.

More often, people are being whipped up over guns and politics, issues related to human sexuality, war, immigration, and welfare. I am staggered by the way church members, preachers, and pastors, led by politicians desperate for votes, are being lured into these controversies and away from the gospel message of Christ.

The great commandment Jesus gave to his followers is perfectly clear and straight-forward. It isn't a puzzle that you must unlock in order to understand. Neither is the great commandment like a mental Rubik's Cube that you have to twist and turn over, hoping that you can finally get all of the shapes and colors lined up as they are supposed to be.

Again, that great commandment is this: "Love the Lord your God with all your heart, and with all your soul and with all your mind . . . and love your neighbor as yourself" (Matt 22:37, 39). These words of Jesus echo the words of God in Deuteronomy 6:5, called the *Shema*: "Hear, O Israel: The LORD our God, the LORD is One. Love the LORD your God with all your heart, and with all your soul and with all your strength."

From the time he was only six, every Jewish boy was to repeat those words daily, and in fact the instructions that follow that command illustrate how important the command was within the Jewish community: "These commandments I give you today are to be upon your hearts. Impress them on your children. Talk about them when you sit at home and when you walk along the road, when you lie down and when you get up. Tie them as symbols on your hands and bind them on your foreheads. Write them on the doorframes of your houses and on your gates" (Deut 6:6-9).

From the beginning of his relationship with the Hebrew people, God set the standard and the path for the Hebrew people, and the path is clearly *love*. The beginning place for the Hebrew people, privileged by the covenant relationship God had established with Abraham, was love for God, and as I read that verse, what gets my attention is that this is "full-person" devotion and all-consuming love directed to Yahweh. It is *fierce love*.

As a little Jewish boy, surely Jesus had been taught that verse and its importance. Surely, because of his relationship with God, the Father, Jesus did indeed have that commandment in every cell of his heart, the center of the human in Hebrew thought.

So it was that when he was questioned by the Pharisees, Jesus wasn't just making something up out of thin air. Instead, he was returning back to the origin of things, the beginning of the relationship of Yahweh with a particular people and the will of God for people.

Love God fiercely and fervently, Jesus said to them, which is harder for some to do than others, but then he added

> *Dear Friend, being the Beloved is the origin and the fulfillment of the life of the Spirit. From the moment we claim the truth of being the Beloved, we are faced with the call to become who we are. Becoming the beloved is the great spiritual journey we have to make.*
>
> Henri Nouwen,
> *Life of the Beloved*

another dimension to the God-human relationship. He said that we are to love our neighbors, whether that neighbor actually lives next door to us or in another country or sits next to us on an airplane or lives in the same family. Jesus left that "neighbor thing" wide open for interpretation, didn't he?

He added one more element to the commandment when he said that we are to love that neighbor, whoever that neighbor might be, *as ourselves*.

Jesus raised the bar for us, didn't he?

Can you believe it? Jesus gave us permission to love *ourselves*.

That big idea challenges the small-minded and closed-hearted ideas about how we treat ourselves, doesn't it? It also calls into question behaviors we call love, which are more like narcissism, self-indulgence, and egocentricity.

Jesus' great commandment invites us take a good, long, and reflective look at just what it means to love God, to love others, and to love our own lives, but that Jesus called this the greatest commandment, superseding everything else, must also call us to take seriously the call to loving and being loved.

The dilemma we face in this twenty-first century is the same one faced by those in the first century who heard Jesus lay out this clear and foreboding commandment, and here is the dilemma:

(1) Loving and being loved force us to face our own self-centeredness and selfishness.
(2) Loving and being loved are at odds with our dependence on keeping external rules, standards, and laws, all of which gratify the need of the ego to feel good about itself. After all, you can measure keeping the law, but how do you measure love?
(3) Loving and being loved require humility, vulnerability, and courage, while keeping the law promotes pride.
(4) Loving and being loved open us up to being hurt and to losing the one you love.

Couldn't God have assigned us an easier way? Maybe, but I don't know what it would have been, given our free will and our "certain recalcitrance." Besides, God designed this force we call love so that it also includes delight and joy, ecstasy and pleasure, meaning and purpose, satisfaction and fulfillment.

Love's rewards are worth the work.

God could have just stuck with the Ten Commandments and a few hygiene and dietary requirements; instead, he chose to create us in his image, which means that we are not only created with the capacity to love and be loved, but it is in loving and being loved that we fulfill our highest calling.

I have come to believe that love is our great assignment while we are on this earth and that while we may whine that we have been wounded so much that we are afraid to love or claim that we didn't have good role models in loving, the great assignment never goes away. In fact, perhaps the assignment is meant most specifically for those who have been wounded most.

There are, admittedly, a seemingly infinite number of ways we humans can hurt each other, and I tremble at the idea of having to decide whose wounds are deeper, whose models of loving more defective, and whose excuses about "not being able to love" are more eloquent or fervent. Thanks be to God that I don't have to sit in judgment over such as that!

My husband often says that if Jesus were to return today with his message and his method of love, he would be crucified again.

At the very least, Jesus would be labeled a liberal.

My friends in twelve-step groups for recovery of addictions tell me that "the hard way is the easy way," and I have learned that they are right. I

> *What is required is to become the Beloved in the commonplaces of my daily existence and, bit by bit, to close the gap that exists between what I know myself to be and the countless specific realities of life. Becoming the beloved is pulling the truth revealed to me from above down into the ordinariness of what I am, in fact, thinking of, talking about and doing from hour to hour.*
>
> Henri Nouwen,
> *Life of the Beloved*

think Jesus mentioned something about that too when he taught us to "enter through the narrow gate" (Matt 7:13-14). He said that anyone who wanted to follow him had to give up everything, and then he said that "no one who puts his hand to the plow and looks back is fit for service in the kingdom of God," which is a kingdom of love.

On a cold March day during a recent Lenten season, my friend Nancy Deforest said to me, "I want you to hear a song."

I have learned to pay attention when someone introduces me to a song I haven't heard before. I wish I had kept a journal of the particular songs that have come to me at just the right time to awaken a part of my mind or heart that has been asleep.

An Episcopal priest, Nancy and I resonate to many of the same issues of the heart, so I was eager to hear what she wanted me to hear. I was not prepared for what she had on her iPod.

In the space of a few bars, Nancy's car became a holy place and, in that moment, a sacred interlude in what was to be a busy few days of Lenten services, sponsored by an interfaith coalition of seven churches in Beaumont, Texas. I was the speaker, and Nancy was in charge of that year's series, which was held at the church where she was the rector, St. Stephen's Episcopal Church.

Whenever I recall that time in Beaumont, I think of the celestial sounds of the singing group Conspirare filling Nancy's car. It was, truly, a "thin place" when the veil between this earthly plane and the spiritual plane was barely there; perhaps the music was the bridge between the two worlds.

Interestingly, the word *conspirare* derives from the Latin *con* and *spirare*, translated as "to breathe together."

Nationally renowned arranger and director of these extraordinarily gifted singers, Craig Hella Johnson has woven the first line of the song "I Love You" by Larry Norman and the words of "What a Wonderful World" into a mesmerizing choral heart-stopper. Looking back, I see now that those words and the music were a perfect inspiration for the beginning of that Lenten series.

The piece begins with renegade songwriter Larry Norman's words: "We can be together now and forever—I love you, I love you"—and these words jolted me to another level.

And when I'm praying, I hear him saying I love you, I love you.

Suddenly, moved down into that secret room of my heart, I realized that this was no ordinary love song, but a prayer.

As I listened, the memory of that moment when I first found the words "I am my Beloved's . . . and my Beloved is mine" came back to me.

There, I realized that this music had a message in it that was for me, but also for me to share with others. This song was the perfect match for the ideas of *fierce love* that were beginning to take root and grow in my mind.

> I am my beloved's and my beloved is mine.
> Song of Solomon 6:3

And then, finally, right before the singers moved seamlessly into the beautiful "What a Wonderful World," were these words that express the concept of this book: "People all over this world are opening up, they're coming together, and they're saying, 'I love you, I love you, I love you, I love you.'"

This music would be the beginning point of my personal work for the years to come, and it would be the inspiration for the Bible study I wrote and for this book. It was inspiration, but it was also challenge.

Little did I know then just what kind of challenge the whole topic and practice of *fierce love* would be.

So it was that I had my beginning to the Bible study I designed around the topic of *fierce love*. Over the summer I read about love and thought about what it means to love. I processed what I read, and I tested out my ideas, comparing *fierce love* with tough love. I explored the various kinds of love—*agape, eros, phileo*—marveling again at how we Americans continue to use the same word, love, to talk about our feelings for another person, peanut butter, or pizza—or God—and on some hard days, I faced the places where the love I was giving was fraught with too much of my own personal needs and neediness. Merely putting the topic of *fierce love* out in front of me forced me to confront my own weakness in loving and being loved.

The Thursday morning Bible study class I have taught for over twenty years now is accustomed to my bringing in all kinds of music to use to make a point. Mostly, they like the connections we explore between the various songs with whatever the teaching is for the day. On the day I began the study of *Fierce Love: Radical Measures for Desperate Times,* I should have had them buckle their seat belts. The least I could have done was provide tissues.

> *In your unfailing love you will lead the people you have redeemed.*
> Exodus 15:13a

They, too, had the kind of hold-your-breath moment I had had when I first heard this arrangement by Conspirare.

To respect the impact of the music on the women in this class, I let them sit briefly in the holiness of the moment, and then I asked these questions. Perhaps you might want to reflect on them as well.

Getting Personal

(1) Is it your experience that we, as a culture, are opening up and coming together, or do you sense that we are shutting down and moving apart into groups that sound like us, look like us, and behave like us?
(2) Is it your experience that people all over the world are saying "I love you" more or less?
(3) What is your personal experience about the prevailing view of the world in our culture—among commentators, in casual conversations, and in the depths of your own heart:
• Do people, in general, see this as a wonderful world? How many people do you know who take the time to notice the skies of blue and clouds of white?
• How many people do you know who would have a cynical response to this musical arrangement? Who that you know would hear the

interwoven words as a message of hope, and who would hear them as sentimentality?

> Little children, let us love one another, for love comes from God.
>
> 1 John 4:7

The last thing I asked on that first Thursday was, "Why did you cry when you heard those words?"

And that question evoked more tears.

The lover in me so wants to believe all the words of this song, as well as the words of Scripture that express God's love for us, but the cynic in me fulfills the definition of a cynic as "one who doesn't want to be disappointed anymore."

It is an act of faith for me, a conscious and intentional act, to accept the words of the writer of John that we often skip over when reading John 3:16 because we are so hurried to get to the part of that Scripture we use to bring people to a salvation moment.

John 3:16 is said to be the most frequently quoted verse in the entire Bible. From the time I was a little girl, I knew that it was a verse used in evangelism, but in recent years I have been moved deeply by those first words that express the reason and rationale behind God's initiative in the world: *"For God so loved the world."*

Take a minute.

Read those words a few times, and then close your eyes and imagine that you are hearing them spoken to you. Imagine substituting your name for "the world" and what difference it might make in your life if you knew in the deepest part of your being how perfectly and unconditionally God, the creator of the world, loves you.

After you have spent some time with that part of John 3:16, move down to the part where it says "that whosoever believes in him," and stop right there and rest for a few moments.

This is the mind-expanding, heart-expanding part of that verse that won't let us form an exclusive little club with Jesus as the den leader. We who dare to call ourselves followers of Christ get in trouble when we start trying to decide who's in and who's out, because it is God's love that is big enough to embrace those who believe in him, and it is God's opinion and definition of what "belief" really means. (Does it intrigue you to ponder whether the pronoun "him" refers back to Jesus or to God?)

I love the way Marcus Borg renders "believing" as more like "beloving," and indeed, if you read the Scriptures with the idea of God's great love for his creation, doesn't "beloving" him seem closer to the nature of God and the truth of the Scriptures than mere intellectual assent?

Here's the foundation of this book, and I will return to it again and again.

God's love is the beginning point of this book, but it is also the beginning point of creation and the starting point of God's relationship with the children of Israel.

My premise is that it is God's love that is revealed in the biblical account, from Genesis to Revelation. I reject the notion that the Old Testament is about a mean, vengeful God while the New Testament is about sweet Jesus.

While it is true that the wrath and judgment of God are depicted in the Old Testament, I believe that if you change your focus, the boundless love of God is more prevalent than the wrathful God. Like everything, you find what you're looking for, and in reading the Old Testament, I see the love of God throughout the story of God's relationship with the Hebrew people.

Granted, God does express anger, but it is the anger of a loving, caring parent toward children who are missing the mark and living and choosing in ways that contradict who they are supposed to be as creatures made in God's very image. God's judgment, I believe, is God's attempt to bring people back to accountability for their choices and to correct those who are using other human beings as objects and arrogantly, willfully, and cavalierly violating the laws of God.

Even in the Greek myths, the one thing "the gods" will not tolerate is human hubris, and the God of Hebrew history has the same attitude toward those who have decided that they can circumvent, ignore, and defy the laws that govern the universe and nature and the God who set things up in the beginning.

A quote from a long-ago poster still intrigues me: "The only thing you need to know about God is that you ain't he."

What I see when I read the Old Testament is that it is God's great love, alive and active in creation, that is at the beginning of Genesis, and it is his *fierce love* that remains faithful, constant, consistent, and active among the Hebrew people through all of their wanderings and in spite of what Walter Brueggemann calls "a certain recalcitrance" that shows up in all people, from the beginning of time.

Out of that foundation, I have come to certain beliefs that both sustain me and challenge me.

(1) I believe that love is God's nature and that God has created us for love.
(2) I believe that if we truly devote ourselves to following Jesus' great commandment, we will treat holy things as they are to be treated, and we will treat others with dignity, respect, and honor, for others carry the image of God, just as we do.
(3) I believe that God would not have given us this great assignment if we were not capable of doing it, though it is likely that we are not capable of carrying it out without the help of God, working in us, and without God giving us the love we need to love as he has asked us to love.

As I trembled before the task of writing this book, a friend told me that I didn't have to practice what I teach or write, but he didn't mean that I didn't have to set my focus on attempting with the best of my ability to follow this great commandment.

I know many of my problems with love and sometimes my failures bring me to my face in humiliation and anguish.

I assume that because you are a human being, there are areas in which you stumble and fall in loving too. Perhaps you even fail. You disappoint yourself and you disappoint others, stretching to live the impossible dream of loving well enough. If you have lived past twenty-five, you have probably been disappointed or betrayed by another person whom you have loved.

Unless you know a greater and better source to begin with than God, I am going to assume these things:

> *The LORD your God will keep his covenant of love with you.... He will love you and bless you...*
>
> Deuteronomy 7:12b-13a

(1) At the very heart of our difficulties in loving is likely a misunderstanding or a misperception of the nature of God and God's love for us.

(2) At the very heart of many of our frustrations in life is not only that we have been looking for love in all the wrong places, but we have been working ourselves like crazy, doing things that aren't so much about loving as they are about trying to survive, trying to please other people, trying to avoid conflict and difficulty, trying to heal old pains and wounds, and doing what we were taught to do or what we saw other people doing.

(3) And at the heart of many of our conflicts with each other is a misperception or confusion about what it really does mean to love ourselves and others because of these reasons and more:

- We are steeped in a culture that promotes narcissism instead of love.
- We are governed by a social culture that says
    - Take care of yourself and what belongs to you.
    - Rely on yourself; don't trust others.
    - Achieve, accomplish, and acquire.
    - Compete and defeat. Win at any cost.
    - The bottom line rules, even in service institutions and professions.

(4) We are now living in a culture in which it is accepted as a social norm to hate, to be rude, to take advantage of others, to manipulate others, and to use others as objects.

I am stunned and terrified at the ease with which people talk about killing others and the frequency of murders. I am stunned and alarmed at the hate people spew about those they don't like, those who are different from them, and the elected officials who don't protect their interests. I am stunned as well that people lie about other people, fabricating stories that will help them get their way, hide their real motivations, manipulate others, win votes and positions with absolutely no regard for what lying does, not only to the one about whom they are lying, but to themselves.

To lie, to hate, to use others for your own selfish gain is an act of violence against yourself.

And yet God's mercy, forgiveness, and grace are part of this glorious impossibility and the grand design God has in mind for us. God knows our frailties and failures, our missteps and our hideous wrongs against him and against each other. God knows that we hurt each other, betray each other, and use others for our own good, but the mechanism is in place for us to return to our knees over and over and ask for forgiveness, for a new start, and for help when we get it wrong.

In his powerful little book *The Wisdom of Tenderness,* Brennan Manning speaks these words about love, redemption, and mercy:

> God cannot not love us. Without the eternal, interior generation of love, God would cease to be love. When we're steeped in selfishness, indifferent to the poor, tormented by lust, wallowing in self-pity, and flattened by depression, God's love continues to carry us. According to John, the essence of our faith lies in trusting that love of God. Salvation happens the moment we accept without reservation what G. K. Chesterton called "the furious love of God."

Manning asks this question of his reader, and I ask it of myself and of you: "Whether your childhood was idyllic or abusive, the challenge still stands: Do you accept yourself as one utterly loved by God?"

My prayer as I write these chapters is that you and I will grow in understanding that there is nothing you can to do to make God not love you or love you less.

And the good news for many of us is that there is nothing any of us can do to make God love us any more than he already does.

We are the beloved of God.

And we are becoming, more and more, the beloved of God.

That is, my friends, good news.

Growing Edges

Once upon a time, someone told a lie about me. I suppose all of us have had lies told about us. It's harder to admit that we've probably all told lies about others, either knowingly or not.

Another time, long ago and far away, someone I loved hurt me deeply. I thought I might die from the pain of it, and I'm not being dramatic.

More than once, I've had to keep calm and quiet in the midst of a storm and allow things to run their course without explaining or defending myself.

I know the pain of blocked communication and broken connections with the people who are most important to me.

"Going deeper into God" has a most practical meaning for me.

As a longtime practitioner of Centering Prayer, the method of prayer taught by writer and Benedictine monk Thomas Keating, I have learned to be vigilant about my twenty-minute "sits." During those times, I use what we call a "prayer word" as my consent to open my mind and heart to the presence of Christ.

The prayer word isn't magic. It is simply a meaningful word that brings my wandering mind back to my intention, and that is to consent to the presence and action of the living Christ in my inner life, the "secret room" of communion and abiding in Christ.

During stressful times or times of personal pain and loss, my "sits" are crucial to my peace of mind.

It is during those times in silence and solitude that I am not problem-solving or seeking answers. Instead, I am opening my whole life—heart, mind, and soul—to the healing presence of who Keating calls "the Divine Therapist," with deep trust that that therapist knows just where my growing edges are and just what expression of love is needed for my healing.

Thomas Keating teaches that when we give the Divine Therapist permission to work at the unseen level, the unconscious, the work begins, and the power and beauty of that work is that because the work is going on at the level of the unconscious, the ego isn't in the mix, interfering with that which God is trying to do.

Keating says that the Divine Therapist, with our consent, begins the process of healing what he calls "the emotional wounds of a lifetime" outside our conscious control.

Over time, this process unfolds.

I have heard Keating teach this powerful concept. I have read his books about what happens when we consent to the presence and action of the living Christ/the Divine Therapist/the Holy Spirit in our inner lives.

What I have experienced has been so incredible that it makes me wonder why everyone in the world isn't accessing the love of God, at work in that inner space, the kingdom that is within.

> *To love another person is to see the face of God.*
> Victor Hugo

Through the mystery of it all, and with the practice of Centering Prayer, I now know that God's love at work does what Jesus did when he encountered people in his earthly mission.

God's love heals the wounds of a lifetime.

God's love transforms all experiences and is capable of working miracles of transformation in our inner lives, as well as in the outer world.

God's love liberates us from the prisons of our own makings, freeing us from bondage to past wounds, afflictive emotions, and self-defeating attitudes and behaviors.

God's love empowers us to live the lives we have been designed to live.

I make no promises as to how God will work in others' lives, and I attempt to let go of my expectations of how God will work in my life. Sometimes the outcomes are far different from my expectations, and sometimes God's work takes longer than I like.

What I have experienced is that God does work in our lives in ways that are mysterious and deep and that Centering Prayer is one of the ways God has worked in my life.

All it takes is surrender to God's processes and faithfulness to the practices of faith, but sometimes that "all it takes" seems to be too much to ask or do.

Sometimes I have to start by asking God to make me willing to be willing, and even at that, surrender is hard.

Chapter 4

God's Fierce Love: Theory or Reality?

"Don't look for the judgment of wrath in the Bible any longer. Instead, find the parts of the Bible that reveal God's love, grace, and mercy, and linger on those verses from now on."

Early in my adult journey, I attended a Bible study in a home in San Angelo, led by a maverick teacher who journeyed to San Angelo once a week to impart his knowledge and gospel of grace to a large group of women. I was young, and he sought me out to give me that message.

That counsel came back to me as I began to prepare to teach the material in this book on Thursday mornings. In the intervening years since I had heard those wise words, the harsher messages of fundamentalism and legalism had swept back and forth across our country in ever-increasing force, polarizing Christians around emotionally and politically charged social issues like abortion and homosexuality, the interpretation of the Bible, and the place of women not only in the culture, but in the home and churches.

"Eve brought sin into the world," a young girl declared in my presence recently, and since it was neither the time nor place for me to talk with her about that, I stayed quiet, choosing instead to deal with that perception indirectly. That point of view, repeated over and over within my particular expression of the church, has created untold damage among women.

"Oh, my!" my spiritual director Bishop Michael Pfeifer said to me when I related those same words from an annual gathering of the Southern Baptist Convention. Obviously, he was troubled by the words and their effect on me, and he quickly responded, "But, Jeanie, the Savior also came into the world through a woman!"

So it was that as I set out to prepare my teaching materials for this nine-month Bible study on love, I began with a personally imposed challenge to prove that God's love could be seen from the beginning of Genesis all the way through to Revelation. No serious student of the Bible would consider ignoring the passages that talk about the wrath of God. They are in there, and so is the concept of the judgment of God, a concept that has struck abject terror in the hearts and minds of young children for centuries.

The teacher who gave me a lifetime assignment must have seen that I needed to experience more of the love and grace of God, but the truth is that while I grew up in a religious culture that did tend to focus more on the badness of human beings than on the goodness of God, in my particular family of origin, there was a prevailing sense of the love of God, communicated through sermons, yes, but also through music and poetry.

"If that person is full of the joy of the Lord, I wish she would let her face know," my dad said one day about a particularly cranky and critical church member who believed it was her calling to point out all the faults and errors of other church members.

My family's history turned on the conversion of my father as an adult, an experience that was so dramatic that it was told and retold by family and friends for all of his life. When the love of Christ captivated my father, the story is told, he was never the same, and so throughout my childhood, I had a strong sense that God's love could transform a human being and reshape his life and his future.

In college, I was exposed to speakers and teachers at Baylor University who were full of the good news that God was a loving God. Perhaps our generation went too far in emphasizing and proclaiming the God of love without the balance of God's sovereignty and justice, and perhaps that was a compensation and an attempt to balance the decades of the tiring, spirit-draining emphasis on our being sinners in the hands of an angry God. Whatever our motivation was in what Dylan Thomas called the "lamb-white" days of youthful idealism, it was good and it was healthy. And it was followed by a volcanic reaction from the other side of the religious world that was determined to keep our focus on the dangers of liberalism and on the coming judgment of God.

I've always loved to recall a sermon of my conservative Baptist preacher-father. Titled "Am I a Liberal?" the sermon had the requisite three points, and knowing my father, there had to have been a poem at the end. In the sermon, my dad passionately proclaimed that he hoped he was known as a liberal, in the manner of Christ. "I want to be known as a liberal," he said, and then after a pause, "liberal in loving, liberal in giving, and liberal in forgiving."

> *God loves each of us as if there were only one of us.*
> — Augustine

My father's life was transformed by the grace and mercy of the living Christ, and my parents lived in a radical faith in the love of God, and for that heritage, I am eternally grateful. Because of that heritage and its profound effects on my development, I've never been able to escape the feeling or the deeply held conviction that I am loved by God.

Thanks be to God for that.

Before you finish this chapter, linger awhile on these words of Henri Nouwen from his book *Bread for the Journey*. Because it speaks to me as poetry, I've reproduced it here line by line instead of as prose:

What can we say about God's love?
We can say that God's love is unconditional.
God does not say "I love you, if . . . "
There are no ifs in God's heart.
God's love for us does not depend on what we do or say,
on our looks or intelligence, on our success or popularity.
God's love for us existed before we were born and will exist after
we have died.
God's love is from eternity to eternity
and it is not bound to any time-related events or circumstances. . . .
God desires to enter into relationship with us, and wants us to love
God in return.

Let's dare to enter into an intimate relationship with God without fear,
trusting that we will receive love and always more love.

You get what you're looking for, most of the time.

Writer Anais Nin said, "We do not see things as they are. We see things as we are," capturing in a few words a reality about perception that can, if we let it, stun us into examining the point of view we bring to everything, including God and what you see when you read the Bible.

Recently, I heard Marcus Borg respond to a participant in a conference at St. Paul's United Methodist Church in Houston, Texas. The woman was determined to counter Borg's message about God's love and grace with bad news about how much evil there is "out there" in the world, totally missing her transparency in declaring her own projections onto the "bad people out there."

Finally, and gracefully, Borg said, "There is the angry God in the Scriptures, but there is the loving God, and at some point you have to decide which is the prevailing God-image for you. And whichever God-image you choose is going to shape your life."

The room was still and quiet as we absorbed the truth of the importance of the God-image we carry, consciously or unconsciously, in shaping how we relate to our own lives and the self-image we carry, the way we relate to others and our own worldview.

When it comes to perspective, it seems to be true that most of us don't take the time to think about how we think and what we think about, but simply react to outer events with opinions, biases, and prejudice. For the most part, it's a rare thing to find someone who is willing to examine his or her own projections to determine what truly belongs to him and what he is asking another to carry for him. We assume our prejudices are based on truth, and when confronted with the irrationality of our biases, we are quick to put up defenses. Increasingly, it seems to me that our culture is one in which finding fault, blaming, criticizing, seeing only the negative, and looking for what is wrong instead of what is right all contribute to a culture in which disrespect of others, hate, and violence are increasing, becoming acceptable and even "smart."

I am reminded how often my father quoted Philippians 4:8, often when I was discouraged or frightened or when he was tired of hearing conversation that was negative: "Finally, brothers and sisters, whatever is true, whatever is noble, whatever is right, whatever is pure, whatever is lovely, whatever is admirable—if anything is excellent or praiseworthy—think about such things" (NIV).

While I love the language of the King James Version and the International Version of that verse, Eugene Peterson's rendition in *The Message* speaks clearly to me: "Summing it all up, friends, I'd say you'll do best by filling your minds and meditating on things true, noble, reputable, authentic, compelling, gracious—the best, not the worst; the beautiful, not the ugly; things to praise, not things to curse."

Matthew Fox, in his book *Original Blessings*, says that "what has been most lacking in society and religion in the West for the past six centuries has been a Via Positiva, a way or path of affirmation, thanksgiving, ecstasy."

Take another moment and reflect on these questions about our culture in general, and then examine your own habits of thinking and the attitudes of your particular social or religious group and see how those attitudes and patterns line up with Fox's quote and Paul's counsel in Philippians. Are we as a culture drawn . . .

more to destruction than we are to creation?
more to what is wrong than what is right?
more to dourness/sourness than to joy?
more to judgment than to encouragement?
more to numbness or aliveness?
more to pessimism than to optimism?
more to faultfinding than to thanksgiving?
more to perversion than to ecstasy?
more to pain than to pleasure?

more to fear than to love?
more to separateness than to blessing?
more to guilt or to grace?
more to war or to peace?
more to anxiety or to serenity?
more to criticism and condemnation than to blessing?
more to what is death-dealing or life-giving?

Getting Personal

1. As you ponder those questions about the culture, what is your personal experience of those forces within our culture? How does the negative energy affect you?

2. As you listen to your conversations with others, are you more inclined to add to the negative energy or to turn the focus to more positive, life-giving topics?

3. What part does the Christian community play in fostering negative conversations?

4. How does the negative focus from the Christian community impact non-believers?

5. How can one person effect change toward a more Christ-like consciousness among friends and associates, family and strangers on an airplane without being obnoxious or a goody-two-shoes?

6. Read Philippians 4:8. What kind of standard does Paul set forth for our conversations? Is he saying we should ignore that which is wrong and live like ostriches with our heads in the sand? Or is he calling us to a higher level of conversation?

7. How does what we talk about reveal our understanding of who God is? How can our conversations shape a more loving, compassionate, and merciful image of God, whether we talk about God or not?

I'm so grateful that I grew up in an environment in which the Bible was the object of love and assurance. Because of that, it is easy for me to take that attitude into an overview of the history of God's relationship with a particular people, the Hebrew people, and with those of us who have been captivated by the story of God's love and grace, which is extended to us whether we are Jew or not, slave or free, male or female.

There are, I am told, at least twenty-seven creation stories that have been discovered in various cultures. This account in the Bible is, for those of us who are within the Judeo-Christian faith, *ours,* and it is beautiful. In fact, I see the story as God's love, poured out in the creative process, delighting in the process, and then pronouncing every part of the creation "good."

Looking at the creation story in Genesis 1–2 through eyes of delight, it is possible to see the Creator God almost playfully creating the world. In those verses, the depiction of God is one of intimate involvement with the creative process.

> We also become the God we connect with. That's why it's so important to know the true God, and not some little, punitive, toxic god, because then you don't grow up, but live in fear and pretense.
>
> Richard Rohr

I love the image of God "brooding" over his creation, as described in the opening lines of this story. God is not depressed or blue, but instead is hovering over that which had no form, until the fullness of time was right for the dividing of the waters from the dry lands, the night from the day, and bringing forth vegetation, animals, and then—humankind. From the beginning, then, there is the feminine aspect of God pictured as a mother hen, "brooding" over her creation.

We who are trained in the Western model of scientific, logical, and rational thinking miss the splendor of the story if we try to literalize the events of God's creative endeavor. Instead, we must understand that the Hebrew language is a language of poetry, and we must understand that when the writer of Genesis says that God "spoke" creation into being, it does not mean that a word, as we understand "word," came out of the literal mouth of a male God-figure, much like the "God" on the Sistine Chapel. Instead, the meaning is much greater, bigger, grander, and more magnificent than that.

The being who was so holy that the Hebrew people would not even speak his name aloud was not a white, male, old-man God, made in our image. Doesn't that trivialize the Holy One?

To understand that creative "word," which is our source and the origin of all that is, we must let go of our inordinate attachment to words as we understand words and expand our minds enough to understand that this "word" spoken by God is the essence of God. To fully appreciate this fantastic event, we have to give up trying to make it all fit into our neat categories and allow both God and love to be verbs. God is, then, the divine creative energy, at work in creation, creating all that is. This story is God "godding," doing what God does, and, in fact, is continuing to do.

Isn't that far bigger than anything we can confine in some contrived system that satisfies the ego's need to *know*, but puts God in a box we humans can manage?

Notice the form and pattern of these verses. In each day, God took the initiative to bring into form a portion of creation. Next, the Scriptures affirm that what God wanted and initiated came into being. Finally, every time, God declared his handiwork "good."

If that isn't pure pleasure and delight, emanating from the Almighty, please tell me what it is.

The amazing thing is that creation continues, then, through us, around us, in us, with us, and sometimes, miraculously, *in spite of us* day after day, year after year, birth after birth? Creation continues, and we humans get to participate with God in creative processes all the time. Made in the image of God, we have within us the capacity to be creative, and when we are allowing that process to unfold and express itself in us, we are revealing a part of God's nature.

I remember the day I began reading the opening pages of Matthew Fox's *Original Blessing*.

My family and I were driving through New Mexico toward Lake City, Colorado, on a long, straight stretch of highway. The longer we traveled on that sunny day, the bigger the blue sky seemed to be. Out in those wide-open spaces, the expansiveness of the terrain matched the expansiveness of my mind and heart. Truly, I felt as if my mind was being liberated as I read. Periodically, I read passages aloud to my husband, always ending with, "This is what I believe!"

Indeed, it was more like I was reading what I had *always* known to be true. It felt to me as if what I was reading about God's blessing on this world and on human beings was something I had always known, but I felt that what I had always known had been trapped behind other teachings, teachings that began with the idea of original sin rather than the original blessing recorded in Genesis 1.

Later, I discovered the writings of John Phillip Newell, former warden of Iona Abbey and a Church of Scotland minister, and the blessing theology that permeates Celtic spirituality, and I found another layer of truth about the goodness of creation and God's love and care for what he made.

Over the years, with influences such as these and others, my understanding of the biblical narrative as a revelation of God's unending love for us and for the world has increased so that what I see in the Scriptures is God's love at work in all things, and my foundational Scripture has become Romans 8:28, but with God as the subject of the sentence: *God is at work in all things, bringing about good.*

That rendition of the Scripture, which I understand is closer to the original language, makes so much more practical, everyday sense to me than the way I learned it as a child. When "all things" is the subject, as in "All things work together for good

> I trust in your unfailing love; my heart rejoices in your salvation.
> Psalm 13:5 (NIV)

for those who love God and are called according to his purpose," you can get into some troubling waters and some terrible platitudes about God when people are suffering.

From the beginning of the Scriptures, then, God pronounced his creation "good," and when it came to the first humans he created, he invested them with his likeness, his breath of life, and an original blessing, which both expressed his love for humankind and also invested in us the power to act within creation, to be good stewards of what God has made, and to care for that which is God's creation.

Starting from that place, instead of the place of original sin, makes all the difference in how you live your life. Beginning from the starting point of "made in God's image" is the place where the Bible starts.

I challenge you to find within the Bible "the doctrine of original sin," and when you do find Scriptures that describe our tendency toward sin, I'd like for you to go back to the creation story. Which is the original state of humans, the blessing or the "original sin"?

It is my discovery that any time God is mad or grief-stricken over our choices, his wrath and his judgment are about how we are not living up to our true nature, our nature of being "made in the image of God." I believe that what we interpret as God's judgment may be that, or it may be the act of a loving God who cannot and will not tolerate our straying from his original design for us and is trying to correct our path.

You might say that God was the first one to think up *tough love*, and the truth is that when I have been brought to my face or my knees in sorrow and humiliation over my actions, my words, my arrogance, my pride, or my outright pettiness or nastiness, there is something in me that wants the tough love of God to bring me back to my original state of blessing. Indeed, the consequences of my choices often bring about suffering for myself and for others that is tough to bear, reminding me of my friend's wisdom that "we are punished more by our sins than for them."

It is the *fierce love* of God that is faithful to me and works within my life to correct my path and restore me to the way he intends.

It is the *fierce love* of God that won't let go of me, even when I think I can make it on my own.

It is the *fierce love* of God that is with me in the valleys and the mountains, the deserts and the lush gardens, as the faithful, providing, protecting mystery I choose to call *God*.

I am writing this book not to enter into any kind of debate about the existence or nature of God. I will leave that to others.

I am not writing this book to answer the questions about how a good and loving God can allow (or cause, from some people's point of view) bad things to happen to good people. It seems to me that the more relevant questions should be around how it is that a loving God can continue to be patient with us, given our recalcitrance and arrogance, and how it is that God can continue to be as gracious and merciful to us as he is when we treat other human beings the way we do.

If "everything is perception," then I am writing from a point of view and perspective of a deeply held belief in the goodness, compassion, and patient *fierce love* of this supreme being I call God, a perspective that has been tested in the hot fires of my own suffering and on the ash heap of a dark night of the soul. My perspective of God, whom I cannot and will not even attempt to define, is of a God of infinite and unconditional love, and while I cannot ultimately define love either, I have experienced enough love and what I believe is God to make these declarations:

(1) It is possible to choose to live from the perspective of love.
(2) It is possible to choose to believe in a God whose nature is love.
(3) Choosing love—as a way of being in the world—will shape the way you live.

It doesn't make sense to me that God would have given us a commandment to love each other if it were not possible to do, so I seek to learn even more about my belief and to share and dialogue with others about this amazing reality of God's great love for us.

Out of that motivation, here is my challenge, an ongoing challenge to myself and to you:

(1) Choose to see a God of love, and you're at least increasing your chances of experiencing the God of love.

(2) Choose to live as an instrument of God's love in the world, and while you will not do that perfectly, you will change the way you live for the good.
(3) Choose to look for evidence of God's love in the world around you, in the faces of people, in random acts of mercy and kindness, and in nature.

My father told me, "People usually find that for which they are looking."

Look for God's love; I think it's easy to find once you begin with an open heart and an open mind.

Growing Edges

When that particular Bible teacher told me to look for evidence of love in the Bible, I took his challenge seriously.

While my toddler napped every afternoon, I read through the book of Psalms, underlining the many verses about God's love and compassion. Then I went to my concordance and tracked all the references to God's love through the Old Testament.

Frankly, I was shocked, but that simple research project changed my way of thinking about God and the Old Testament.

Later, when I began a lifelong study of the life of Jesus, it was his love that grabbed me over and over, for everything Jesus did was for the purpose of extending love to individuals by healing them and teaching them a more loving way of being in the world.

> Go after a life of love as if your life depended on it—because it does.
> 1 Corinthians 14:1 (*The Message*)

Now, years later, when I bump into situations that discourage me or hurt me in one way or another, I return to those underlined verses about God's love and read them over and over.

When I am frightened about the future or anxious about a loved one, a scary world crisis, or a conflict with another person, I return to those verses about God's unfailing love.

Going to those Scriptures helps me reaffirm the source of life, and "going there" is like going to a deep, refreshing well of sweet water.

Reminding myself of God's patience and compassion is like rebooting my brain.

Archimedes, the Greek mathematician, scientist, and engineer, famously said, "Give me a firm spot on which to stand, and I shall move the earth."

God's love is a steady place to stand, and from there, it is amazing what can happen.

It's a risk to test this simple practice of going deeper into the heart of God through meditation, but the truth is that I have nothing to lose and everything to gain by doing so.

Recently, a person with whom I share a lifetime of memories said to me, "No matter how low I got or how hard my life was, I never lost my foundation."

Grounded in God's love for you and with that love as your starting point, you are strengthened and empowered from within to face life and each day's challenges with confidence and courage.

This isn't theory for me. I have tested the premise and found that it holds.

Chapter 5

The Great Romance

I'll never forget the moment when I heard Keith Hosey say that the most important romance of our lives is our romance with God.

Frankly, I was shocked. How could he use the word *romance* to talk about a relationship with God? My young mind was shaped by Hollywood and adolescent fantasies about romance. I couldn't fathom what he meant, and yet at some level I knew he was speaking truth. What Keith said resonated with something I had been learning in a Yokefellow spiritual growth group about how a block in a human relationship was likely a reflection of a block in my relationship with God.

The problem with our understandings of the word *romance* and even of the word *love* is that we have such superficial interpretations of both words. In his book *The Paradox of Love* and in lectures at the C. G. Jung Education Center in Houston, analyst and writer Pittman McGehee states that you can assess the sophistication of a culture by how many words that culture has for an important concept. McGehee points out that the English language has only one word for *love*. We say we love pizza and we love our children. We love holidays and we love God, using the same word to express one of life's greatest mysteries and challenges.

The Greek language has at least four words for love.

It seems to me that there should be some word reserved only for our love for God and God's love for us, but I cannot think of a word that could possibly capture that reality fully. *Reverence* and *awe* come close, and yet the word *love* indicates an intimacy that the other words may preclude.

Understanding the Bible begins, for me, with the understanding of two important ideas. First, the main character is God. The story from Genesis through Revelation is about God's relationship with a particular people, and all of the stories reveal the nature of God.

Second, the acts of God toward the Hebrew people are acts of redemptive, consuming, and faithful love. Even his acts that we call "the wrath of God" are expressions of God's fury over the refusal of the people to accept his love; the misunderstanding, misuse, or outright perversion of his love; or their refusal to return his faithfulness to them with love.

> *In your unfailing love you will lead the people you have redeemed. In your strength you will guide them to your holy dwelling.*
>
> Exodus 15:13-14

"It's a love story, after all," Pittman McGehee said at the end of a question-and-answer session following a lecture, remarking about the Bible. That statement, too, stunned me. It also brought tears to my eyes.

The Bible as *love story* works really well for me.

Putting on the lenses of love to read Scripture affects what you see. If you're looking for love in all those places and stories, you're going to find it.

God's love, expressed as delight and provision, is all through the creation story in Genesis. His pronouncing all that he made as "good" and humans as "very good" reveals a creator intimately involved with his creation. As I look at the investment of dignity and responsibility God gave humankind in giving us the ability to make choices and assigning us the task of oversight and care for the creation, I see both his love for us and his desire for us to grow up into the full measure we are intended to be.

Why else would God have given us such huge responsibilities and the freedom to choose how we would use our abilities if he had not intended for us to grow into the tasks we faced? Would it really have been love if he had left us infantile, sucking our thumbs in the garden of Eden, as naked as the moment we were born?

Even when Adam and Eve chose to defy the rules God had set out in the garden, there was no time he told them how bad they were.

Instead, you see God providing garments for them before their big exit from home. I find Genesis 3:21 and the idea of God's making garments of skin for his children as they set out into the grown-up world to be one of the most tender verses in the Bible. He knew that from then on, nothing was going to be easy again. While the Scripture does describe how their life will be outside the innocent state they had been in, God extended his love toward them with protection, provision, and covering.

It seems to me that throughout all the stories recorded in Genesis, the most important thing about God is that God never abandoned his people. In fact, he continued to reach out to them, attempting to work for good within the confines of the messes and mistakes of ordinary people who were trying to figure out how to live in a covenant relationship with Yahweh.

Always, God's faithful, fervent, pursuing love was with the children of Israel.

Moving deeper into the story of the Hebrew people, we see a pattern developing with the people. They would follow God for a while and then, like Adam and Eve, decide that they wanted to do things their own way. They would fall away a little here, neglect God a little there, break a commandment here, forget a ritual there, and suddenly they would have fallen so far away that they were in bondage to some bad ruler. Suffering under abuse or outright danger, they would cry out to God, and he would hear them. Rescued, they would return to God and the worship of him, but soon somebody would forget the order of things, and then someone else would follow suit, taking God's love for granted, and the cycle of obedience-rebellion-oppression-deliverance-promises of faithfulness would begin again.

The people kept wandering off, but God stayed faithful.

I am reminded of the cliché "the more things change, the more they stay the same." Are we really any different, as people or as groups and nations, from the children of Israel?

In the story of the Hebrew people that is recorded in Genesis and Exodus, I am captivated by these events that reveal God's tenderness and fierceness: In the story of Abraham, Sarah, Hagar, and their dysfunctional family, an angel of the Lord "found" Hagar in the wilderness after Abraham had banished her from the family not once but twice, provided for her, and sent her back to the family (see Gen 16; 21:8-21.) In the first account, Hagar responds to God's initiative by saying, "You are the God who sees me" and "I have now seen the One who sees me" (Gen 16:13).

Is there anything more important and transformative in loving another person than truly seeing and being seen for who you are? Is there anything more faith-building than knowing that you are seen by God, that you are not invisible, but seen by the Almighty?

As a child, I sang the children's song "Oh, be careful little feet where you go, for the Father up above is looking down in love" with more than a little trepidation about being careful *enough* what my eyes saw, my hands did, my mouth said, and my ears heard. In fact, that song almost crippled my courage about making choices and living, and the line about the Father looking at me, sung at the end of every verse, made me feel that at any point, I was going to be *caught* seeing, saying, doing something that, as my mother would say, "I had no business doing."

It's interesting to me now, thinking about how I missed the part about his looking at me *in love*. I wish someone had interpreted that song with an emphasis on the Father's love and delight in me. It might have changed a lot of things for me, and I'm pretty sure I would have had more fun!

Later, as a teenager, I stood in the sanctuary of First Baptist Church in Amarillo, craning my neck to see the "eye of God" in the center of the ceiling. As I looked at it, the words of that song and my image of God "keeping an eye on me" so he could catch me doing something I shouldn't have been doing came rushing back to me.

It was only later, when I read the words of Hagar, when I understood what it was like to be *seen* for who I am and seen with the eyes of delight and approval that I understood that that children's song could just as easily have been interpreted by my teachers as God's loving gaze toward us and his protective, caring, watchful, and seeking "eye" keeping us within sight out of love.

Perception really is important, isn't it? Some say that perception is everything.

It is important as well to note that when Abraham died, both of his sons, Isaac and Ishmael, went together to bury him. Apparently, the writer of Genesis thought that this fact, following the conflicted beginnings these two brothers had, was worth noting.

How would the world be different if we brothers and sisters in the human family might get over our differences and learn how to love each other with respect and tolerance? What if we repeated these words of blessing to our children and our children's children in such a way that the blessing of God's love were transmitted to their young minds and hearts through our touch, our gaze of delight in them, our actions toward them—"The LORD bless you and keep you. The LORD make his face to shine upon you and be gracious to you; the LORD turn his face toward you and give you peace" (Num 6:24-26)?

> *If you want to make progress on the path and ascend to the highest places you have longed for, the important thing is not to think much, but to love much, and so to do whatever best awakens you to love.*
>
> Teresa of Avila

God's love is at work in the stories of the patriarchs and the women of the early history of the Hebrew people, and in spite of what Walter Brueggemann calls "a certain recalcitrance" in them, God continued to provide for them and attempt to guide them and show them the way they should go.

Joseph's life was checkered with drama; sometimes he acted like an arrogant, spoiled child and at others, with unusual maturity and mercy. His brothers had thrown Joseph into a pit to get rid of him, so great was his sense of specialness. Then they lied to their father, Jacob, about what had happened to Joseph!

Joseph had risen to power in the Pharaoh's house in Egypt and had been given much responsibility during a time of famine. Joseph's brothers, seeking food, found themselves asking for help from this brother they thought was dead. In a dramatic moment in the twists and turns of a family drama, the brothers threw themselves down before him, declaring themselves to be his slaves.

Joseph's response to them was evidence of God's deep work of mercy within the heart and soul of Joseph: "You intended to harm me, but God intended it for good" (Gen 50:20).

The *fierce love* of God working in Joseph over decades of hardship, feast, and famine freed Joseph to be an instrument of love and mercy to his siblings, the ones who had caused him the most trouble.

I see God's love in his setting out the rules of engagement for life with him for the Hebrew people in the Ten Commandments. Those commandments, examined through the eyes of love, can be seen as protectors of the relationship with God and with each other. Like a loving parent, God provided guidance for his people by setting boundaries and practices of what to do and what not to do in order for them to live together to live well with each other.

God's infinite patience has to be one of the primary characteristics of his *fierce love* for us. To wonder and exclaim about how God has not given up on us is indicative of my limited perception and projections of my conditional and flawed love onto God, whose love seems to have no end.

I sing with my church family about God's love that goes from "east to west," and "what wondrous love is this" always brings tears to my eyes. I need to be with people who understand the "deep, deep love of God" and his amazing grace.

God's pattern in these stories is to work through someone whom he has prepared in a special way to be a liberator, such as Moses, or a prophet, a priest, or a king to be his instruments in restoring the Hebrew people to the covenant relationship with him.

It always stuns me when someone talks about how they don't like the Old Testament because of "that mean God" that deals with people with such rage and wrath.

It makes a lot of difference who teaches those Bible stories, and my Baptist friends and I joke about how some of the more R-rated stories in those Old Testament pages were left out of our Sunday school classes when we were young.

I will be forever grateful that the people—teachers, professors, pastors, and friends—who emphasized God's constant, redemptive love and made sure I knew that the worst thing any one of us has done is somehow covered by God's great love.

This Easter, I heard about a woman who kept proclaiming that she talked to God and that he talked back to her.

Offended by the presumption of an unlearned and unsophisticated woman, the bishop went to this woman and challenged her statements and asked her to stop saying that she talked to God and he talked to her. "People will think you are crazy," the bishop told her, implying that her craziness might reflect back on his teaching or his authority within his ecclesiastical world.

Finally, the exasperated bishop approached the woman one last time to demand that she stop making her outrageous claims about talking with God. "The next time you talk to God," he said to the woman angrily, "ask him what my sins are."

The next week, the bishop approached the woman and demanded to know if she had talked to God that week.

"Yes, sir, I did," the woman replied, simply and humbly.

"Did you ask him what they are?" the bishop sneered, and the woman replied, "I did, sir."

"Well?" he asked, waiting to trap her in her own ignorance.

"He said he doesn't remember, sir."

Fierce love knows when to forget.

Fierce love knows what to remember.

Fierce love is full of mercy and tenacity.

"I don't know that I believe in this God of love you talk about all the time."

Were those words, spoken with bitterness, a challenge? Did this angry woman want me to convince her that God's nature is love and that I believe God loves her specifically? Maybe her bitterness and anger was only my interpretation. Maybe she was hanging on to her last thread of hope and crying out for reassurance.

Later, when I heard this woman's story, I understood why she couldn't believe in a God of love. Raised in a religious culture that preached only the angry, punitive God of wrath, judgment, and punishment, she told me about how frightened she was in church, listening to the peril that she wasn't sure she could avoid since she was such a bad person.

> *The LORD, the LORD, the compassionate and gracious God, slow to anger, abounding in love and faithfulness, maintaining love to thousands, and forgiving wickedness, rebellion and sin.*
>
> Exodus 34:6-7a

"How do you really know that this God you talk about so easily is about love?"

This time, the sarcasm was hard to miss. I had to decide in about two seconds whether to take the question seriously or move on. Sometimes people like to stir things up not because they really want honest dialogue or answers, but because they just like to see what happens when they challenge the speaker.

Even to talk about God is to evoke an array of responses, for everyone has his or her own individual idea of who God is. For the most part, that image is based on one's earliest caregivers or authority figures, our first "gods," and until we take seriously our God-image and whether or not it is serving us or hurting us, most of us live with a God-image that is an artifact of childhood we project onto "God."

To presume to know anything about God or to offer one's views about who God is and what God does is itself presumptuous. Author, speaker, and teacher Rob Bell opens his book *What We Talk About When We Talk About God* with this searing question: "Is there a more volatile word loaded down with more history, assumptions, and expectations than that tired, old, relevant, electrically charged, provocative, fresh, antiquated yet ubiquitous as ever, familiar/unfamiliar word, God?"

The interplay of conflicting words amuses me, for even that reveals the complexity of trying to capture any idea of who God is. In fact, there are times when I wish we could return to the Hebrew practice of not even speaking aloud the name of God, for the abuses and misuses of God are sometimes so sacrilegious and full of one's own personal projections, all of which perpetuate ideas of God that are too small, too biased, and too self-satisfying.

You may think that Bell is going to explain why he doesn't use the name of God, but he surprises us. After his opening declaration about the use of the name *God*, Bell turns our minds again with one simple sentence: "And that is why I use it."

We use the name *God*, and we talk about God even when we flounder with what it is we are trying to express. Even when we are doubting the existence of God or debating the nature of God, we are doing so because there is something in us that is connected to God or yearns for God.

Perhaps all of us want to believe in a God who loves us unconditionally and is benevolent toward the world and one's own life.

The first time I read Augustine's words about this "God-shaped" vacuum we have within us, I knew he had discovered a deep, inalterable truth, and when I read that our hearts are restless until we find our rest in God, I knew that my restlessness had an object and a reason for its churning away inside me.

Indeed, I speak from the perspective of a God-image of love because I grew up around people who saw God as loving, merciful, and compassionate, but as an adult, I have chosen to shape my theology, my faith, and my way of being in the world around my belief in a God whose name and character are love.

It is a fact that there are people who never experience that God-concept and, in fact, grow up in environments and traditions that run counter to that perspective and even are ruled by hatred, violence, abuse, and cruelty. And yet I know that even in those circumstances, the God of love sometimes reaches the heart of a child, a rebel, a doubter, or a killer.

In my adulthood, I have chosen teachers whose understanding of God is one of love, forgiveness, and faithfulness.

Regularly, I read about those whose entire lives have been spent around people who teach the opposite of love, respect, tolerance, and forgiveness. I read about murderers and rapists. I hear about religious leaders who violate the bodies, minds, and souls of their followers. I know about the acts of cruelty inflicted by human beings on other human beings.

The hard, cold, unbearable truth is that we live as imperfect beings in an imperfect world. We can either keep announcing the problems, focusing on the wrongs, showcasing the evil, and destroying each other with our words, our actions, and our negative mindsets, or we can "be transformed by the renewing of our minds" (Rom 12:2), a concept articulated, incidentally, by a murderer, who, by an encounter with the living Christ, was knocked to the ground, blinded, and changed. It was Saul-who-became-Paul who would be so overtaken by the love of Christ that he was able to write some of the most powerful and beautiful hymns to love, grace, and mercy in the entire Bible.

Growing Edges

I was introduced to the "place to stand" idea of Archimedes in a Yokefellow spiritual growth group, a life-changing experience for me. The ideas that formed the process of that group experience came from the writings of both Paul Tournier, Swiss psychiatrist and student of Carl Jung, and Quaker author and theologian Elton Trueblood, who was also chaplain at both Harvard and Stanford Universities. It was Trueblood's book *A Place to Stand* that shaped much of my thinking about the importance of choosing wisely what will be the foundational principles that determine your decisions and your life.

I've learned that if I start my theology by observing human beings and their foibles, I am starting at the wrong place. In other words, if I look at human beings to decide how God is or if there is a God, I'm going to be in trouble from the outset. Furthermore, if I look at the institutions of religion to form my ideas of God, I may become cynical, discouraged, and even disdainful.

On the other hand, if I start my theology with God and a God-concept that is life-giving, I have a place to stand that is firm and stable.

Because I attempt to be a follower of Christ, and because I believe that Jesus is the best picture of God that we have, my theology is going to be a Christian theology, and the teachings that I try to carry out in my personal, daily life are going to be the teachings of Jesus.

> Love is the epiphany of God in our poverty.
> Thomas Merton, *A Letter on the Contemplative Life*

My chosen position is Christo-centric, meaning that my place to stand is on the life and teachings of Jesus and my lived experience of the mystery of the presence of the living Christ, or the Holy Spirit of Christ.

With all of that said, my challenge is to carry out my chosen way of being in the world in my everyday life, which is ordinary, sometimes mundane, but never boring, full of conflicts over all kinds of trite and irritating issues. The people with whom I attempt to live this life of love are just like I am. We are all ordinary, imperfect saints, attempting to live more than we are able.

Thanks be to God, the adequacy of God meets us at the points of our inadequacies with grace, mercy, and love.

God's eye is on the sparrow, and it is on me too, and it is the eye of love.

Chapter 6

The Beloved in Search of the Beloved

Every morning when I sit down to write, I face two impossibilities that are strong enough to make me run from my task.

On the one hand, I am faced with the largeness of love and the ever-increasing understanding of the immensity of love. With my desire to capture what is impossible to define, contain, or explain, I am intimidated by the call to the ideal and the deepening and growing awareness that the desire to love and be loved is a constant shared by all of humankind, even and perhaps especially those who have buried that longing under layer after layer of defenses against the pain of lost love, unrequited love, or unfulfilled desire.

On the other hand, my task brings into sharp focus the places and times in my daily life when either anger or other afflictive emotions, conflicts, or the emptiness of indifference force me to face my own inadequacies and imperfections. Indeed, the desire to be more loving and to love more faithfully seems sometimes to stir up my own complexes, those states of being that are relics from my past still acting out in the present, often disturbing and contaminating what could be a lovely moment with fears, memories from the past, defense mechanisms, and behaviors that suggest I don't want to love or be loved, when that is precisely what I need and want.

I understand that the more personal something is, the more universal it is. This understanding helps me to hold two opposite realities—the enormity of love and my imperfections—in creative (if uncomfortable) tension until what Carl Jung calls "the transcended third" emerges.

The transcendent third is another possibility that can emerge from allowing both realities to co-exist simultaneously in my mind. Instead of "either/or" thinking, holding two opposites in tension allows a back and forth between both realities in a creative and open process. Instead of rejecting either the bigness of love (it's so hard, so imperfect, so why try?), allowing "both/and" thinking can bring forth strength, solutions, and growth.

Even as I write this book, I sense that transcendent third as a more gentle holding of the two opposites, the ideal and the actual.

I write, then, with a consciousness of my flaws and inadequacies in loving, but with a call toward love, which I believe is full of grace and mercy.

On a bright, sunny morning, I gathered in the Great Hall at Laity Lodge Retreat Center with members of our church. The retreat leader began the session by leading us in a responsive reading of Psalm 136, with the leader reading the verses and the participants responding with "His love endures forever."

I recall that experience for two reasons. I remember that among our Baptist group, largely unfamiliar with responsive readings and often resistant to them, there was an awkwardness to the process. Reflecting on that through the years, I am astounded that we would not/could not/did not, as a group, move smoothly and easily into the fervent and enthusiastic declaration, "His love endures forever." Shouldn't we/couldn't we/why didn't we grow stronger and more bold with each of the declarations, moving to an almost "Hosanna" with the twenty-sixth and last affirmation of God's very nature?

> *For the LORD watches over the way of the righteous.*
> Psalm 1:6

However, the experience made such an impression on me that since then, that particular psalm has had deep meaning for me. Perhaps that awkward moment was a turning point from which I moved away from feeling awkward about declaring the truth of God's love to an understanding of the deep importance of speaking those words about God, repeatedly and often.

After that morning worship, someone complained to me about the experience, stating that the Hebrews' history was not our history. I gently responded that though Christians may have tried to cut ties with our Jewish roots, we are Judeo-Christian, and our heritage is permeated with the reality that God's love endures forever.

> Love affects more than our thinking and our behavior toward those we love. It transforms our whole lives. Genuine love is a personal revolution.
>
> Thomas Merton, *Love and Living*

Yes, the Hebrew history is our heritage, and so is everything that has happened in the family of humankind, either directly or indirectly. We are all connected, in ways small and large.

Perhaps *fierce love* is best defined as enduring love that never ends.

When I was growing up and learning the books of the Bible, we were shown how the book of Psalms was right in the middle of the Bible. Once you had that starting place, you could more easily navigate among the books of the Old and New Testament, especially if you memorized all the books of the Bible.

That the psalms are in the middle of the Bible had meaning for me, even as a child, and throughout my entire adulthood I have turned to the psalms countless times for comfort, reassurance, and perspective. They remind me that there is no human emotion that I cannot express to God. Even more helpful to me is the stunning and sometimes startling expression of the ambivalence of human emotion. The psalmist lays out his praise and adoration of God in one psalm and then in another his rage and fury, his sense of hopelessness and fear, as well as his demands that God vanquish his enemies!

I can relate to the full range of human emotion that is expressed in Psalms and, at the same time, rest and refresh myself with the psalms that relate the love and mercy of God to his children. It's all there, thanks be to God, and for the rest of my life I have turned to the psalms for comfort and inspiration.

Going to the psalms for an understanding of the rich mix of powerful and conflicting emotions, laid bare before God himself, comforts me and frees me to speak with radical honesty to the God who is, apparently, big enough and gracious enough to tolerate whatever it is I need to get off my chest.

Getting Personal

That Bible teacher who suggested I go through my Bible and underline the verses that declare God's love suggested that I start with Psalms. These psalms, listed in Lesson 4 in the "Questions for Reflection" section at the end of this book, speak of the love, compassion, mercy, and grace of God. You may want to take a look at them and see which ones particularly speak to you and then respond to the questions that follow the list. If you want to go deeper in the Psalms, you may also want to read my book *Ancient Psalms for Contemporary Pilgrims*, which is designed to facilitate personal reflection and contemplative prayer.

I teach what I call "relational Bible studies," and every year there is a full-page explanation of what that is in the notebooks each person receives. The following paragraphs are taken from that explanation:

> A relational Bible study is built on the premise that it is possible to have a personal relationship with God, through the activity and mystery of the Living Christ, and that the study of the Bible is intended to nurture and enhance an individual's relationship with God, with oneself and with others. In a relational Bible study, there is a focus on deepening the connection between God, as revealed in the Scriptures, and the individual, and to nurture a vital, personal love relationship between people and the Living Christ.
>
> At the same time, the primary relationship between God and the individual impacts a person's relationship with other human

beings, starting with the relationship with oneself, and so there is dialogue, shared discovery, interaction and koinonia that develops among class members and facilitator.

The emphasis, then, is not on finding "the answer" or "the solution." No one person is "dispensing truth." Instead, there is an emphasis on the shared process of exploring and discovering life-giving truths and principles within the Scriptures that impact, nourish and strengthen individual faith and, as a result, one's relationships. These truths are believed to heal and transform, liberate and empower the individual to live up to his identity as a person, made in the image of God.

Facilitating the class, I combine small-group discussions around tables, large-group discussions, and lectures. Over the years, I have discovered that the benefits and gifts from this style of teaching are powerful. In this process, I take full responsibility for preparing the lessons and the lecture each week, but we are in a shared learning experience together. As a result of that, everyone receives pearls of wisdom from the people in the class on a weekly basis.

> Give thanks to the Lord, for he is good, his love endures forever.
> 1 Chronicles 16:34

One Thursday morning, after we had been discussing God's great love for us and the ways in which the Hebrew people had wandered away from God's love and the covenant relationship God had established with Abraham, my longtime friend Charlotte Sullivan raised her hand. She spoke about how many times the Hebrew people had done the opposite of what God had guided them to do. She talked about the mistakes, the failures, the difficulties that were the results of their choices and the suffering they brought on themselves by their own choices.

"And yet," she said, "no matter what, God was there."

I will never forget the effect of Charlotte's words that morning. We were silent before the simplicity of deep truth and just let that pearl sink deep into our hearts and minds.

That silence was the only appropriate response to Charlotte's words.

No matter what, God—Emmanuel—is there, and God is here with us.

No matter what.

Never, not even once, were we in the Sword Drills asked to locate a verse in the Song of Solomon. I am confident, however, that there were adolescents in my youth group who could, if asked, find the more tantalizing verses for the rest of us. As the preacher's daughter, I might have been the one finding the Song of Solomon, but I was too scared of what would happen if it turned out that I was the one pointing out such verses!

When asked how he would teach the Song of Solomon to a Sunday school, a longtime teacher and preacher said, "When it comes up in the schedule, I leave town."

How on earth the Song of Solomon got into the canon, I cannot imagine, but as I have continued to love and study the Old Testament, I have to ask how on earth it is that we who expound on how we love the Bible have managed to ignore this beautiful book. As I was teaching this "Fierce Love" on Thursdays and making my way through the Old Testament, how could I possibly pass over the Song of Solomon?

> Dare to love and be a real friend. The love you give and receive is a reality that will lead you closer to God as well as those whom God has given you to love.
>
> Henri Nouwen

I'm guessing there is no other book that has had a greater variety of interpretations or opinions, and there have always been and still are considerable discussions about whether it should be studied or not. My thinking is that we would all be better off if we gave it serious study. A rabbi in the second century, Rabbi Akiba, called the book "the holy of holies" and said that "no day outweighed in glory the one in which Israel received the Song of Solomon."

Some have believed that Solomon was the king and the maiden and the shepherd are two lovers. Some give it a love-song interpretation, and others say it was a wine song in banquet halls, but from early Jewish writings, it is evident that it was used liturgically in the eighth century and was to be read on the eighth day of Passover, at the beginning of the new year. Apparently, it was read both privately and publicly and is still prescribed to be read at the conclusion of the morning service on the intermediate Sabbath of Passover.

Set among other books that contain stories of warfare, incest, multiple wives, killings, and outrageous acts of violence inflicted on the Hebrew people and sometimes enacted by them, this is a book of lyric poetry of exquisite beauty, full of sensuous symbols and images.

There is no monologue or dialogue, but the words of the book are expressed by an unknown speaker. We have to guess who the speaker is.

Found in the Talmud in 150–500 CE, the earliest interpretation of the book that has prevailed throughout both Jewish and Christian circles for centuries has been that it is an allegory. Some have interpreted the bridegroom as Yahweh and the bride the Jewish nation. It has been interpreted as the experience of the nation in its relationship with God.

Another old interpretation with Jewish mystical thought is that it represents the union of the active intellect with the passive, and among Christians, Christ is seen as the bridegroom and the bride. According to Origen, an early father of the Christian church, the church is to be seen as the bride of Christ. Others interpret the lovers as God and individual person, while some see the sacred marriage of the feminine and the masculine within an individual.

> *His love endures forever.*
> Psalm 136

That people through the centuries have been scandalized by the book and its language and horrified that such a thing has gotten into our sacred Scriptures at all both amuses me and reminds me of hard realities of the church's history. Throughout the history of the Christian church, sexuality and erotic love have been censured, repressed, and oppressed.

There is hardly anything the organized church and the church's independent offshoots has gotten more wrong than the issue of the vital, necessary, and beautiful gift of human sexuality, and we've gotten it wrong in just about every way imaginable. In doing so, the church has pretty much discredited itself in the process and has almost totally lost its voice of influence. As a whole, we are blazing hypocrites when it comes to the issues of sex, making our prissy pronouncements about what is forbidden and what is not when we all know now that all manner of things have been going on since the beginning of the church, and often by the ecclesiastical leaders themselves.

I long for the day when we can have honest and healthy conversations about human sexuality. I do know that our children are confronted daily by sexual messages and images. Very little—if anything—is still considered sacred, and children see and know and experience things that they cannot interpret. I do know that our children are, like we were, confused because they get conflicting messages, and I hurt for them. Surely we can do better than we have done.

When I was fourteen, I sat in my bedroom window of the parsonage where my mother and father and I lived in Dallas, Texas, looking at the full moon. In that moment, which has become a sacred memory for me, I knew that sexuality and spirituality had their source in the same place and that they were both gifts from God. I didn't have the language at fourteen to articulate that, but I would say now that both—sexuality and spirituality—are essential forces in our nature or of the essence of our human nature. At least in my lifetime, we within the church have not done a good job of giving reverence and dignity to the life-force put into every cell of our bodies by the God who made us.

God has given us this exquisite gift, but we have not been good stewards of the gift.

> *When I write to you that, as the Beloved, we are God's chosen ones, I mean that we have been seen by God from all eternity and seen as unique, special, precious beings.*
>
> Thomas Merton,
> *Life of the Beloved*

The Bible does have rape and incest, prostitution, adultery, and polygamy in it. It has raw and terrible brutality, and it has the consequences of such, and so do we.

All of that makes me wonder about just what brave soul it was who spoke up for Song of Solomon when it was included in the canon, and what he was up against, arguing for it. I wish I could somehow "listen in" on those discussions among those who must have believed, as do I, that the book and its sensual imagery is a gift. If you have not read it, give yourself the gift of a slow and careful reading of this treasure. Whether you receive it as a beautiful expression of a man and a woman and their love for each other, or whether you see it through the eyes of the mystic and interpret it as God's search for his beloveds, the book speaks of a view of God as love.

The more I have read the book and thought about it, the more I wonder if the people who insisted that it be included in the canon might have wanted to elevate sexuality back to the place it was meant to be, to redeem the brutalities that are recorded in the Scriptures, to show us the blessing of romantic and sensual love, to reveal God as a lover in search of his beloved. I'm comfortable with the book's being both about our love relationship with God and the love that is possible between two human beings.

Whether it is allegory or not, whether it is a wine song, a love song for a wedding feast, or a liturgical song, I know this one thing: it is about love. And if it is about love and if God is love, I'm thinking we can learn something important from immersing ourselves in the Song of Solomon.

Chapter 7

Love in the Hard Times (or Love on the Rocks)

On this beautiful spring morning in 2014, the sports world is rocked by racist comments purportedly made by the owner of the Los Angeles Clippers basketball team to his biracial girlfriend. Those comments are like cannon balls, shot around the world, further unsettling the unsettled world of racial tension.

I would love to distance myself from this ongoing problem, but I cannot.

Televangelists are exposed for their corruption and immorality, their greed and avarice. What they did, in the name of God, has seeped into the collective unconscious and conscious minds of Americans and is then projected onto local churches and their pastors, undermining the respect of people toward ministers everywhere.

A man betrays his wife or a wife betrays her husband, and suddenly the social, professional, or religious cultures in which those two individuals have lived their lives are forced to shift and change to accommodate the broken loyalties, the subsequent fallout with friends and family members, and the toxic fumes of bitterness, guilt, confusion, and sometimes grief.

"I didn't have anything to do with this," my friend lamented over lunch, relating the latest in a string of failed marriages among her group of friends, "and yet it is affecting how our children relate to each other, our friendship with both spouses, and is even making me doubt my own judgment about people!"

A respected older man related a conversation with a person who had been instrumental in the overthrow of our denomination. With tears in his eyes, he told me about expressing his heartache over the fallout of the actions of those who had led the mission to "purify" what they believed was a rapidly leaning trend toward liberalism within our denomination.

"Churches have been split," the man told this party to the overthrow. "Reputations and fine careers have been ruined. Families and marriages have been broken, and friendships are irreparably broken. People have had health crises, and some have died from the stress of it all, and a whole generation of our children wants nothing to do with church, or at least our churches, because of the infighting, and I ask you why. Why?"

Of course, there was no satisfactory answer given, but only a vague and cold evasion of a response.

I didn't start the denominational war, but I have been profoundly affected by the actions of others, inflicted on tens of thousands of innocent churchgoers, misled and misinformed to their detriment by religious people who used secular political means to gain power and control.

In order to get along with each other and thrive, human beings need to have guidelines, laws, and standards. In fact, we seem to operate best when we know what the rules are and, however rebellious or reluctant we are, we are made to stay on our side of the road, stop at red lights, and mind our own business.

It would be such a wonderful world if all of us were mature and responsible enough to do the right thing without laws and without punishment for breaking those laws, just because we care about ourselves and about other people enough to watch out for each other.

God gave the Ten Commandments to the children of Israel in order to protect them and show them how to live with God and with each other. Through their history, more and more ritual laws, health and cleanliness laws, and punishments for not following those rules were added to the daily life of the people as they struggled with their own human nature and how to relate, as humans, to Yahweh.

In the books of the Bible labeled "major and minor prophets," the problems concern collective sin. Repeatedly, the Hebrews would begin neglecting first one and then more of the Ten Commandments and the codes of ethics, and that would lead to abuses of power in daily life. Soon, having gotten away with the breaking of the laws and having strayed from a relationship with Yahweh, people began abusing other human beings. As corruption and violence increased and as moral weakness followed, the Hebrew people were easy prey to be taken over by bad leaders.

> I led them with cords of human kindness, with ties of love.
> Hosea 11:4

Over and over, the Hebrew people repeated the cycle of oppressing others followed by becoming the oppressed, and what happened to them clearly exposes the truth that separation from God leads to the use and abuse of power. Separation from God makes people behave in less-than-human ways and makes them tend to give in to a lower, sometimes almost animal nature. Sin makes us see other humans as objects and makes us prey on others, using God and others for our own gain.

Caught in the grips of lawlessness, people often fancy up their worship, but according to the prophet Isaiah, fancy worship by people who break God's laws is a stench in God's nostrils.

The prophets were men who had an unusual sensitivity to the times in which they lived, and they spoke and wrote the truth to their people, speaking for God. It took a lot of courage to be a prophet, and those who would seek to be a prophet must be willing to take the prophet's reward. It isn't an easy road, telling the truth to your own people.

Basically, prophecy in the Old Testament is not about foretelling the future, as in fortune-telling. Instead, biblical prophecy speaks the truth about a situation. It is a rigorous and bold declaration of just what the sins of the people are.

Biblical prophets spoke unrelenting truth to the people and told them what would happen to them if they continued in their current behavior. Prophets could see the logical consequences of continued sinfulness of people against God and each other, and for the most part biblical people didn't want to hear about their sins or where their sins might lead them any more than people of our day want to hear the truth about their sins.

The part of prophecy that often gets overlooked, however, is that while all of the prophets have the same theme, the sinfulness of the people and where it is taking them, they also all contain the fervent, fierce plea of God to his people: *Return to me.*

The repeated longing of God for his people to come back to him contains within it the essence of the nature of God and the *fierce love* he had for his people. It was the prophets' job to be the mouthpieces of God in heralding over and over the invitation for people to return to the vital, dynamic love relationship God had set up with his people when he established the covenant of love with Abraham.

This theme of God's redemptive, pursuing love is what biblical scholars call the "scarlet thread of redemption" that runs throughout the biblical narrative. That scarlet thread reveals God's very essence and nature. God cannot stop pursuing us with his love. He cannot stop grieving for us to return to him, and he will apparently stop at nothing to bring his children home to his heart, his presence, his ways.

Underlined and starred in my Bible are these words from the book of Lamentations: "Because of the LORD's great love we are not consumed, for his compassions never fail. They are new every morning; great is your faithfulness. . . . For men are not cast off by the LORD forever. Though he brings grief, he will show compassion, so great is his unfailing love" (3:22, 31-32).

One of the most beautiful expressions of God's unfailing love is found in the book of Hosea, which always surprises people with its subject matter.

"What was God *thinking*, telling Hosea to find himself an adulterous wife and have children with her?" a woman asked indignantly during our discussion of the book.

"Why haven't I ever even heard of this book?" another woman demanded. "I've been in church all my life, and not once have I even heard Hosea's name mentioned. Now I know why!"

It is true that this strange little book includes an amazing R-rated story about Hosea and his adulterous wife and their children. I, too, grapple with the verse that says God *told* Hosea to do such a thing, but taking the story literally only trivializes the power of the real story, the backstory.

What better way could the people understand God's faithful love toward them than to tell the story of unfaithfulness within a marriage? Who among the adults in the group wouldn't be able to connect the dots between marital unfaithfulness and the unfaithfulness of God's people, often referred to as his bride, and God?

Of course, the story is counterintuitive. We are schooled and programmed to react to adultery, betrayal, and unfaithfulness by throwing stones at the people out there who have done such deeds and flagellating ourselves with self-condemnation, guilt, and shame when we are the "guilty party," whether our unfaithfulness is toward another human being or toward God. Look, however, at the words of God to Hosea, words that reveal God's nature. Look at what God is teaching Hosea about the nature of true love in this verse, Hosea 3:1, *after she has committed adultery again*: "Go, show your love to your wife again, though she is loved by another and is an adulteress. Love her as the LORD loves the Israelites, though they turn to other gods and love the sacred raisin cakes."

I love this story, largely because I love what it teaches and reveals about a kind of love my world needs to learn.

The book of Hosea is a beautiful portrayal of the Hebrew word *hesed*, which is simply the unconditional faithfulness of God.

Hesed means there is nothing I can do to make God stop loving me or love me less, and so I can stop beating myself up for all the bad things I have done.

Hesed means there is nothing I can do to make God love me more, and that means I can stop my endless striving to earn God's love, prove my worth to God, or try to curry a special place at the head of the line with God.

Here is how God describes his love in Hosea 2:19-20, even as he is clear, direct, and often uncomfortably honest about the sins of Israel: "I will betroth you to me forever; I will betroth you in righteousness and justice, in love and compassion. I will betroth you in faithfulness, and you will acknowledge the LORD."

It has been my experience that the people who love best are people who have come to terms with their own brokenness and their own character defects, have taken responsibility for them, and have been given forgiveness, grace, and mercy.

To be aware of my sin, then, is a gift and a grace, even though it is sometimes terrible to come to that level of awareness.

It is so hard to fall from grace in your own eyes, to see the filth inside the cup that you have polished so well.

It is so hard to withdraw your projections from others. Most of us prefer for someone else to carry the flaws and the faults we so easily see in them than to find that the flaws and faults are in ourselves. "It takes one to know one" speaks to our ability to see in others what we hate to see in ourselves.

It is hard to remove the plank in your own eye, and so much easier to pick at the specks in others, and yet it is God's nature to wake us up and help us become aware of our own sinful nature and our own wrongs and sins. It is so much easier to do another's moral inventory than to have to do my own, but it is necessary for me to bear the burden of my own sinfulness in order to bear the beams of God's redemptive love.

> *Those who love you are not fooled by mistakes you have made in the past or dark images you hold about yourself. They remember your beauty when you feel ugly; your wholeness when you are broken; your innocence when you feel guilty; and your purpose when you are confused.*
>
> Alan Cohen

To be aware of our own sin is a moral obligation. To take responsibility for what is ours is a moral obligation.

What we do not work out or talk out or confess, we will take out, project out, or act out on innocent and undeserving people.

An unswerving truth in daily life is that children blame and adults take responsibility.

Sin is a serious issue, and the books of the prophets take up a lot of space within the Bible. That which separates us from God also separates us from each other. Within our Judeo-Christian heritage is a picture of our reality: We will always have a tendency to choose down instead of up. We will always have the capacity within us to choose darkness over light, selfishness over generosity, falsehood over truth, deceit over honesty, and, perversely, death-dealing behaviors and habits over life-giving practices and patterns.

That is part of the human condition, and yet the good news is that we also cannot escape the other reality: we are made in the very image of God, created just a little lower than the angels.

When we forget who we really are, God has a way of calling to us and waking us up to the truth that we were meant for more than the far country of the prodigal son of Luke's Gospel.

My great friend Frank Pool once said to me, "The goodness and greatness of God's mercy and forgiveness are greater than all the badness of all of us, wrapped up together."

God's *fierce love* sometimes expresses itself as mercy and sometimes as grace, but always God's love is available as compassion, tenderness, and passion for us.

Sometimes I wonder if what we experience as God's wrath and fury is our projection of how we would behave onto God. Sometimes what I feel as God's anger toward me is actually my anger toward myself, my shame, my disappointment in myself.

Underlying everything I wonder and speculate about God, I know that this one thing is true: God is fiercely in love with us.

In my study I have my books arranged by subject matter, and I have jokingly said that for every problem I have had, I have at least one shelf of books devoted to that particular problem. It is probably a defense against pain that I want to know everything I can about whatever my current challenge happens to be, but being informed isn't a bad thing.

Being informed, learning new coping skills, becoming educated about the things that I'm facing may be a defense, but ultimately I also have to face the situation, feel my feelings about it, and perhaps go through some deep valleys to the other side of the problem. Sometimes I deal with a problem I know I'll never solve, but must learn to live with it in a different way.

I've learned that denial is the first and most primitive form of defense in facing things you don't want to face. Avoiding the problem, acting as if it doesn't exist, distracting oneself in a variety of ways, and coming up with euphemisms that soften the blows of the problem are all common behaviors when life hands us something unpleasant or even tragic.

It is *hard* to face unpleasant realities. It is *painful* to be slammed up against things you cannot change, and it is *difficult* to learn new ways of coping with an old problem.

One of the amazing things about the life of Jesus is that he was transparent about his own dark nights of the soul. Read the story of his temptation in the wilderness following his baptism, and you see his struggles against the Adversary, who would have him become a lesser Messiah, carrying out his mission on earth in a way devised and defined by him. For Jesus to sweat through those forty days was grueling, but the fruit of the wrestling was a clear and focused sense of what kind of Messiah he was to be and a mission statement that he read in the synagogue when he returned home.

The difficulties Jesus had with the religious establishment are all in print. Nothing is hidden. Nothing is sugar-coated, including the long, hard night he had in Gethsemane when his suffering was so great that it was as if he sweat drops of blood.

How must it have felt to him for his closest friends to go to sleep while he wrestled with his fate? How terrible must it have been when Judas betrayed him and he was arrested and tortured through Peter's betrayal of him, the trials, the beatings, and ultimately the crucifixion.

There are many things we can glean from Jesus' suffering and struggles, and one of the most riveting to ponder is his transparency and vulnerability in his most terrible hours.

To call our sufferings by their precise names, to tell the truth about our feelings about our sufferings, and to allow ourselves to be seen and known in our suffering without having to hide behind euphemisms and platitudes is a healthy response to life's hard times.

Jesus did not run from the inevitable events. He faced them head-on, and the closer he got to the crucifixion, it seems, the more vulnerable he was.

Jesus was on that cross, as a criminal, and yet that is not the end of the story.

I love the interpretation of the cross event that says that the human Jesus had to die in order for the living Christ to be born, for that is something I can take into my own sorrows and dark nights. Whenever I face something straightforwardly and honestly, I am allowing something in myself to die—an old dream, a relationship, a time in my life, an old way of being in the world that is no longer serving me—and if I have loved that particular person, place, time, or thing, I suffer when I let go of it.

However, when I am finally able to let go of that which I have loved, there is finally room for new life to come forth. The longer I live, the more I am aware that at some point, the big lesson in life is that life is about letting go and then letting go some more.

I have long felt that Jesus' cry from the cross—"My God, why have you forsaken me?"—was not an expression of the absence of God. Instead, Jesus' cry was *evidence* of the presence of God, the Father, with him.

I have written about the sacred act of forgiveness in other books, but during this last year I learned something new about the process of coming to forgiveness when it seems that the hurt or the offense is too great to release.

There have been times I have wanted to forgive, but the hurt continued to come between myself and the act. There have been times when the hurt has been so great that I haven't wanted to forgive, seemingly thinking at some level that holding onto it somehow prevented me from being hurt by that person again.

At other times I've said the words of forgiveness too quickly, before I have had time to process the pain of it all. I've said those words too soon either because I've been so scared I would lose the relationship that I wanted to hurry up and get to forgiveness so that we could put the whole thing behind us and move on or because I've thought that that was what "a good Christian" should and must do.

From the cross, the human Jesus taught us a great lesson about forgiveness. In his agony, he must have looked down at the crowd with unbearable sorrow, not only for his own separation from the people and mission he had loved, but also because he knew that what they had done to him was a far greater violence inflicted on themselves than on him.

Any time we abuse another person, we perpetuate a cycle of hate: we hate the other person for letting us do it, and we hate ourselves for doing it. If we allow another person to inflict violence on us (and by extension on themselves), we are participants in a cycle of hate. Be clear that I am not blaming victims for being abused; instead, by identifying their position in the cycle of hate (hating the abuser for the abuse, hating themselves that it happened) victims can be empowered to take steps to change that role and to stop the cycle.

Jesus, full of sorrow and pain, prayed for those who had done this heinous deed, "Father, forgive them," essentially handing over to God the ultimate task of forgiving those who had betrayed and convicted him, tortured and beaten him, crucified and mocked him.

There have been times in my life when I could not let go of a hurt that had cut deep into my heart. No matter how many times I prayed for the grace to forgive, the hurt still lingered, festering and tormenting me.

There have been times I have prayed, "I want to forgive, but I cannot forgive. Please help me," and that prayer has helped me.

However, when I can hand over to God the task of forgiving, something happens that is like release and relief. I know forgiveness is God's will, and I know that God has more practice at it than I have and is far better at it than I am.

Somehow, giving God my pain and surrendering the forgiveness part to him frees me in a way that nothing else does. "Forgive them for me" has an unusual way of helping me move toward forgiveness.

There is one more aspect of Jesus' surrender that has eased me through some difficult times with people who have hurt me, and times when I have hurt others. Jesus also said, when he asked his Father to forgive the ones who had stripped him of his work and brought to a halt his mission on earth, "for they don't know what they are doing."

Carl Jung said that *unconsciousness* is a sin. Think about it, and remember how many times you have said or have heard another person say, "If I had *known* what was going on, I wouldn't have done that!" or "If only I had *known* what would happen, I wouldn't have done it!"

Being unconscious keeps you from knowing what another person is feeling, thinking, wanting, or doing.

Being unconscious prevents you from seeing the consequences of your actions.

Being unconscious thwarts your awareness of what is important, what is going on, perceiving nuances in communication, behavior, and circumstances.

Being unconscious keeps you infantile, gullible, and "guileless," all of which leave you open to being a participant in evil.

All of the world's great spiritual traditions define spirituality as "waking up, and then waking up some more."

Jesus forgave the thieves on the cross. Their sin was clear, and they were direct about it. The sin of unconsciousness of the enormity of their act was such that Jesus asked the Father to forgive them.

What a terrible thing it must have been to have awakened the day after the crucifixion or the week after to the realization that you had participated in the crucifixion of Jesus.

Forgiveness is one of the costliest parts of love, and most of us, at one time or another, have to look into the eyes of someone we love deeply and say, "I am so sorry. Please forgive me." And most of us, if we live long enough and authentically enough, have the opportunity of looking into the eyes of someone who has betrayed us or hurt us and saying, "I forgive you. Now let's learn a new way of being together."

Forgiveness is one of the rarest expressions of love, but perhaps it doesn't lose its force if it is used more freely. Perhaps forgiveness helps love grow stronger and more valuable.

Getting Personal

1. When was the last time you held a grudge for a long time? What effect did that have on you? What secondary gain did you get from hanging on to that grudge?
2. When was the last time you asked someone to forgive you? What was the result?
3. What is the hardest thing you have ever had to forgive?
4. Who needs your forgiveness?
5. What is the difference in forgiving and excusing?
6. Why is it necessary to change the dynamics in the relationship as part of the forgiveness process? What will happen if you don't change them?
7. Is there anything in your life today that is unforgiven and is like a piece of gristle, never going away? What might happen if you asked God first for forgiveness? What would happen if you accepted his forgiveness?

Growing Edges

When I was first introduced to the Twelve Steps of Alcoholics Anonymous by a friend who was in Al-Anon, I was especially drawn to the Fourth, Fifth, and Sixth Steps as a practical way of making things right between people who had harmed each other.

The idea of making a thorough moral inventory of my actions and feelings that had caused problems in the past appealed to me. My sponsor guided me to make an inventory of my strengths as well, and then she gently encouraged me to confess my sinful actions to God and to another person, and she taught me the appropriate ways to make amends to the people. I saw the whole process as liberating, and as I began, I prayed for the wisdom to see myself with courage and with clarity.

Admittedly, I found the idea of the process to be more engaging than the actual carrying out of it, but as my sponsor led me step by step, the benefit of confession was liberating and healing. In fact, I have said on many occasions that if I were running the world, I would provide a way within the churches for people to have access to this kind of process.

> *In your love you kept me from the pit of destruction; you have put all my sins behind your back.*
> Isaiah 38:17b

Perhaps if each of us confessed our own sins to another person and heard the words "You are forgiven; now go and sin no more," we might not have such a backlog of sins that we project onto each other and onto the bad guys in the world.

As I worked the Twelve Steps and since I was so enamored and helped by the Twelve Steps, as a codependent, I thought others would gladly receive my explanation of "the program" and join me in the process of recovery. I was wrong. In fact, some of the people in my life didn't really even want to know that I had found those steps, and they most certainly didn't want me announcing to the world that I was working a recovery program for whatever that strange disease—codependency—was.

Like my friend and mentor Keith Miller, I thought that everyone could benefit from the program, and in my zeal I probably turned off more people than I enticed into working the Twelve Steps. Later, I would realize that my need to have everyone do what I was doing was not only childish, but it actually was the manifestation of codependency and the need to control.

Over a long time, then, I dealt with a broken relationship that, no matter what I did, I could not repair, until finally there was an opening between myself and that person that was large enough for the fresh breezes of mercy and grace to blow through, sweeping out the cobwebs of resentment and bitterness.

I had thought we would have to have a *long talk* for forgiveness to work itself out between us. I had assumed each of us would have to own our part of the problem, and I had imagined that there would be crying for all the hurt each of us had inflicted on the other.

I was wrong again.

Forgiveness came about through the mercy and grace of God and perhaps because I had finally had to hand over the problem to God and allow God to work it out.

"It isn't as if the past didn't happen," I told my spiritual director.

"It did happen, and it was hurtful beyond belief, but somehow, now, it is as if the past has lost its death-grip on us."

We forgive, I hear, not to change the past, but to change the present and the future.

We forgive so that God's *hesed—his unfailing love for all of us—* has room to move in and among us, between us and for us.

Interlude

I wrote the confession and absolution below as part of a worship service designed around the theme of reconciliation. It appears in "Worship Service," *Women in the Bible*, Christian Reflection: A Series in Faith and Ethics 47 (Waco: The Institute for Faith and Learning at Baylor University, 2013) 64. Used by permission.

Confession

God of creation, we know that we are made in your image, male and female, and yet we acknowledge that we have too often failed to honor the dignity of each other.

Lord, have mercy.

We confess that we have confined and constrained each other by holding each other to small roles and identities, based on gender.
Lord have mercy on us.

We confess that we have given disrespect to each other. We have labeled each other, and we have treated each other as stereotypes.
Lord, have mercy on us.

We confess that we have valued one gender over another—either by cultural conditioning, habit, bias, or prejudice. We have sinned against each other by carelessness, ignorance, or willful intent.
Lord, have mercy.

We confess that we have turned blind eyes to the abuse, the slander, the flippant insult or the blatant disdain of one gender by the other.
Lord, have mercy.

We confess that we have not honored the mystery of those who are different from us.
We confess that we have closed our minds and our hearts to each other.
We confess that we have used each other for our own gain.
We confess that we have punished each other for not fulfilling our expectations of the other.
We confess that we have, instead of loving each other, tried to change and control each other.
We confess that instead of loving each other, we have feared each other.
Lord, have mercy.

We acknowledge that where love is lacking, power and control rule.
We know that where power and control rule, love dies.
Forgive us and help us, Lord, we pray.

Pastoral Absolution
May the God who created each of you

have mercy on you and forgive you of your sins.
May God heal the separations between you
and restore the fragmented, alienated parts of your lives.
May the God of love who made you in his image
grant you pardon, give you deep peace
and uncommon love for each other.

Silence
The LORD your God is with you, he is mighty to save.
He will take great delight in you, he will quiet you with his love,
he will rejoice over you with thanksgiving.
Zephaniah 3:17

Chapter 8

Song Sung Blue

Periodically, a new version of "What do you see?" goes around on the Internet. A current version depicts what appears to be half the face of a young man, but then, suddenly, the image appears to be the profile of that same young man. If you ask "Which is it?" you must be willing to answer "both." In these tricky images, the viewer must be willing to accept that the image is both/and instead of either/or.

In my process of depth analysis, I learned early on that "ten things can be true at the same time" and that "perception is everything." What I "see" from my position and perspective is one point of view, but it is only one, and while that is frustrating for my ego-self that insists on being right, it can be liberating and even life-saving. Certainly, allowing more than one way to look at a situation can save a relationship.

When it comes to the big problems in my life, learning to broaden my perspective, see from another point of view, and even change my mind has been comparable to taking the chains off the situation as well as my mind. Being willing to expand my thinking and open my heart frees me to problem-solve with greater flexibility.

The model of working with openness seems to reflect God's love for us, for over and over God's spirit is required to work in the messes we make, the detours we take, and the barriers we put up, even between ourselves and God. When the Bible declares that God's mercy is as far as east is from west and that his love for us is faithful, unending, and constant, then I have to factor in the possibility that one thing that never changes about God is his flexibility in dealing with us!

So it is that when I come to another problem, one that I have created or one that has been thrust on me by the actions of another person, I find it helpful to ask myself some hard questions such as these that follow. I ask the question "What if?" in order to engage the imagination.

What if the problems we have in relationships, either with God or with others, are invitations to grow up and deepen our capacity for love—giving it and receiving it?

What if we could begin to see the mistakes we make in relationships as opportunities to make corrections? What if those mistakes are *not* death-blows to the relationship? What if they are *not* permanent scars? What if those mistakes did *not* become the weapons we use against each other?

What if there is something within us that engineers challenges for us in our life of faith in God to help us grow to the next level of faith? What if we, like Hosea, choose big challenges, albeit unconsciously, so that we can discern more clearly?

What if our biggest failures in life are the necessary stepping-stones to a richer, more rewarding life?

Is it possible that there are times in our lives and in our ongoing maturing process when God allows us to experience heartache and loss, not to punish us, but to help us grow?

Please note the language of that last question. I did not say that God *causes* us to experience heartache and loss; I wrote that God *allows* it. Again and again, I return to one of my foundational Scriptures that forms a basic tenet in my belief system: *in the midst of our pain and anguish, God is at work, attempting to work for good, even in the biggest messes and failures of our lives* (see Rom 8:28).

After we have railed against our pain or our problem, after we have wept and mourned our losses, after we have come out of the shock of a tragedy, and after the feelings of anguish or anger, grief or

---

I fled Him, down the nights and down the days;
I fled Him, down the arches of the years.
I fled him, down the labyrinthine ways
Of my own mind;
and in the midst of tears I hid from him.

Francis Thompson, *The Hound of Heaven*

despair, or any other feeling that accompanies a painful experience, then it is possible to begin to open our minds and our hearts so that we can look for the ways God may be at work in the midst of our suffering.

My affirmation of faith is that God does reveal himself to us, if we are willing to be open to his work. My life experience is that comfort, answers, directions, solutions, and other resources do come at the right time, if we are willing to receive them. If I cannot or do not see where God is at work, then my response is to wait, and in the fullness of time, God shows up.

The True Self/*imago dei* that is within each one of us has the assignment of helping us mature and grow. That part of us (call it the soul, the God-within, Christ-in-you) is the drive, impulse, energy that is creative, transformative, and regenerative. As I imagine that place where God dwells within me, the image of the vine and the branches the Gospel writer portrays in John 15 comes to my mind, reminding me of the intimate connection between the human soul and God.

Taking the view suggested in those "what if?" questions above changes the way we experience our failures and our flaws, our mistakes and our losses. If life is a lifelong school in loving, then whatever happens can be surrendered to God for him to turn that which is broken into something useful.

The tender words of Barbra Streisand's "Leading with Your Heart" remind me of the risk it is for any of us to keep opening our hearts to life and to love, yet I have learned that when it comes to big issues in my life, my heart can be counted on, most of the time, to be trustworthy: "Believe your heart, trusting that it knows, as the dark of night will always find the light of day. Listening with your heart you will hear it say, leading with your heart you will find your way."

Of course, it is the romantic in me that loves that song and loves the idea that we can trust our hearts to guide us. If you won't take Streisand as an authority on such matters of the heart, consider what C. S. Lewis said: "The heart never takes the place of the head, but it can, and should, obey it."

The street wisdom is that "hurt people hurt other people" and that "we use our wounds as weapons." My life experience has proven those simple commentaries to be accurate.

With the change of focus that includes the truth that God is at work in all things, my belief is that God is loving enough to take our deepest wounds and, performing his healing work, turn them into medicine that can heal someone else. If brokenness is inevitable, and it seems to be, then my belief is that that is the very place God does his best work.

Songwriter and poet Leonard Cohen says it perfectly in the beautiful "Anthem": "Ring the bells that still can ring. Forget your perfect offering. There's a crack in everything. That's how the light gets in."

The Bible is not a record of perfect saints or pure and undefiled characters. In fact, if you're looking for sinless perfection in any of the great heroes of the faith, you'll have to develop selective vision.

The stories of the patriarchs and their families are fraught with deceit and lying, manipulation, and seemingly endless ways of using other people as objects to satisfy one's desire for greed, power, and control. How often people have looked to the men and women in the Bible for guidance on raising children and staying married, only to find one dysfunctional family after another.

Through the years I have heard people try to win elections touting "Bible-based family values." I have heard people declare that theirs is a "Christ-centered marriage" or a "Christian marriage," and while I might have one idea of what that means, I have learned to ask people who use those terms to tell me. Sometimes I discover that the person has not really thought about what that means, but the words sound good or comforting. Sometimes in the Christian community it seems to me that we use the jargon of our particular group in order to fit in. I've learned to be sensitive to those who may not know the jargon.

I've also learned to pay attention when my jargon or "God-talk" offends or alienates someone else.

If it is true that you can tell how sophisticated a culture is by how many words it has for something, how is it possible that we have only one word for *love*?

Native tribes in the far north of Canada and Alaska use about fifty words to refer to snow and ice, and in Sanskrit, I am told, there are more than seventy words for love, including the love of a teacher for his students and the love of students for a teacher.

Jungian analyst and Episcopal priest Pittman McGehee, author of *The Paradox of Love*, writes about how limited we are in discussing love since we have only one word. He laments the impossibility of understanding the psychology of love and coming up with words that are adequate to talk about love. McGehee defines *eros* as "a non-rational desire to connect, relate or create." *Eros* is what draws us to particular people, and it draws us to places, areas of interest, and even to God. It is the "spark" of attraction, the fire that can either enflame us with passion or consume us with its power. McGehee writes that "Jung believed that Eros may be the kind of energy or power that creates new consciousness."

> The demands which the difficult work of love makes upon our development are more than life-size, and as beginners we are not up to them.
> — Rainer Maria Rilke

In other words, *eros* draws us toward new experiences, awakening us to broader perspectives and to new revelations, knowledge, and inspiration. If that is true, then it is *eros* that draws us to particular people and relationships and perhaps even challenges that have the power to transform us. Jung said, "The meeting of two personalities is like the contact of two chemical substances; if there is any reaction, both are transformed."

We seem to be drawn by an invisible force to people who have something to teach us about ourselves, life, and love.

It was also Jung who said that "everything that irritates us about others can lead us to a better understanding of ourselves," reminding us of the power of projection. Could it be that the very problems we experience with other people contain an invitation to look at ourselves more closely, to wake up to some of our own immature or self-defeating ways, to become more fully conscious of our own motivations and behaviors that keep us distant from others? Is it possible that our greatest conflicts with loved ones or strangers provide us a way of becoming more aware of our own broken and wounded parts, bringing them into the light so that they can be healed?

Recently, I experienced an extremely painful leg and back injury. A friend, probably weary of watching me limp, sent me to her yoga teacher. Convinced that she could help me, my friend kept pushing until finally, when I was sick and tired of hurting, I consented. I never dreamed how much I would learn from this masterful teacher.

One of the first things Ann Hyde taught me was that "we don't cure pain with pain," and so I have been learning important lessons about patience with pain and with what seems to me to be a painfully long process of healing. In that process, Ann is teaching me about incremental steps in change and in healing. What I wanted was instant relief from the pain; what she has shown me is the power in careful, attentive practice over time. Tiny gains add up over time, and now tiny gains thrill me.

One of the most important things Ann has taught me is the power in the breath, that mysterious life-giving and life-revealing force within us. Breathing into the place where the pain is, being conscious of deepening both the exhale and the inhale, has opened my mind to a resource I had, at best, taken for granted. Mostly, I had ignored the power of breath.

In the same way, we have the capacity to be aware of the painful parts of our lives, and then consciously, intentionally, and repetitively, we can direct love to the very places where we are constricted and in conflict. Focusing on the love of God, we can be conduits of God's love to the people and situations that are causing us the most pain, thereby becoming instruments of peace and love in those situations.

Philia is the Greek word that represents the love of friends for each other, or what is called "brotherly love," indicating the kind of love about which one would say, "I love him like a brother." I am curious about how it was that the city of Philadelphia, "the city of brotherly love," came to be named such. William Penn named it, supposedly, because he wanted it to be a town of religious tolerance. Also, he bought the land for a fair price from Native Americans, with whom he wanted to live in peace. Penn must have understood the power and blessing of love among friends enough to bestow that designation on a new city.

In a previous book, *Dance Lessons: Moving to the Beat of God's Heart*, I emphasize the possibility of friendship as one of my most valued spiritual practices. I do believe that we are changed by the people with whom we enter into friendship, and I know for sure that my friends are an essential part of my soul's well-being. I take seriously the care and nurture of my friendships because I know that they are vital to my life, and I hope that the love I have for my friends is vital, nourishing, and refreshing to them.

Such a thought about the value of friendships reminds me of my mother's caution to use care in choosing one's friends. She sometimes irritated me about her standards, but she was far wiser than I was in understanding that friends affect us deeply. It is an unfortunate truth that there are relationships that are toxic and even can be life-threatening, especially to young, naïve, and vulnerable adolescents.

According to McGehee, there are those who see *agape* only as God's selfless love for us, citing writer and Swedish theologian Anders Nygren, who said that *agape* is not a natural possibility for humans. McGehee disagrees, holding the idea that *agape* is a possibility for humans, especially when it is defined and experienced as "the love that lets be." It is the love that allows the other person to be who she is in the moment, without attempting to coerce, manipulate, overpower, or change her. It is the love that accepts a person as she is, which, in my experience, is one of the essential factors in the person's transformation.

The image that comes to my mind when I think of this kind of love is that of the womb, where the life that begins at conception grows, changes, and develops at its own pace. Of course, there are things that go wrong in that womb, but that is not the point. The point is that the container of the womb is the place where the fetus can reach its potential, following its own trajectory. McGehee writes, "The greatest love God can have for me is not to have a plan, but to let me be and become."

> *We're all like sheep who've wandered off and gotten lost. We've all done our own thing, gone our own way. And God has piled all our sins, everything we've done wrong on him.*
>
> Isaiah 53:6

It is of no small import that the room in which depth analysis takes place and the dynamic that occurs between an analyst and an analysis is called a *container*. In Jungian practice that container is called a "temenos." What I have experienced in that process is the paradox of the transformative energy of *agape* love. As I have been allowed to be however I am in the moment, somehow that allowing—the letting be—has empowered me to access the energies for change and transformation within myself. I am fascinated by the truth of Carl Jung's view that we cannot change anything unless we accept it. Jung says, "Condemnation does not liberate; it oppresses."

I've been on both ends of that condemning stick. I've borne the brunt of criticism, and I've given it, a fact that makes me ashamed, but thanks be to God, I am learning the truth of Jung's wisdom. Acceptance, patience, mercy, and grace are far more effective change agents than criticism, judgment, or condemnation and more accurate mirrors and expressions of God's *agape* love.

Through the years, I have sought counsel from spiritual directors, friends, teachers, family members, therapists, and analysts along the way, but the advice, counsel, and teachings that have had the most effect in lasting change for me have come as *suggestions*, giving me the dignity and respect of grappling with them and deciding for myself if they fit the process of growth that I believe is orchestrated, designed, and guided by the spirit of God, operating through that True Self within me. The suggestions that come with a wagging finger, a shaming tone, or a judgmental or punitive threat may cause me to do any number of things to avoid censure or punishment, but they don't work very well in creating a desire in me to make life-changing choices.

"The love that lets be," far from being an indifferent stance or a "whatever" attitude, is like the rain and sun, necessary nurturance, on my weak or withered spirit. As I see it, we are God's instruments. We are God's hands and feet, his arms, and his conduits of love. We humans, reflecting the image of God, have the capacity and capability to be channels of his blessings to others. I tremble when I consider what might happen if individual, local churches might consider extending *agape* love to each other as a mission statement.

Gordon Cosby, founding pastor of the Church of the Savior in Washington, DC, writes about *agape* love. I have contemplated each sentence deeply, longing to integrate the truth of Cosby's words into my heart and hoping that what is in my heart will be manifested outwardly in acts of love. Consider his words:

> Agape love is the power to love the unlovable. It is the power to love people we do not like. Jesus commands us to love our enemies in order to be like God. We are not told to love in order to win our enemies or to get results, but that we may be children of God, who sends the rain on the just and the unjust, who looks after both the good and the evil. The predominant characteristic of this agape love is that, no matter what a person is like, God seeks nothing but his or her highest good.[1]

"Why is it," I asked my husband, "that people often treat each other so badly within the life of a church?"

I admit that my life has been unusual, for I have spent it all within the context of the minister's home, as the daughter of one minister and the wife of another.

"I like the idea of church better than the reality of it," a minister told me. "It sounds good on paper, but working it out in daily life is *hard*."

What if we within the church, the body of Christ on earth, began taking as our one objective the tasks of learning how to love each other with *agape* love?

What if we within our individual communities of faith began to see ourselves as instruments of peace and love to each other within the community first, and then to those we encounter in our daily life?

I understand that we have been given the great commission, as it is called, with our mandate to go to the corners of the earth with the gospel, but there is a cry from the church for us to practice the other teachings Jesus gave us, including his great commandments to love God, our neighbor, and ourselves.

I know a lot about the inner dynamics of church life, yet I continue to hold on to the vision of the healing, transformative, maturing, redemptive instrument "church" can be, just as I hold to the vision of what marriage and all our other relationships can be. I may not be as romantic or idealistic as I was when I left Baylor University as a graduate, longing to "drink life to the dregs," but perhaps my idealism is better, tempered with realism and practicality by a life lived in long-term relationships with friends, family, and the church.

The biblical model for relationships is so much more than "one man and one woman for life." Isn't it about loving each other with *agape* love that accepts and allows each other to be and become who each one is? What did Jesus do, but enter into people's lives, accepting them as they were, but also healing them in ways that would set them free to live more fully into who they were intended to be?

We are transformed the most by connecting soul-to-soul, honoring the *imago dei* in each person, valuing and respecting the uniqueness of the other, and allowing each other the freedom to think and feel what each person thinks and feels. It seems to me that what Jesus modeled in his closer relationships was deep respect, mutuality and reciprocity, vulnerability, and honesty.

People flocked to Jesus because they felt safe with him, and doesn't love foster that safe container where people are safe from any form or taint of emotional, physical, sexual, spiritual, or intellectual abuse, overpowerment, or ridicule?

Love flourishes when people feel valued and heard, seen and validated. Love's opposite, whether it is the cold killing of indifference or the suffocating fumes of power and control, destroys the relationship and the people who cannot or will not break the insidious and often hidden dynamics of toxic patterns.

Love flourishes when it is possible for people to make mistakes without being condemned for life, where people are allowed to grapple with their character defects without being labeled as "the black sheep," "the problem," or "the addict," and where people don't think it is a sign of weakness to say "I was wrong" and "I am sorry." Love flourishes when forgiveness is taken seriously and practiced often, for we all need the healing waters of grace and mercy.

> *Be energetic in your life of salvation, reverent and sensitive before God. That energy is God's energy, an energy deep within you, God himself willing and working at what will give him the most pleasure.*
>
> Philippians 2:12-13,
> (*The Message*)

Love flourishes when we delight in each other, when we give thanks for the gift each is to our lives, and when we, by lighting up with joy when we see each other, spark the flame of life in others, just by being glad to see them.

When my friends or family members have a birthday, I always say, "I am so glad you were born," and then add, "and I am glad I get to share life with you."

It's a blessing I give; admittedly, it is a blessing I crave.

Love is hard work, but it is the very mistakes we make, the losses we suffer, the failures we endure that can be the places where the spirit of God, whose name is Love, can do his best work in us, for us, and through us.

I am touched by the story of Henri Nouwen, one of the most influential people in the area of spirituality in my life and in the lives of countless others. Nouwen wrote that he often delivered lectures to hundreds of people who came up to him by the throngs, telling him how much they had learned from him and been inspired by him. He described how people would pour out their appreciation to him, but how often no one would ask him to go for coffee afterwards. He said that he would go back to his room, alone, and weep because he was so lonely.

Aren't we all, at some level and at particular times, that lonely?

Aren't we all in need of someone who can simply be there for us?

And aren't we all less lonely when we reach out and touch someone else, being an instrument of God's great love merely by being present, available, attentive, and accepting?

Growing Edges

It took me some time to understand what Pittman McGehee meant when he lectured about *agape love* as *the love that lets be*. That felt too much like apathy to me. I had also heard him taught about *detachment* in relationships, and that concept really took me some time to understand. *Detachment* sounded too much like *indifference.*

Over time, however, a light began to come on in my mind, usually around a relationship in which I was holding on too much or trying to get another person to do what I wanted, all out of "love," you understand.

Enmeshment describes a relationship that is too close, too codependent, and perhaps even smothering. *Enabling* is a term that describes behaviors that help another person stay stuck in self-destructive patterns. Much has been written about these patterns and the problem of *symbiosis*, a condition in which both people "benefit" from the close relationship, though perhaps not in a healthy way. Symbiosis is a connection formed out of need; at first, the need-attraction may be satisfying, but eventually a relationship based on need only brews a toxic mix.

Khalil Gibran counseled about relationships, "Let there be spaces in your togetherness," and that wisdom fits with the practices of agape love and detachment. Agape love, then, is one of the highest forms of love in that it sets the loved one free to be who she is and do what she was sent here to do. In fact, in that willingness to set the other free is a profound belief in that person and a blessing of the person's individuality and gifts.

In agape love, there is no using of the other for your own benefit. Everyone's needs matter. In agape love, the art of detachment allows each person to solve his own problems and carry his own responsibilities without interference from the other. Neither letting the other be nor detachment is about apathy or indifference, but it comes from the higher place of respect for the other's choices and actions. Even God lets us solve our own problems, which is sometimes the opposite of what I want. Sometimes I want him to wave a magic wand over my problem and repair it instantly.

Jesus taught a beautiful lesson about love when he said to Mary Magdalene when he appeared to her after the resurrection, "Don't cling to me." It is often our nature to want to cling to those we love, to hold them to us, which may hold them back. We want to protect our loved ones from hurt and harm, and often what we do is protect them from the opportunity to solve their own problems.

It is natural, more for some of us than others, to be overly involved and overly invested in what rightfully belongs to the other person, thus the slogan of Twelve Step groups: *Mind your own business.* Love, however, is a lifetime of learning the delicate art of letting go. It is also the high art and skill of minding your own business.

Note

1. The original source for this passage has since been lost, but it is widely believed to have come from a sermon Crosby gave at the Church of the Savior in Washington, DC.

Chapter 9

Life's Big Secret

If there is anything on earth that will expose your flaws, your self-centeredness, and self-concern more than attempting to love another person, I don't know what it is.

I stood at the altar with Martus Miley and vowed my love for him for the rest of my life. At twenty-two, I had no idea about what that would mean or that loving him would expose such flaws in my own character.

Most likely, my ideas about loving him were shaped by the Hollywood fairy tales and my adolescent yearnings for romance. To further complicate things, I am confident that I had an idea of how he would love me, meet my needs, and carry me over the thresholds of one grand adventure after another. Later, when we led marriage enrichment events, it all came out that he expected a combination of Betty Crocker, Raquel Welch, and Florence Nightingale.

I thought my heart would burst with love as we welcomed each of our three daughters into our lives. I loved them so much, in fact, that it scared me, and yet parenting, like marriage, introduced me to fears I didn't know I had, weaknesses, fatigue, impatience, and self-doubt.

If I had known how hard it was to love, I'm not sure I would have had the courage to set out on the journey. Thanks be to God, I took the risk and the chance.

Part of the problem in loving, I've learned, is in reconciling the ideal and my expectations with reality. Another big part has been giving up my childish ideas of love and taking on the challenge of love that is self-giving instead of self-seeking, gift-love instead of need-love, and real love instead of the crazy love of codependency.

When I was a child, there were a few Scriptures that gave me a lot of trouble. One of them seemed to show up every year on the "Memory Verse Card" handed out in Vacation Bible School. I cannot adequately describe the pressure I felt trying to live up to it, and since I could not do it, I was doomed from the beginning. That Scripture is found in Matthew 5:48, and the version I memorized struck terror in my young mind and heart: "Be perfect, therefore, as your heavenly Father is perfect."

That the words were printed in red indicates that they were spoken by Jesus, and if they were spoken by Jesus, they had even more power to my child's mind. Unfortunately, my understanding of "perfection" was more a reflection of the social mores, prejudices, and biases of my parents, my Sunday school teachers, and my peers than what Jesus taught! I was to learn the hard way that every person who quoted that Scripture had her own idea of what "perfection" was.

> In a word, what I'm saying is, "Grow up. You're kingdom subjects. Now live like it. Live out your God-created identity. Live generously and graciously toward others, the way God lives toward you."
>
> Matthew 5:48
> (*The Message*)

Through the years of my childhood and adolescence, I could make two responses to those words, which I interpreted as a commandment. I could either ignore them as an impossibility, or I could spend my life trying to achieve perfection, which actually was all about external perfection, eternal striving, and always falling short of whatever idea I had of what it meant to be a perfect daughter, a perfect Christian, and then, later, a perfect wife and a perfect mother. Frankly, it was exhausting, but it also forced me to compartmentalize my everyday life apart from my life with God.

Most of all, I wanted to love "perfectly." I wanted my relationships to be "perfect," and I worked hard at that, thinking that my efforts and my yearnings would make happen what was in my head as a picture of what "perfect love" meant.

However, I was not left in that straitjacket of striving for perfection. Early in my adulthood, I heard Keith Miller speak about how Jesus set out to place the ideal, perhaps even Don Quixote's "impossible dream," like stars in the sky to guide us on the journey. Grace, he said, is always available for us along the way, for no one of us can perfectly fulfill the grand vision Jesus had for our lives.

At the same time, I heard my husband teach a lesson on this troubling verse, using the Greek to beam a light on this verse and in our collective darkness of misunderstanding. Apparently, the original language has movement and process in it when it is more accurately translated as "be on the way toward becoming." Furthermore, the word for "perfect" is best understood as "whole," so the verse actually is more accurately rendered as "be on the journey of becoming whole."

I still remember the relief I felt when I was liberated by that understanding of the language. Finally, with my new understanding of the real meaning of that verse, I could unshackle myself from the past and move into the mercy and grace of the journey.

Today, Eugene Peterson's rendition of the verse from *The Message*, printed at the first of this chapter, makes even more sense to me. Becoming and growing up indicate movement, change, transformation, and I think that is what Jesus was about.

However the words of Jesus filtered through to my child's mind, I must grapple with them as an adult, especially if I am going to consider myself a "follower of Christ."

As a follower of Christ, however frail and fumbling I may be, I am living out my faith within the context of a large, richly textured heritage of the Judeo-Christian faith and the speckled, checkered history of "the church" of Jesus Christ.

That Jesus gave us his greatest commandments to love God, our neighbor, and ourselves is foundational in this journey of faith, and those commandments are grounded in an understanding of John's naming of God as *Love*.

Moving out of the brief overview of God's love recounted in the Old Testament and into the teachings of love found in the New Testament, I am reminded that it is God's faithful, persistent, unconditional (*fierce*) love that is the main "story line" of the Old Testament and, in fact, the entire Bible. This *is* an account of God's pursuing love for his people, and that love is the scarlet thread of redemption; it is God's trying to woo his people back to his heart and buy them back from lesser gods that is the love story that informs my faith.

The Bible is indeed a love story after all.

One of the biblical concepts I love most is the concept of "the fullness of time," a concept that speaks to my impatient nature over and over when I am trying to force things to happen, manipulate things according to my timetable, and coerce others into fitting in to my story of how things should be.

I've had a hard time learning to wait on God, and I've complained that while he is never late, he has missed many opportunities to be early! That, I admit, is my impatience and my immaturity that insist that things happen at my speed. I've been frustrated more than once that he works on his own timetable, bringing events together at just the right time.

God, on the other hand, seems to have a larger, wider, and more thorough grasp of the whole of things, and that is understood best in the incarnation. When the people of God were ready, which means that when they had exhausted their resources, tried all their plans, and had come up short, Jesus was born to be the best picture of God humankind has ever seen.

> *I know of no other means to reach perfection than by love. To love: how perfectly our hearts are made for this!*
>
> Therese of Lisieux

When what God was trying to reveal about his nature through the priests, the prophets, and the kings didn't accomplish what he wanted, *in the fullness of time*, God came in the man named Jesus to show all people who he was and what he wanted to do. The human

Jesus lived, then, as a rabbi, having a human experience and revealing the nature of God, whose name is Love.

Jesus taught love, and he exhibited love. He acted toward others with the kind of love that healed, transformed, liberated, and empowered people, and then he left us with this challenge to love each other as he had loved those entrusted to his care while he was having his human journey. His message was simple but profound. It was simple but not easy, and it was that we were to love God and each other fully and passionately.

> Love is the first ingredient in the relief of suffering.
> Padre Pio

The church, the body of Christ on earth, has been trying to figure out what it means to be a follower of Christ for over 2,000 years, but I fear we still struggle to accept the secret of that message Jesus entrusted to us: "Love the Lord your God with all your heart and with all your soul and with all your mind. This is the first and greatest commandment. And the second is like it: Love your neighbor as yourself. All the Law and the Prophets hang on these two commandments" (Matt 22:37-40).

Throughout my life, my group of Christians has stumbled and faltered over the secret of life and the challenge of faith. Some have tried to make church all about being good enough, behaving well enough, and following the rules fervently enough to get us into heaven when we die. Some have tried to make it only about meeting human needs, which is hugely important but misses the important piece about loving God first.

Others have tried to exclude various parts of humankind from the fellowship of the church, and still others have made church all about being an entertainment complex, when the truth of the matter is that the one thing Jesus asked us to do that he himself counted as "the greatest commandment" is love.

It's that simple, but it's actually so hard, so impossible to measure and calculate, and, frankly, so scary that we prefer our lesser ways to the hard way that leads to fullness of life.

Love *is* the narrow way, and it is the way of wholeness, health, salvation, and the abundant life. Love really is the answer. It is the cure. It is the secret of life in the kingdom of God.

Here is what I believe with all my heart: If I can surrender to this power called love, open my mind and heart to it, and be willing to risk that love really is the secret of life, I will find these things:

(1) My own wounds of a lifetime can be healed.
(2) The chains of my own making—or perhaps those I collected growing up—can be broken.
(3) My spiritual vision can be restored so that I can see life and myself and others more clearly, and so that I can see the handiwork of God more often.
(4) My relationships will change dramatically, to be life-giving to everyone.
(5) My purpose for living will be made clearer, and I will see what I do as a gift of love to God and for others.
(6) The problems and burdens I cannot repair or remove from my life will be lightened when lived and carried with love.
(7) The sorrows of my life will be consoled with love, often in mysterious ways and often through human instruments.
(8) Life itself will become richer with meaning, experienced through the filters of love.

I could go on and on, but you get the picture. Love changes everything, and mostly it changes the people who are willing to surrender to its power and risk becoming lovers of God and lovers of each other.

The words of songwriter-singer Leonard Cohen often make me catch my breath, and I always want everyone to hear his music and love his work as much as I do. In his song "Come Healing," I hear words that resonate with my experience of having tried and failed in loving. It is a penitential hymn, actually, that acknowledges the failures of our mistakes, and its theme is similar to the hymn "Softly and

Tenderly," which my group of Christians often sang at the end of a service as what we called an "invitation" hymn.

Cohen invites healing to the mind and body, the spirit and the limb, to the "gates of mercy," admitting that none of us is worthy of the healing or the grace, a truth that reminds me always that God loves and God forgives not because of who we are or what we have or have not done, but because it is his nature to love and forgive.

"Come Healing" riveted me to its melody and words from the beginning, and I've pondered every line in my heart over and over. Leonard Cohen isn't from my religious tradition exactly, but somehow his words resonate with my understanding of love that transcends religious and cultural lines. When he sings these words, I know exactly what he is talking about: "O solitude of longing, where love has been confined . . . Come healing of the body, come healing of the mind." As I reflect on my own life and the barriers and obstacles that still remain, I see that I have confined love behind walls of fear.

> *The LORD your God is in your midst, a mighty one who will save; he will rejoice over you with gladness; he will quiet you by his love.*
>
> Zephaniah 3:17

When I observe the broken relationships around me, I yearn for the longing for love to be met by love that is liberated from the prisons of mistakes and failures of love. When I look at the church, the larger entity of the body of Christ, and shudder at the brokenness within individual groups who are attempting to follow Christ, I long for the love of Christ to be set free so that there can and will be a healing of "the body."

And so I am brought to my knees over and over to pray, "Come, Lord Jesus, do for us what we cannot do for ourselves. Free us from our fears so that we can be healed with your love, body, mind, spirit, and limb.

What might happen if we could get over ourselves enough to collaborate freely and fully with God and his passionate love for us?

Getting Personal

1. What is the scariest thing to you about loving another person?
2. Do you block others' love for you? If so, how do you do that? How do you think that makes the other person feel?
3. In your personal history, who was it that taught you the lesson about love that has most profoundly shaped your life? Was that lesson liberating or constricting?
4. What keeps you from being spontaneous in loving others?
5. What keeps you from being generous in loving others?
6. Do you know when you are enabling someone and when you are loving?
7. How do you feel when someone tries to control or manipulate you in the name of love?
8. If loving is one of the ways we express our image of God, what do your habits of loving reveal about your God-image?

Growing Edges

For over twenty years, I have gone back to Bishop Mike Pfeifer's counsel to me when I first met with him for spiritual direction. What I did not know at the time was that he was giving me one of the keys to the kingdom of God, here on earth, now.

If I had known how powerful his suggestion was, I might have been too scared of it, or my ego might have seized control of the very idea of sitting before God for twenty minutes once or twice each day and just loving him. I might have gotten pompous about knowing one of the secrets of the kingdom life.

On the other hand, my ego might have whispered or yelled in my ear that what Bishop Mike was suggesting to me was way too simple for me. After all, I had been in church all my life. I could handle bigger, harder, more complex and difficult assignments for the spiritual life than that simple—deceptively simple—practice.

Bishop Mike was always on point in his counsel. Always, his guidance was direct and simple, and in its simplicity it was life-changing.

I had no way of knowing at first that Bishop Mike was tapping into a powerful principle of life: when you give something to another, you are giving to yourself. Loving God—mindfully, thoughtfully and intentionally—sets in motion the principle of reciprocity. There was no way I could love God without being loved by God in return.

By giving me a simple exercise, Bishop Mike also respected the common human difficulty of making changes. He must have known that if you try to change a behavior too fast, the ego gets scared and will likely find a way to sabotage your efforts.

Looking back, I stand in amazement at the way that simple practice has built a reservoir of love somewhere deep in me, a reservoir that, when tended by the practice, never runs out because its source is God himself.

> *When one does not love too much, one does not love enough.*
>
> Blaise Pascal

Keep it simple, another slogan from the Twelve Step program, comes from that same wisdom that teaches that it is the simple things—the mustard seed, the yeast, the smallest step—that has the potential to grow into something powerful.

Bishop Mike taught me in that moment how to do what Jesus asked in John 15. Quietly, gently, he gave me the first step in learning how to abide in Christ and remain in his love.

Chapter 10

Jesus' Mandate: Love YourSelf

It's a small thing, I suppose, when people begin a sentence with "Me and James are going somewhere," but it annoys me. I shouldn't let the small stuff bother me, but truly "me and him" is like fingers scraping down a chalkboard. (Remember those?)

The first problem, of course, is that "me" cannot be used as a subject of a sentence. It should be "I." The second problem with this construction is that my parents and my English teachers always explained that one puts *the other person* first when constructing a sentence. "James and I went" was drilled into me from early on in my education, so much so that I almost wince when someone, especially an adult, begins his sentence with "Me."

I'm sure I may be pressing a point to suggest that such language is symptomatic of a shift in the culture of the "Me" generation, but every time I hear that grammatical error, I'm reminded of the groundbreaking book *The Culture of Narcissism*, by Christopher Lasch.

More recently, author Sam Vaknin has contributed to the understanding of narcissism in his acclaimed book *Malignant Self-Love: Narcissism Revisited*. Vaknin's theory is that those with narcissistic personality disorder have lost their true self and are identified only with the false self, the roles, the image they present to the public.

It is no wonder that author and Jungian analyst Dr. James Hollis calls narcissism "a suffering of the soul."

"We all have some narcissism when we are children, " Hollis said in a lecture at the Jung Center in Houston, "but we do hope to grow out of it!" We laughed, weakly, but then Hollis grew more serious.

"Unfortunately," he said, "American religion with its emphasis on fundamentalism and entertainment religion not only does not address this suffering of the soul, but it colludes with it."

This isn't a chapter about narcissism. It isn't about egocentricity, egotism, self-absorption, or self-centeredness, but I have discovered that when I write or speak about the love of oneself, I have been challenged to define just what it is I mean and how the authentic love for oneself is to be differentiated from self-indulgence or any of the other personality or character disturbances mentioned above.

This chapter also isn't about the current emphasis on self-compassion, though it is time for that valid spiritual practice to be brought before our consciousness.

I'm not writing about "claiming your power," "finding your bliss," or "speaking your truth." I'm not writing about building self-esteem either, but I am writing about one of the most important concepts Jesus taught, the love of one's self.

As followers of Christ and as human beings, we may be comfortable with the idea and practice of loving God and loving one's neighbor, but we stumble on the other part of Jesus' commandment, loving oneself.

Growing up, I heard a lot about the "soul" of a person, and so I had no trouble expanding my childhood understanding of "soul" when I participated in a Yokefellow spiritual growth group, the content of which emphasized accessing "the kingdom within."

> *When we keep claiming the light, we will find ourselves becoming more and more radiant.*
>
> Henri Nouwen,
> *Life of the Beloved*

In our Yokefellow group processes, we were made aware of the work of Dr. Carl Jung, who is largely responsible for the development of the idea of the false self, also called the ego self or the small self, and the True Self, capitalized to indicate its importance.

When I first heard Jung's theory explained, I knew that what I was hearing had the potential to be life changing for me. Our leader taught us about that which we present to the world, the ego self, and the True Self, the part of us that is hidden within, like the great treasure lying in a field that Jesus used as a figure of speech.

Through years of attending classes in Jungian psychology, doing extensive depth analysis, practicing Centering Prayer, and reading countless books, I have come to an understanding that is, amazingly, consistent with what I learned as a little child, growing up in my parents' home: *There is a reality at the core of every person, and you can call it the soul, the True Self, or the imago dei.*

I understand well that when I teach about the True Self in retreats, workshops, and classes, I am speaking to a group of people or a particular demographic, most of whom are inclined to be either aware of or open to the reality of this inner realm. Normally, people with whom I speak are people who are neither resistant nor hostile to nor ignorant of the reality of spirituality. For the most part, people with whom I converse are either wanting to experience their own spirituality, seeking to believe, overcoming bad religious training, or hoping to find spiritual answers to hard questions.

My experience is that when I talk of the True Self that is at the core of every person, a quiet reverence settles over the group. No one argues with the idea that there is something in us that I call the *imago dei*, the image of God, and people are instantly accepting of the idea of the sacred nature of our lives, by virtue of the fact that there is this part of us where we dwell with God and God dwells with us.

Sadly, though, many people jump to the conclusion that the True Self is the part of oneself that must be kept hidden. People conclude that it is the "bad self," the part that, if made known, would be rejected, criticized, or shunned by others.

"If people really knew me like I am," I've heard people say on many occasions, "they wouldn't like me any longer."

This chapter is about authentic love for one's True Self, the Self that God made, and as I teach this concept and write about it, I stand in reverence and awe before the reality of that spark of divinity within each of us. I seek, therefore, to "fan the flame" of love for that part of us that is eternal, the inner being or "place" within that Thomas Keating calls the "secret room of prayer."

> *Let your light shine.*
> Matthew 5:16

I believe that when we sing the children's song "This little light of mine," we are singing about the True Self that is at the heart of every human being.

While all the Gospel writers refer both to the kingdom of God and the kingdom of heaven, it is Luke who locates the kingdom as an inner reality. "The kingdom of God *is within*," he writes (Luke 17:21b).

Jungian analyst and author John Sanford writes in his classic book *The Kingdom Within*, "The kingdom was not something coming upon man from outside of himself, but was a reality within himself, the very foundation of his personal existence, and something which could be experienced by the individual" ([New York: HarperOne, 2009] 42).

The very concept of an inner kingdom had to have been shocking to the ears of the people of Jesus' day who were looking for a Messiah to set up an earthly kingdom with a king and potentates and positions for the followers of the Messiah in the halls of power. Perhaps that concept is just as shocking to some of my contemporaries who keep insisting on the same kind of power-based structure where there is a hierarchy of importance one must hustle to get in, in order to be "in the kingdom of God."

Sanford continues:

> When we find and realize the kingdom in ourselves, we experience a growing wholeness, an increasing sense of the meaning of our individual personality, a realization of new and creative energies, and an expanding consciousness. . . . The kingdom involves the realization of our personalities according to the inner plan, established within us by God; hence the unfolding of a Self which predates and transcends the ego. (42)

So just what is it that Jesus means when he says that we are to love our neighbor as we do ourselves? How does that fit in with the JOY rule I learned as a child, a rule that insisted I put Jesus first, others second, and myself last?

Why have we emphasized loving others first, to the exclusion of loving our own "wild and precious lives," as Mary Oliver so poignantly refers to our uniqueness, our individual souls?

And could someone please tell me why I cannot remember a single sermon, in my long life in a minister's home, about how it is that we follow that teaching of Jesus and appropriately love our own lives?

How is it that the appropriate, healthy, and *scriptural* interpretation and application of those few words in Jesus' great commandment slip by us so easily?

Why aren't our children being taught, from an early age, what Self-love really is, in a way that is age-appropriate?

Love of the Self, as Jesus taught us, is the love of the True Self, the innermost design and the imago dei.

Loving Self is not about polishing up our outer image. It isn't about working to build up our confidence or pump ourselves up with a false affection. It is about a deep, holy reverence of the soul within. Loving the Self is caring for the person that God created, supporting that True Self so that each of us becomes what we are intended to be and does in life what is consistent with who we are.

What I know for sure, from my life experience and from deep conviction, is that this True Self within us is like an inner GPS, invested with the tasks of generating life for the individual, from the inside out. The True Self is about integrating, creating, and connecting. It is the Self within us that generates growth and transformation. It is the Self that pushes us toward maturing and autonomy.

> *If I make you light-bearers, you don't think I'm going to hide you under a bucket, do you? I'm putting you on a light stand. Now that I've put you there on a hilltop, on a light stand—shine!*
>
> Matthew 5:14-16
> (*The Message*)

- The True Self is mystery, and it creates mystery.
- The True Self is "Christ in us, the hope of glory" (Col 1:27).
- Connecting with the True Self is a matter of becoming conscious, and it is the key to a meaningful life.
- To connect with the Self-within is to connect with God-within.

- To "abide in Christ" as he abides in you is to participate in a life-changing mystery; it is to be faithful to that which is holy within you.
- To connect with the Self is to connect to the Source of Life, the power source.
- To connect with the Self is to be connected to unconditional love that is within the inner well of your being.
- To love your Self and to connect with it is to partner with God. It is to commit to becoming who you are created to be. It is to discover and do what you were sent here to do and to fulfill the purpose that is in the design of your life.

These "mysteries" must be some of the keys of the kingdom to which Jesus referred, although he never outlined them in a formal way.

In his last class taught at the Jung Center in Houston, before moving away from the city, Pittman McGehee said, "The Self loves you—all of you, including the ego, the shadow, and the complexes." McGehee's statement introduced a life-changing concept that has the power to liberate and empower us from the defects, flaws, and burdens of our lives.

I lived for a long time thinking that God only loved the cleaned and polished-up parts of my life, the parts that were suitable for public viewing, and the parts that were very religious. What a shock to learn that God loves my phoniness, my falseness, and my pretenses, my faults and my failures and my deepest, darkest secrets that I try to hide even from myself. In fact, if you read the Gospels carefully, it may be those very parts—the outcast, the leprous, the fallen—that the living Christ loves most.

What he said in psychological terms, and uniquely in the language of Carl Jung, is the same as saying that God loves you. It locates God within, in the flesh-and-blood "temple" that Paul speaks about in Romans 6:19 when he says, "Do you not know that your body is a temple of the Holy Spirit, who is in you?"

I do not understand God as a glorified male figure, sitting "up there" in some heavenly place, nor can I understand God as "the man upstairs." Instead, my concept of God is grounded in a belief that

God is everywhere and that God dwells within me. God also dwells within my neighbor and the people I may not like; whether those people know that God is dwelling within them, I do not know, but what I do know is that the locus of God in the individual belief system determines the relationship with God.

Believing that God is far away affects how you live your life.

Believing that God is near and within you also affects how you live your life.

McGehee continued, "Agape love is Self-to-Self (as opposed to ego-to-ego, role-to-role, mask-to-mask), and when we are loving another Self-to-Self, we are loving God."

To many, these words are radical.

To those of us sitting in that classroom, they were gospel, good news.

I'm wondering if adequate loving of oneself might be the antidote or cure for many of the ills that plague relationships, including the addiction to "putting others first" and caretaking that our culture knows as "codependency."

It was shocking and humiliating to me as an adult to learn that my people-pleasing was not about loving other people, but it was an attempt to get them to love me, approve of me, or at the very least, not disapprove of, criticize, or judge me!

How troubling it was to learn to differentiate between caretaking and caregiving. It was hard for me to admit that sometimes my caretaking of others was actually a way of taking care of myself. Unconsciously, I believed that if I took care of others' needs well enough, surely they would return the "love" I had lavishly given and love me back in the same way. What I thought was concern for others was motivated by a concern for myself.

The key to understanding this sneaky little problem is to tell the unflinching truth about your motivation. When helping others, ask, "Just what is it I'm trying to get out of this?"

You know you have been trying to take care of yourself by putting others' needs ahead of your own when you're frustrated that you don't seem to be getting what you need. You may feel others are taking advantage of you or don't appreciate all you have done for them.

What a hard awakening it was to admit to myself that much of my caretaking of others' feelings was to protect myself. How liberating it is to learn how to give authentic, loving care to others in ways that met their authentic needs and still protected my boundaries and limitations. How challenging it still is to sift and sort through "what's mine" and "what's yours" to know when I am actually helping someone and when I am enabling them to stay stuck in their self-limiting and self-destructive patterns!

How hard it was, and still is, to wake up and change the focus of my "loving" from codependent patterns, which included living through other people, expecting others to generate life for me or do for me what I should and could be doing for myself, and worst of all, masking my true feelings, stifling my valid needs and desires, and putting on a variety of masks in order to be acceptable and accepting.

I have learned the hard way that codependency reflects a tendency to be overly identified with a particular role, image, or ego-position in life, thereby creating a kind of hypocrisy, and that all smacks of "it's all about me" narcissism.

I have had to make lots of amends about this, in order to change, and as it is often said in recovery groups, "I'm not where I want to be, but thanks be to God, I'm not where I was." Life is about progress, not perfection.

The fact is that all of these ego-based ways of relating to people are enemies of authenticity and integrity, and sometimes they may even look like hypocrisy. Scratch below the surface of those dysfunctions and you see not authentic love, but a gaping chasm of need, a bottomless pit of dependencies on someone out there to fill the hole with an endless supply of "love."

Jesus' love for others was liberating love, and not consuming, possessive substitutes of this holy fire that can change lives.

Jesus' love for others changed them not because he tried to control or manipulate them and not because he wielded power over them, but because he healed them where they were sick or afflicted. Jesus transformed their lives from a limited place to one of expansion and usefulness. He liberated them from all kinds of prisons, both inner and outer, and he empowered people to become who they were intended to be and to do what they were intended to do.

Indeed, it is in holding each other close with open arms that provides enough space for love to flourish and grow, as well as to nourish and replenish each other. Each person, then, can participate in the health and well-being, the growth and maturing into wholeness of the other person, whether the other is a soulmate, a spouse, a relative, or a friend, a fellow companion on the spiritual path within an organized church or in a one-on-one relationship, as the individual takes responsibility for his own soulwork.

> *Let there be spaces in your togetherness.*
> Kahlil Gibran, *The Prophet*

I believe that loving oneself begins by waking up, becoming conscious, and making choices that support the growth and health of one's own True Self.

What did Jesus mean about loving ourselves? What would that look like? I believe that if we love ourselves as we love our neighbors, we would . . .

- Love God with all our hearts, minds, and souls, as a starting place.
- Seek that primary relationship with him, first, in that kingdom that is within.
- Care fully and appropriately for ourselves.
- Model healthy compassion for our limitations, our mistakes, our wounds.
- Take seriously the call to live the life we have been made to live.

- Take seriously the gifts and talents invested in us—and the purpose for which they were given to us.
- Be a good steward of our gifts and talents and both the development of them and the use of them.
- Set good boundaries with other people.
- Encourage others to connect with the True Self/soul/*imago dei* within them.
- Guard our hearts with all diligence, becoming emotionally intelligent and responsible for how we manage our emotions.
- Learn what it means to live the kingdom life from Jesus' teachings and example.
- Be intentional in finding the specific treatment plan for any childhood wound we have.
- Take responsibility for the "toxic waste dump" of baggage that is within us so that we don't act it out, take it out, or project what is in us on others.
- Learn to love our fate—the factors that were given to us at birth that have shaped us.
- Free ourselves from the control, manipulation, and power of people or systems that keep us bound in any way.
- Recover from our own addictions, whether to religious systems, other people, behaviors, or substances.
- Relieve ourselves from the unrealistic expectations we place on others and others place on us.
- Commit to being fully alive for all of our lives.
- Accept our limitations, whatever they are, realistically and with grace.
- Learn how to let go of obsessive needs to have, be, or consume anything or anyone.
- Dare to live authentically—and be more than a role, a person. or image, a small self.
- Take responsibility for our own choices.
- Give up blaming others for our predicaments or choices.
- Assume responsibility for our own personal power and never give it away.

- Be a good manager of the particular problems we have.
- The list could go on—you might add to it.

My sisters were fourteen and eighteen when I was born, so I grew up without the benefit of having some of my rough edges smoothed down or away in the ordinary and, I assume, natural and necessary tussle of sibling interactions. (That is a euphemism for "fights.")

One day, one of my grandchildren yelled out at his sibling, "You are not the boss of me!"

I could hardly contain my amusement, and though I was about to intervene to settle whatever argument was taking place, I decided that those two siblings could jolly well work it out themselves. Perhaps I don't need to add that my (in)action was one way of freeing them to love each other as they learned how to duke it out on their terms.

> *Baby you're missing something in the air*
> *I got a name but it don't matter*
> *What's going on, it's cold in here*
> *You have a life but it's torn and tattered*
>
> Elton John

I've had to learn who "the boss of me" really is. Ultimately, of course, it is God.

On most days, on the playing fields of my life, I do better when I take full authority of my life, seeking first the kingdom of God within where, if I listen, the still, small voice of God will nudge me in the right direction.

I do better allowing God to be the boss of me and accepting that I can partner with God as long as I let God lead as I take responsibility for living my "one wild and precious life."

It is a sacred task, learning how to love mySelf, the Self that is made in the very image of God.

Getting Personal

1. How does self-reflection feel to you? Is it a valuable process, or does it stir up memories or feelings you'd rather keep buried?

2. Are you aware when you cross from self-care to self-indulgence? How does that feel?
3. How do you feel about the way God made you?
4. Are you able to say "The Father is very fond of me" and mean it?
5. What did you learn about loving yourself when you were a child?
6. How are self-respect and self-love connected?
7. If you could really love, honor, respect, and care for your True Self, what might change in your life?
8. Is it possible to keep only two parts of Jesus' great commandment, loving God and loving others, and ignore the part about loving oneself?
9. A simple directive helps me put my priorities straight when it comes to love, and it is this: *Worship God. Love people. Use things. In that order.*

I am assuming that "loving people" includes the love of your own Self. What kinds of problems would following this directive prevent?

(I have explored more of the ego and Self concept in my books *Joint Venture: Practical Spirituality for Everyday Pilgrims* and *Dance Lessons: Moving to the Beat of God's Heart*.)

Growing Edges

On that beautiful spring day as I was completing this book, I paused in my writing and looked out the window at the lush green of my lawn and shrubs, the thick green leaves on the tree that has grown higher than the second-story window of my study, and the clear, blue sky.

What I really wanted to do was abandon my project for a moment and head for the outdoors, but with a deadline ahead of me, I decided to stay at my desk and finish this chapter. I had puzzled for a long time about what it meant to "love oneself," especially in the context of all of Jesus' teachings.

Suddenly, like a gentle awakening, I saw that to love oneself is to honor and respect the original design of my life, the design fashioned by God, the part of my life I've learned to call the *True Self*.

To love myself would be to try to have "the mind of Christ" toward who I am, at my core, to attempt to see myself, not as others see me and want me to be, but as Christ might see me. I think that begins with seeing who my natural self is, which includes my temperament, my strengths and weaknesses, my abilities and my limitations. Perhaps loving myself is what Paul means when he calls us to come to a "sober estimate of ourselves," a point of view that is clear-eyed and honest.

Because I am capable of highly advanced self-delusion, the work I have spent in analysis has not been mere "navel-gazing." Instead, it has been an exercise in serious study of how God made me so that I can spend my life in alignment with God's idea of who I am to be and what I am to do instead of taking off, blindfolded and unconscious, down a road paved by others' expectations.

As I sat there, looking out at God's masterpiece in my backyard, it felt as if I had entered a holy place in which the veil between my understanding and the heart of God was momentarily lifted. It felt, as well, as if more of the scales had fallen from my eyes and I could see meaning and purpose in my history as never before.

And then the wonder of another reality swept over me when I understood at a deeper level that authentic love of another person is the love of that person's True Self as well. With that thought, I understood what Pittman McGehee was talking about when he lectured about meeting soul to soul and the mystery of the True Self's love for the True Self of another.

> *It's a sure thing: you will love others as you love yourself.*
> — Pittman McGehee

I don't fully understand the practice of Centering Prayer that is so much a part of my life, but I do know that when I sit in the silence, consenting to the presence and action of God, who dwells within, I am connecting with the very source of life and love, the one I choose to call God, and in that connection, I love God and God loves me.

Whether I "feel" something or not in that sacred time, I know that my consent to God's love matters. Whether a particular "sit" has immediate results or not, I trust that in the silent and unseen exchange of love, I am loving God and loving myself.

And when I leave my sacred room and go out into the world, I can better love whatever neighbor I meet in the world because I have taken the time to receive God's love.

How God appropriates that love is an amazing thing to see.

Chapter 11

Out of the Shadows, Into the Light

I like the idea of loving my True Self. I like the idea of loving the True Self in other people as well, and I love to think about how beautiful it is when people connect with each other, soul to soul, True Self to True Self. Surely that is what heaven on earth and probably beyond is all about.

It's the false self, the contrived self—my ego self—that gives me trouble.

Sometimes my ego self tries to talk me out of loving myself. In fact, my ego self loves the status quo so much that it can convince me that the lies that defeat and discourage me are the truth.

In Jesus' temptation experience in the wilderness after his baptism, the Adversary tested him mightily. My ego self operates very much like that Adversary who kept coming at Jesus with alternate ways Jesus could carry out his mission. The True Self/the soul is ruthless in accomplishing its purpose, though, and the Adversary was no match for Jesus' identity or his mission. The Adversary has an easier time with most of us humans.

Each of us has our own reasons for giving in to the temptations to go the easier way, to take the quick fix or the simple solution. Each of us is susceptible to those forces that would discourage us or make us choose that which would soothe the ego instead of that which would fulfill our purpose in life.

It is meaningful to me to know the struggle Jesus had in his temptation experience (recorded in Matthew 4, as well as in Mark and Luke). Whether the Adversary that went after Jesus right after his baptism was an external voice or whether this was an inner battle necessary for the human Jesus to know his calling clearly and fully doesn't matter as much to me as the fact that Jesus lets us in on his struggle to define his mission.

The ego loves predictability, sameness, and familiarity. It loves comfort and the status quo, and the ego's biggest problem and grand delusion is that it thinks it is the center of our psyches. Thus, the term *egocentricity* helps me understand what we mean when we say someone "has an ego." The Adversary's temptations for Jesus would have made Jesus fit right in with the status quo of his culture. Having an ego is necessary for getting around in the world. It is what gets us to work and keeps us paying our bills, doing our jobs, etc.

The True Self, however, is the part of us that is primary. It is God-within, operating through the uniqueness of the personality, temperament, and gifts and strengths. It is the growth mechanism within us.

The triumph of the True Self is always experienced as a defeat of the ego self.

I like baby Jesus, all cuddled up in the manger. I like sweet Jesus, meek and mild, too. I like the way he taught us to love and the ways he healed people, set them free, and gave them new life. What scares me a bit is the other side of Jesus, the side when he got out of control,

> *Knowing your own darkness is the best method for dealing with the darkness of others.*
> *Everything that irritates us about others can lead us to an understanding of ourselves.*
> *There is no coming to consciousness without pain.*
> *People will do anything, no matter how absurd, in order to avoid facing their own Soul.*
> *One does not become enlightened by imagining figures of light, but by making the darkness conscious.*
>
> Selected quotes from Carl Jung

wildly turning over tables and scattering animals and coins in the temple.

I can spiritualize that scene in the Gospels and make it all okay by telling myself that he was purifying the temple of the bad influences and snarky people who were misusing the temple, his Father's house of prayer.

That scene becomes more personal and pertinent to my life when I imagine that the living Christ/the Divine Therapist, working within my inner life, somehow sets in motion a series of events that is similar to a "cleansing" of my life. Sometimes trouble on the outside or turbulence on the inside indicate that my false gods are being challenged, hurtful belief systems are being shaken loose, and the emotional programming of a lifetime is being transformed. When Paul said that we are to work out our salvation "with fear and trembling," he knew what he was saying.

What scares me too are the "woes" Jesus pronounced on the religious leaders of his day. When I read Matthew 26, I tremble. I've been on the inside of the religious establishment and of church for my whole life. I hate to admit it, but when I read Jesus' indictment of those leaders of his day, I shudder to think of my own hypocrisies. I tremble when I think of the inconsistencies in my own life of faith, and I turn away in fear of facing the parts of myself that are not true or authentic.

Jesus scares me too when he says that for some who call out "Lord, Lord," he will say, "I never knew you!"

I take those Scriptures seriously.

It is true that there are all kinds of "bad people" out there, the crazies out there who will get you. You know where "out there" is, don't you? It's wherever I'm not. It's where you aren't hanging out, right?

I was stunned the first time I heard someone say that whatever any one of us is capable of doing, all of us are. I take that very seriously. There is a Hitler in all of us, I am told, and a Judas. Given the same circumstances at the same time, any of us might be what we most hate in another.

Yet that same Jesus, whose words cut through our defenses in Matthew 26, also counseled his disciples to love each other as they loved their neighbor.

> *Continue to work out your salvation with fear and trembling, for it is God who works in you to will and to act according to his good purpose.*
> Philippians 2:12b-13

What if your neighbor is one of the bad guys? And who is my neighbor, anyway? Could it be that my neighbor is a part of me or my history that causes me pain or embarrassment, shame, or guilt? Is it possible that I am being called to love that part of me that is broken, wounded, and an embarrassment to me and to my family?

The truth is that to go out into the world, planning on loving everyone and everything without the ability to be discerning, set boundaries, and define what love really is and what it is not, is to set yourself up for trouble.

Loving each other as Christ loves us has to be defined and understood. Don't forget that the same Jesus who told his disciples not to judge also told them to "shake the dust from their sandals" when they were not accepted in a particular place.

Following the teachings of Jesus requires good common sense, doesn't it? Somehow, part of the challenge is discerning when to follow which teaching.

Applying the teachings of Jesus in my everyday life gets complicated, frankly, and sometimes it is so hard, I decide it isn't worth it.

The day someone told me that you cannot change anyone but yourself was a most important day. In fact, that nugget of truth changed my thinking forever.

Unfortunately, I've found it harder to put into practice than I ever imagined. Sometimes, failing to change myself has led me to increase my efforts to change others, and so I keep being taken back to that important lesson: Change begins with me, no matter how much I want it to begin and stay with others.

I'll never forget the moment someone told me that I needed to love the part of myself that I had rejected and shunned for a lifetime. It took my breath away to hear that the way to wholeness and healing was to learn how to love my faults, my shadow, my complexes, and the part of myself that gives me the most trouble. I didn't have a clue what that meant or how to do it, but the truth of it kept getting louder and louder in my head until, finally, I had to pay attention.

The world seemed to stand still when someone suggested that I couldn't move forward in my personal transformation until I faced the part of myself that caused the most shame and embarrassment.

"You have to look in the mirror," that brave person said, "and you have to see if what you cannot stand in others is also in you."

Of course, Jesus' saying about not judging others popped into my mind, and of course, I felt ashamed for having judged another person. I may have been right, but I was missing Jesus' point and the point that my guide was trying to make: What you see in another person may be a reflection of your own shadow or defect that you are projecting onto that person—so that you don't have to face it in yourself.

Jesus made it clear: As you judge, you will be judged. It's a hard truth, isn't it? And it's an amazing thing how often we swing right past that truth of Jesus'—a truth that could change relationships forever.

"Your shadow is that part of yourself you don't want to see," yet another brave person said to me. "You need to know your shadow, though, if you're going to be free." Your shadow is the part you work hard to keep down in the basement of your unconsciousness, hoping that "out of sight, out of mind" is a reliable principle.

Unfortunately, what we do not own about ourselves has a way of slipping through the cracks of our defenses the things we say or behaviors that we hope no one sees.

What I refuse to own about my inner life, my attitudes and motivations, my character traits and defects, my behavior and my habits owns me. That which I

> **Make friends with your opponent quickly.**
> Matthew 5:25-26

refuse to accept in myself can be guaranteed to turn up the volume until I finally am willing to see who I really am.

Most of us hide our flaws from others, especially from the people we most want to please. If we can face whatever it is that we are hiding, call it by its real name, uncover the ways it sabotages our relationships and our happiness, we can begin to know what it is to live in grace.

The power of Jesus' great commandment can be unpacked and examined for all of one's life, and it does begin with loving God with all your heart, mind, and soul. I am still learning what it means to love my own life; here is what I learned and experienced in attempting to follow that great commandment so far.

First of all, loving God sets in motion the reciprocal energy of love between God and oneself so that truly loving God and being loved by God become a dynamic movement. In other words, loving God is never a one-way street. The love of God is dynamic, active, life-giving, and in constant motion, and it is laced with mercy, grace, and compassion.

> *Let your enemy be your teacher. . . . In the spiritual life, your enemies are really your friends, and that is not just doubletalk. It is very often true.*
>
> Adapted from Richard Rohr, *Falling Upward*

Secondly, the love of God begins all kinds of processes within a person. Thomas Keating says that Centering Prayer gives God permission to heal the emotional programming of a lifetime at the deepest level—in the shadows, actually, where we cannot see and where the ego cannot impose its imperial ways on the process.

Self-improvement plans are all about the ego taking charge of polishing up the outer self, the ego, to be more acceptable, desirable, marketable, or popular in the outer world. Even some of what we call our spiritual disciplines and our character development can be taken over by the ego's agenda to make us look more Christian and less flawed either in our own eyes or the eyes of the ones we are trying to impress.

If we allow God to work at the unseen level—in the shadowlands, if you will—then God ("the Divine Therapist" says Thomas Keating), will show us the flaws and failures, the sins that separate us from God and others. If we become aware of our own *stuff*, wake up to the responsibility of managing our own defects, are convicted of our own brokenness, God can help us learn how to love our own wild and precious lives.

Who knows? Perhaps removing the plank from our own eyes will help us see with different eyes the splinter that is in another's eyes.

In a lecture at the Jung Center in Houston, Pittman McGehee said about how we see each other, "We are all alike, basically, so it seems that we might have more compassion for each other, doesn't it?"

In another setting, speaking to a group of young priests, McGehee said,

> We all know that you are going to have troublesome people in your parishes. You will have people with personality disorders like narcissism, borderline personality disorder and other disturbing disorders. You will have people who cause you trouble and who are trouble, but when you get up in the morning and look in the mirror, take a close look. You are looking at the person who, for you, is the biggest problem in your parish—unless you become conscious of your own shadow.

The hard part, but the hope, is that when we are looking in the mirror, we are also looking at the one person we can change, if we can let love drive the change.

How does that begin? How can you ever love yourself, as Christ might love you if you were one of his followers? I don't have the answers, but here are some questions that might lead you in the right direction.

Getting Personal

(1) Remember that child in you who didn't feel accepted or loved?
• Whose love did that child need?
• What prevented that child from feeling loved? Take some time every day to recall that child, as if you were the parent, loving that child tenderly. Write a letter to that child, expressing love for that child that is still within you.
• What does the unmet need of the child you were cause you to do now? Imagine ways you, as a loving parent to yourself, can meet that need.

(2) Remember that big mistake you made when you were a teenager?
• Imagine yourself talking as a loving parent to your teenage self, telling that teenager that you love him or her, mistake and all.
• Imagine that the teenager tells you what he's felt about that mistake. Can you listen with compassion?
• Imagine what God would say to that teenager to offer understanding, forgiveness, blessing. What would happen if God released you from the bondage of that mistake and set you free to love yourself?

(3) Bring to mind your biggest faults, character defects, failures, and mistakes.
• Call them what they are, and by their real names. Don't use euphemisms.
• Make a list of the people who are hurt by the things you do, and state exactly how they are hurt. Ask yourself what causes you to keep doing these things. Imagine that God wants to talk to you about these flaws and that his voice and face are full of compassion for you.
• What if God's love, accessed regularly through prayer and meditation, began to transform those flaws? What could be different if you started loving yourself with a renewed sense of compassion?
• How would your life be different if you gave up hurting yourself and others and started loving others the way God loves you?

Here's the catch: We do love others the way *our concept of God* loves us. If our concept of God is that of a punitive, punishing God, we will be punitive and punishing toward others. If our concept of God is that he is an abandoning or distancing God, we will be abandoning and distancing of ourselves and others.

Whatever the God-concept is that we hold, either consciously or unconsciously, it will manifest itself in our relationships with ourselves and others. Whatever our understanding of God's love and God's forgiveness is, that is what we will act out and live out in our daily lives.

"I've come to see that we experience grace the most," McGehee stated in his lecture on love, "when we have been dis-graced." That is biblical, and knowing it is life-changing.

We love to love when it's easy. We love romantic love, when we are all jazzed about the other person. We love a new project or the possibility of a trip.

Some of us love newborns and babies, until they grow up to talk back and act up and take off for parts unknown, to do their own thing.

Love is tested and tried, however, in the hard times when wills collide and needs are left unmet.

"Expectations," a friend told me, "are premeditated resentments."

Indeed, we all have expectations of other people in relationship, whether at home or out in the various arenas of our daily lives. Sometimes having expectations is appropriate, as in a job where performance equals pay or promotion. At other times, when the boundaries are not so clear and defined, we can torture each other with our agendas we expect others to meet.

The truth is that managing our relationships is a full-time job, but fortunately there are countless courses to take, articles and books to read, workshops to attend, and life-enhancing therapies to help us learn how to relate and communicate with each other.

In every relationship, there are issues to work through. Part of the challenge of any relationship is to work through them, however, and not just let them fester and grow out of avoidance or unacknowledged power issues.

Sometimes, too, we are called to tell hard truths to each other. At other times, we go through terrible suffering that calls us to draw on strengths and love we didn't know we had to help a loved one through a bad time. Ultimately, too, we all have to bear love's hard tasks of letting go, either through death, separation, or the simple and difficult reality of geographic distance.

Now and then, we do have to shake the dust from our sandals and move out of a relationship because the dynamics between us are toxic or destructive.

I have quoted Carl Jung countless times, reminding myself and others that "when love is lacking, power and control rush in." My experiences have led me to the painful flip side of that truth: when power and control rule, love dies.

Love dies as well when there is too little attention given to the relationship or to the other person so that indifference and apathy set in. Physical or verbal violence are terrible acts against each other, and the "violence of silence" is a particularly insidious abuse.

All of us bring baggage from the past into the present moment. We either repeat the patterns we learned in childhood or rebel against those patterns. Some of us spend our entire lives trying to repair the damage done by those who, whether out of ignorance or willful intention, wounded us deeply.

There are situations in which continuing to engage with a particular person is life-threatening. There are those who do intend to hurt others, even within the organization we call "church," and it is naive on the part of good-hearted church members to try to deal with certain pathologies with inadequate methods.

In my experience, I have watched people with serious personality disorders do incredible damage within a church, seeking power or seeking attention. I have seen such people manipulate, control, and intimidate others within a church, and I have watched others excuse those behaviors or gloss over them, often simply because it is too hard to tell the truth about what is going on.

I know of a church that had repeated disturbances in their morning worship services (people wandering in from the street and shouting warnings, obscenities, or gibberish). Finally, because one such person disturbed the service repeatedly, a policeman trained to manage public disruptions was called in to guide the members to discern the difference between an unhappy show-off and a disturbed person who might do actual harm to others.

I've heard of studies that attempt to help churches discern the ways people with personality disorders and more difficult pathologies can be recognized. The intent is not to label those people, but to protect the church from being destroyed by the tactics used by those whose intention is to divide the church. Obviously, laypeople cannot diagnose, but behavior patterns that are disruptive and dangerous must be acknowledged and dealt with appropriately.

Calling things by their actual name with discernment and compassion is a way of loving the enemy, whether that enemy is within ourselves or from our outer world. Stopping harmful behaviors or patterns in ourselves or others is a way of loving as Christ loved. Stopping those behaviors can be done better when they are in the beginning stage or when the problems are small; continuing to deny that the problem exists is unloving and even careless for oneself and the larger community.

When we think about horrific events like what happened in a movie theater in Aurora, Colorado, or in an elementary school in Newtown, Connecticut, we have to wonder what might have been different if the young men's problems could have been recognized, acknowledged, and treated? How many lives could we change or save if we have the courage (and resources) to identify and help the people with obvious mental and emotional disorders get the treatment they need?

"I love you enough to let you be mad at me" is one of the most loving things a friend can tell a friend whose behavior is damaging herself, her relationships, and the people around her. The most loving thing we can do for our neighbor and ourselves is to face the darkness that is within us, to confront our character defects with radical honesty and bold courage, and to tell the hard, unvarnished truth about our own evil.

We must face our wrongs, speak the hard, unvarnished truth to ourselves and to others, take responsibility for the violence in our lives, and recognize the ways we cover up our faults. If we can do these things, we take care of our part of the toxic fumes that poison other people, our relationships, and our lives. Think what violence might end in our society when, instead of killing the energy "out there," we helped each other face the enemy within our own lives.

Richard Rohr, in a recent meditation from his website, writes about "Salvation from the False Self" in a series he has called "Shadowboxing." These words are full of grace: "Love holds you tightly and safely and always. It gives you the freedom to meet the enemy and know the major enemy is 'me.' . . . Shadow work literally saves you from yourself (your False Self, that is), which is the foundational meaning of salvation. For then "You too (your True Self) will be revealed in all your glory with him" (Col 3:3-4)."

Growing Edges

When I teach Centering Prayer workshops, I issue a warning in the first session. The practice of Centering Prayer, in which you speak a prayer word that expresses your consent for presence and action of the living Christ/the Divine Therapist to work at the unseen, interior level of your life, can be revolutionary. The practice of Centering Prayer can change your life, set you free, and heal the wounds of a lifetime. Sometimes, believe it or not, we frail humans are not ready for such!

The practice of Centering Prayer, like nothing in my life, has required me to trust a process I am not controlling, to allow God to work without my dictating how and when and in what measure change

> *The more you have cultivated and protected a chosen persona, the more shadow work you will need to do. Conversely, the more you live out of your shadow self, the less capable you are of recognizing the personal you are trying to protect and project. It is like a double blindness keeping you from seeing—and being—your best and deepest self.*
>
> Richard Rohr, adapted from *Falling Upward: A Spirituality for the Two Halves of Life*

will happen, and to let go of the fantasy that I am in charge of the depths of my soulwork.

The practice of Centering Prayer has become one of the most necessary practices of my life, for in it I am able to surrender the biggest battles, my most obstinate attitudes and habits, and allow God to change me from within at his pace.

Centering Prayer has helped me trust God's timing and it has helped me be patient with what feels like an interminable process of change.

Centering Prayer has placed me in a mode of receptivity to God's love and grace as I am instead of the old way I feeling that I had to earn God's approval by working harder and harder.

Centering Prayer has acquainted me in brief, mysterious moments with my True Self, and I have learned to listen for and to the voice of the True Self.

Centering Prayer is a resource that helps me discern the difference in the voice of the Adversary and the voice of the True Self/God, speaking from within.

Centering Prayer also strengthens my connection with the True Self. It builds resources of courage and love so that when I am tested to give in to my ego's whining and to the tyranny of my complexes, I can access those resources. I can draw from that well I cultivated over time to meet the challenge of the moment.

(Other resources necessary for the strengthening of that inner wellspring are the Welcoming Prayer, lectio divina, and the labyrinth. These and other resources are described in my book *Dance Lessons: Moving to the Beat of God's Heart.*)

Chapter 12

Love as Blessing

"Why didn't you write this book first?" my friend Jim Nelson asked me over lunch.

"I had to live first," I responded. My answer didn't satisfy him, however, so he asked me again.

I grew more somber for a moment, thinking more deeply about my response.

"I had to learn what not-love was," I told him, "before I could write about love."

Life has convinced me that choosing to be a person who loves—a lover in the world—is one of the most important decisions of one's life. Is it too much to say that choosing to love is one of the prerequisites if you are going to call yourself a follower of Christ?

Given Jesus' great commandment and his teachings about relationships, I think that committing oneself—giving one's heart to Jesus—means that you are enrolling in a lifetime school of loving. Perhaps being a disciple of Christ is not so much about being good, as it might be defined by our religious culture, as it is about loving deeply and loving well.

Seen through the eyes of that perspective, it is possible to understand Jesus' teachings as the radical, life-giving guidance for daily life that they really are.

> *I am the light of the world. Whoever follows me will never walk in darkness, but will have the light of life.*
>
> John 8:12

Jesus' primary message concerned love, and that message remains. It is a simple message—"love one another as I have loved you"—but it isn't easy.

It is the simple things that can transform our lives.

Following the teachings of Jesus will turn your life upside down because love will force you to the limits of your own self-centeredness and self-concern. Love will expose you to yourself, and it will introduce you, if you let it, to the radical grace and mercy that the living Christ provides in abundance. The choice to be a love-giver in the world is the key to the abundant life, and it begins when you choose to see yourself as a learner about love for the rest of your life.

The great Kenosis passage in Philippians 2 speaks of the humility of Jesus as he "emptied himself" in order to become human and show us the extent of God's love for us. Emptying, for us, is destructive if we interpret it to mean that we are to "become a zero," as some religious teaching has misled us. Emptying isn't about having no will, no opinion, no self and becoming nothing. It is not a degradation of oneself or false modesty.

To the contrary, the emptiness we are called to if we are to love out of gift-love instead of need-love is a yielding to the will of God, whose will for us is that we receive his love for us and then, full of that love, are able to give love. We surrender our small agendas so that we can be filled with God's love for ourselves, for others, for the world.

The love that heals begins with a surrender of one's ego self for the higher purpose of being guided from within by the True Self. This surrender makes it possible to align oneself with the will of love. It is giving up the need to exert power and control over God or others for the sake of love.

We don't empty ourselves to be empty, but we empty ourselves of all that we want to cling to for the purpose of being filled with God's love, purpose, and power.

> *My dear children, let's not just talk about love; let's practice real love. This is the only way we'll know that we're living truly, living in God's reality. It's also the way to shut down debilitating self-criticism, even when there is something to it. For God is greater than our worried hearts and knows more about us than we do ourselves.*
>
> 1 John 3:18-20
> (The Message)

Emptying oneself, surrendering, yielding, and letting go all require humility, and that state of being is necessary if one is going to be filled with God's love and purpose. Because you cannot give what you have not received, it takes a leap of faith to open oneself up to receive what the living Christ has for us instead of what we decide we need.

In this love relationship with God, we don't define the terms, and this is never more true than when we hit the wall in a relationship and don't know what to do next.

We can choose to surrender to God's love, however.

When I use the beautiful account of Jesus' washing of his disciples' feet (John 13), I usually engage participants in a discussion about whether they are more comfortable giving love or receiving it. It is probably no surprise that most people say they prefer to give love. Most people prefer to wash others' feet than to have their own feet washed. Our culture prizes self-reliance and independence, so it is no surprise that most people are uncomfortable being on the receiving end of others' love or care.

When I think of the spiritual practices available for us, it sometimes occurs to me that each one is, figuratively speaking, a way of allowing the living Christ to wash our feet, to nourish us with spiritual food, or to open our blind eyes, heal our wounds, and love us.

Our spiritual practices are not given to us to build some resume of righteousness; instead, they are given to us so we can draw closer to God and cooperate with his work within us. We do it so that we can be filled with God's love and his purpose and power, joy and peace and all the other fruit of the Spirit—rather than greed, pride, avarice, self-will, hate, anger, resentment, bitterness, envy, insecurity, shame, or guilt.

I practice Centering Prayer not to earn points with God and not to control results, but to live more in alignment with Truth, instead of our lies, and Love, instead of not-love.

I consent to the presence of God so that I can experience God's love as a present, near reality. I consent to the action of God within us so that we can be transformed from within.

Opening my mind and heart to the presence and action of Christ-within is a way of allowing the Spirit who dwells within to go to work, doing what needs to be done instead of what I decide I need.

The prevailing rules of engagement for contemporary culture look something like this: Take care of yourself first. Compete and defeat. Don't forgive; get even. Do unto others before they do it to you. Win, whatever it takes. Don't let them see you cry. Watch your back.

Sometimes I am dismayed at how far we have drifted from basic respect for others; using other people—and disposing of them when they are no longer useful to us—seems fairly normal. We manipulate one another as if humans, made in the very image of God, are checkers on a checkerboard.

Why do we do what we do?

Sometimes—perhaps most of the time—we do what we do out of ignorance, laziness, or thoughtlessness. Sometimes we do what we do because it's what we know to do, and if we *knew* better, we'd *do* better. Sometimes we are repeating the past or trying to settle a score from the past as if getting even will assuage the hurt in our hearts.

> Love, love changes everything, how you live and how you die. . . . Love, love changes everything, pain is deeper than before. . . . Love will turn your world around and that world will last forever. Love, love changes everything . . . and Nothing in the world will ever be the same.
>
> Andrew Lloyd Weber

People use others because they believe that they are entitled (due to position, power, prestige, gender, or a simple inflated sense of self) to whatever that person can provide. And there are those among us who have enormous unresolved issues that laypeople do not have the means or the power to address.

We can observe the problems around us and choose hopelessness and despair, thereby joining the ranks of those who choose the lowest common denominator of interaction. Or we can choose, day by day, the Jesus way. It isn't easy, attempting to love like Jesus loved, but the way of self-centeredness and meanness is harder in the long run.

The Jesus way can be seen in the Beatitudes, which are not rules or commandments to follow, but a description of the mindset and heartset of a follower of Jesus. Putting on the lenses of love and seeing the Beatitudes as guidance for living in relationships with each other provide a map for us as we take off down the path of loving each other and ourselves.

Getting Personal

Take a look at the Beatitudes, listed here from *The Message*, by Eugene Peterson, and reflect on the questions that accompany each beatitude.

(1) "You're blessed when you're at the end of your rope. With less of you there is more of God and his rule" (Matt 5:3).
• When have you been shocked/surprised to discover something about a loved one that you didn't know? Did that discovery delight or disappoint you, confuse or mystify you?
• When did you have to admit to yourself or to another that you don't have it all together, you don't know "the answer," and you don't have a clue how to solve a relationship issue with someone you love? How does that feel?
• What is the difference between humility and being humiliated? Which is harder for you?
• Have you ever fallen from grace in your own eyes? Why could that be a good thing?

(2) "You're blessed when you feel you've lost what is most dear to you. Only then can you be embraced by the One most dear to you" (Matt 5:4).

- What if that which is most dear to you is your pride? When has your pride been hurt the most?
- Are you able to feel and express your most tender feelings to the ones you say you love?
- How well are you able to feel empathy and compassion for others? Are you comfortable with others' sorrow and grief, or does it scare you away from them?
- Can you relate to others' feelings of loss, helplessness, despair, and loneliness?
- Do you feel honest remorse and sadness for the ways you have hurt others, or is your focus more on how you've been hurt? Do you know how you have hurt others?

(3) "You're blessed when you're content with just who you are—no more, no less. That's the moment you find yourselves proud owners of everything that can't be bought" (Matt 5:5).

- Are you able to accept yourself as you are, not thinking either too highly of yourself or too little, but coming to a "sober estimate of yourself" (Rom 12:3)?
- Can you be a conduit for agape love, the love that "lets be," accepting another just as he or she is?
- Are you able to collaborate and cooperate with others, or must you always be the leader?
- Do you have a teachable spirit and a mind that is open to others' wisdom and knowledge?
- Do you know how to be interdependent within relationships, balancing both dependence and independence?
- Do you feel you must give up you to be loved by others?
- Do you think, secretly, that others should conform to your image of who you want them to be?
- Do you try to manipulate others to change? Do you ever withhold love in an effort to get a person to do what you want?
- Would others say that you try to make them over in your image?

(4) "You're blessed when you've worked up a good appetite for God. He's food and drink in the best meal you'll ever eat" (Matt 5:6).

- How seriously do you take your responsibility in nurturing and sustaining a vital, personal love relationship with God?
- Do you really place your top priority on your relationship with God?
- Do you idolize others, making them carry the burden of your idolatry, a burden no human should have to bear?
- Do you require that others make you a God-substitute?
- How well do you "abide in Christ"? What does that mean to you? (See John 15.)
- Can you "go the distance" with God, being as faithful to him in hard times as he is faithful to you when you forget all about him?

(5) "You're blessed when you care. At the moment of being 'care-full,' you find yourselves cared for" (Matt 5:7).

- Most translations of this verse speak of being merciful, which may be implicit in the understanding of caring for each other. An attitude of mercy does make one more likely to care for others. In what ways do you extend mercy and care to others? How hard is that for you to do? In what ways have mercy and care come back to you? Did you feel you deserved that?
- What does this beatitude say about the law of reciprocity?
- Why is it important to give mercy and to care for each other?
- Paul wrote to the Christians in Ephesus, "And be kind to one another, tenderhearted, forgiving one another, even as God for Christ's sake has forgiven you" (Eph 4:32 KJV). What would happen if you took that injunction into your most difficult and problematic relationships? What risk would that be for you? What kind of payoff might you have?
- What do you get when you withhold kindness, mercy, and compassion from others?
- One of the worst features of narcissism is that it cripples a person's ability to feel with or care about another human being, and when that happens, people become less than fully human. In the grips of narcissism, a person becomes an automaton, incapable of relating to the needs and concerns, much less the soul, of another human being. Narcissism in any of its forms destroys relationship and kills love.

(6) "You're blessed when you get your inside world—your mind and heart—put right. Then you can see God in the outside world" (Matt 5:8).
• Jesus lived from his own center, from the inside out. He was not controlled by the adulation of others or their outright denial of who he was. To the end, he remained true to who he was and what he was sent here to do; he was clearly the best example of individuation we can find. He knew who he was, and he acted with that inner authority that comes from having his mind and heart in perfect alignment with God.
• In your most awake and aware state of being, you know who you are and what you were sent here to do. How easy is it for you to "be your Self—your True Self"?
• If you are too much controlled by others and allow others' approval or disapproval to affect your sense of well-being or happiness, why is that?
• Who is it you try to change? How is that working for you?
• When was the last time you tried to manipulate someone to do what you wanted?
• How do you react when others try to manipulate you?

(7) "You're blessed when you can show people how to cooperate instead of compete or fight. That's when you discover who you really are, and your place in God's family" (Matt 5:9).
• Where is it most easy for you to cooperate with others, instead of competing or fighting?
• What do you do when you don't get your way?
• Do you get your way in relationships all of the time, none of the time, or most of the time? What is the ideal balance?
• What is the difference between cooperation and concession?
• What skills are necessary for cooperating with others?
• Do you believe God loves the other people in your world as much, more than, less than he loves you?

(8) "You're blessed when your commitment to God provokes persecution. The persecution drives you even deeper into God's kingdom.

Not only that—count yourselves blessed every time people put you down or throw you out or speak lies about you to discredit me. What it means is that the truth is too close for comfort and they are uncomfortable. You can be glad when that happens—give a cheer, even!—for though they don't like it, I do! And all heaven applauds. And know that you are in good company. My prophets and witnesses have always gotten into this kind of trouble" (Matt 5:10-12).

- Beside this beatitude should be printed a warning sign, for its message must be handled with great care, discernment, and wisdom.
- This beatitude does not give wholesale permission to be a martyr, and it is not about being obnoxious with your expressions of faith. It is not about walking around with a chip on your shoulder or an attitude of superiority because you are a Christian and then kicking up a storm and claiming to be persecuted for Jesus.

I believe these words express that if you live the Jesus way, as Eugene Peterson calls authentic discipleship, you will be living counter to the culture whose rules are written at the first of this chapter. It may even mean that you live counter to the norms of the circle of people you love most. You may, in fact, experience criticism and resistance and perhaps even ostracism if you choose to change the dynamics of the interactions of your social, religious, or family groups.

You may be judged as being naive or foolish, but here's the point: This "persecution," however it may present itself, is not intended to be worn as a medal of honor. It is to be seen as an opportunity for you to fall on your knees in humility, to examine your motives at an even deeper level, and to trust more. Perhaps the lack of understanding about who you are and what you are doing may be seen as an invitation to commit more fully to an even more radical level of tolerance, forgiveness, acceptance, and *fierce love*.

This beatitude must be handled with great care and discernment because our egos want us to get

> I hold this to be the highest task of a bond between two people: that each should stand guard over the solitude of the other.
>
> Rainer Maria Rilke

inflated about how mistreated and misunderstood we are. Perversely, we may even get inflated about how persecuted we are, and that is in direct opposition to the Jesus way.

Any resistance or so-called persecution must be seen as an opportunity to examine oneself, and any feedback or criticism should be held in prayer to see if there is any truth in the criticism. Counsel with another person who understands soulwork can illuminate the truth or untruth of the criticism, the fairness or unfairness of hurtful comments.

- In what relationships is it hardest for you to love authentically?
- In what relationships do you feel free to live from the True Self, from the inside out?
- How do you feel when people you love are making attempts to change and grow? Do you impede their growth, or do you encourage and celebrate it?

Growing Edges

"How are you?" I asked a man I hadn't seen in a long time.

"I'm blessed," he responded, and I remembered how he always said that.

I looked deep into his eyes, and what I saw was despair and disappointment in the way his life had gone. The truth was that he knew and I knew that he was trying to keep himself going, one foot in front of the other, declaring that he was blessed. He wanted to believe it, and I wanted his declaration to be true for him.

When I was a child, my father often said, "We are not saved just for our own sake. We are saved in order to serve, and we are blessed in order to be a blessing." The practice of *blessing* in the Bible must not be understood as "You are special." Blessing is not a declaration of entitlement or of privilege, and it was never intended to communicate that "you are more special than others." My friend learned that he could not will himself to feel blessed.

The desire to elevate oneself or another above others, either by natural abilities, achievement, power, or position, is part of our human tendency. The fact is that some *are* brighter, cuter, richer, or more talented or athletic than others. Like it or not, some people are "more equal" than others when it comes to outer world characteristics. Football coach's Barry Switzer's quip that "some people are born on third base and go through life thinking they hit a triple" rings sadly true.

Let's face it: Some of us are born luckier than others, which begs the question for me, "Is it luck, or is it blessing?"

Being born lucky, however, doesn't speak to God's valuing of each of us or his love for all of us. I believe that in the eyes of God, all of us are of equal value.

Blessing, in the history of the Hebrew people, had great significance. Blessing was the passing of empowerment from one person to another. Blessing carried with it the good wishes for the life of the blessed one; the father, the king, the authority figure gave blessing to empower the blessed one to fulfill his or her responsibility in life.

To be blessed, from a biblical perspective, might be synonymous with the language of the New Testament when it is written that someone is "filled with the Holy Spirit," another concept that our egocentricity wants to seize and make over as a statement of someone's super-spirituality.

My ego so wants to be in charge of my spiritual life, but somehow—and I think it is God's mercy at work—I keep being reminded that to be filled with the Holy Spirit means that I am filled with the fruit, the qualities of, the manifestation of God himself: "But the fruit of the Spirit is love, joy, peace, patience, kindness, goodness, faithfulness, gentleness and self-control" (Gal 5:22).

If I am truly blessed, then I am blessed to give what I have received, to pass on the goodness and love of God, to be an instrument of love, joy, and peace where I am.

I might want the salvation of God just for my own personal benefit, but that isn't the gospel message.

I am saved in order to serve.

I am blessed in order to be a blessing.

Chapter 13

Can You Drink This Cup?

The risk and burden of love is, I suppose, what makes people close their hearts or never dare to open them. The great irony is expressed in the words of Padre Pio, "Love is the first ingredient in the relief of suffering," and the poet Rumi's declaration that "love is a jail!"

Whoever has loved deeply knows the irony that life's greatest gift, love, can bring life's greatest ecstasy and joy and life's greatest suffering and burden.

For a lifetime, I've interpreted Jesus' question about "drinking the cup" as his reference to the coming crucifixion, and that interpretation still has meaning to me. In recent years, I've understood his life as an expression of God's love for us and his mission on earth as one of love. The response, then, that Jesus made to the mother who wanted power and position for her boys takes on new meaning with relevance to our own lives and our own attempts to live with love.

Jesus warned the disciples about the cost of following him. He said that following him had to come first and that "no one who puts his hand to the plow and looks back is fit for service in the kingdom of God" (Luke 9:62). Eugene Peterson renders that warning this way in *The Message*: "No procrastination. No backward looks. You can't put God's kingdom off till tomorrow. Seize the day."

Jesus was willing to go the distance because of love, and he wanted to make sure that the disciples didn't take their commitment lightly. In today's language, Jesus asks a follower to be "all in."

I can leave Jesus' life and teachings flat on the pages of my Bible and be unchanged by whatever happened to him, what he said and what he did. On the other hand, I can reflect deeply on his teachings and "ponder them in my heart," as Mary his mother did, and be challenged and changed by them. I can, if I choose, see Jesus' entire work as a curriculum of love.

To integrate the imagery of "drinking the cup" into my inner landscape, I imagine what that image might mean in my daily life and in my relationships. It's easy to understand that Jesus was asking the disciples if they were willing to suffer, but the truth is that on the front end of something big, we may think we know what it is going to be like to suffer. In the midst of paying the cost of something, we may tremble and quake. Consider these possible interpretations of "drinking the cup" for your own life.

> *The hour has come for you to wake up from your slumber.*
> Romans 13:11

(1) *Can you stand to be conscious, fully awake, and fully alive?*
Once Adam and Eve ate the fruit of the tree of knowledge, they awakened to the terrible burden of knowing the difference between good and evil. The price for them was becoming conscious and being burdened with the responsibility of conflicts and choices.

When I began a lengthy process of depth analysis, I desperately wanted instant relief and quick and easy answers for the difficulties of my life. My analyst said two things that seemed, at the time, almost trite. I have reflected on those statements repeatedly, shaking my head at how little I knew about the journey of knowing myself.

"Where do I start?" I asked, sort of innocently and certainly naively.

"Awareness, awareness, awareness," he said.

I had waxed eloquent about how "spirituality is about waking up, and waking up some more" in the past. (Well, maybe it wasn't eloquent. Maybe I was merely repeating what I had read and heard.)

Excited about what I might discover, I jumped eagerly on the invitation to become more aware.

"Buckle your seatbelt," my analyst said to me quietly, and then he added a quiet, simple statement that got my attention. "I don't romanticize the spiritual journey."

He didn't warn me away from the journey. He didn't paint a hard road ahead, but neither did he paint a rosy picture that would have stroked my ego's need to be "conscious" any more than Jesus did when he talked to his disciples about the cost of following him.

Again quoting Carl Jung, he said, "There is no coming to consciousness without pain. People will do almost anything, however absurd, to avoid facing their own soul."

Looking back on the rigorous and painful process of analysis, the goal was to discover and become the True Self that God created me to be and to fulfill my purpose in life, a process Jung called "individuation." However, a major part of that process was discovering where love was blocked, where fear had overtaken love, and to bring those parts of myself that were lurking in the shadows of my unconscious mind into the light.

Carl Jung said, "One does not become enlightened by imagining figures of life, but by making the darkness conscious." The writer of the epistles of John said, "If we claim to have fellowship with God yet walk in the darkness, we lie and do not live by the truth. . . . If we claim to be without sin, we deceive ourselves and the truth is not in us" (1 John 1:6, 8).

Becoming conscious means that you are able to bear the burdens of seeing the truth about your life, telling the truth, and choosing to make changes. Becoming conscious—drinking the cup of consciousness—means that you are willing to face your own demons, your shadow, your flaws, and your defects, neither blaming others for them nor flogging yourself for your mistakes. Owning your dark side is one of the most powerful ways I know of making the transition into the light.

Waking up means waking up to your own "wild and precious life" and accepting responsibility for your gifts and your purpose in life. Becoming conscious can also be about waking up to the power of love. And perhaps that is its most important gift.

(2) *Can you stand to become your own person, to love your one "wild and precious life"?*
All of us arrive at adulthood with adaptations and accommodations to the outer world and to the people who are in our world. It is natural that we spent at least the first half of life cooperating and conforming to others' expectations and to the rules and norms of the particular culture into which we were born and grow up.

There comes a time, however, when the True Self pushes us to become our own person, demand to be heard, accepted, and expressed. To learn to listen to the "still, small voice" of God, speaking through the uniqueness of your own True Self, is both obligation and opportunity, and I have learned that the True Self is relentless in accomplishing its purpose.

We need courage, stamina, and perseverance to respond to the demands of the outer world. Until we begin feeling heavy resentment, we may not be conscious of the weight of the world's expectations. Once I am conscious of the burden, though, I must notice the places and times when I behave out of duty instead of delight, when I please others instead of myself, or when I meet others' needs and neglect my own. I must notice when I feel guilty for thinking for myself and acting with authority from a sense of authenticity.

To individuate doesn't mean that I become individualistic, arrogantly ignoring others and their needs or "doing my thing" to the expense of others. Indeed, to choose to individuate may necessitate a period of adjustment while the old patterns are confronted and changed, and sometimes people resist and push back against the efforts of one person to become free.

I am reminded that Jesus' family went to talk to him about what he was doing. Perhaps they too questioned who he was and what he was trying to do, actions that precipitated Jesus' disturbing words: "Who is my mother, and who are my brothers?"

Pointing to his disciples, Jesus said, "Here are my mother and my brothers, for whoever does the will of my Father in heaven is my brother and sister and mother," forever differentiating for his followers one's family of origin and the family shaped by a common mission.

The model Jesus set for us is one of radical authenticity. He answered first to God, and for us to do that, we must discover what it is that God is speaking to us. First and foremost, I believe, God is urging us to be and become the person he designed us to be.

(3) Can you risk being authentic?
I confess a point of view that is not popular: I dislike school uniforms for children. I admit another prejudice. I protest the "neutralization of America" by the trend toward cars of the same color.

Does anyone still remember that one of the first questions asked by someone who had just purchased a new car was "What color is it?" Remember the rainbow of colors that cars used to be, each revealing a personal preference? Remember pink and black Chevys? I recall a bright yellow MG my brother-in-law had, a maroon car my dad brought home for me to use my senior year in college. I remember when cars came in various shades of blue and green, and now, I love my red car, especially when I'm looking for it in a sea of gray and white, black and taupe in a parking lot.

> *When you are no longer center stage, you can allow others to breathe alongside you; you can appreciate their existence as being equal value to your own. No longer are you the star in your own movie, you can feel a kinship with others that naturally gives rise to a sense of belonging.... Your suffering will not turn you in on yourself; it will turn you outward, to the world.... To suffer with: this is the meaning of compassion.*
>
> Roger Housden,
> *Ten Poems to Open Your Heart*

What is to keep us from becoming so neutralized that we too easily drift into thinking that we must all think alike, act alike, vote alike? Isn't there room for more than one point of view?

My bias against uniforms and beige cars may be unreasonable and irrational, but it's mine, and I love it because it comes from that place that resists the cookie-cutters that little children and adults must fit into in order to be accepted.

I understand that it's easier for parents if their kids wear uniform, but I also know that it is easier for everyone if children behave according to a set standard of expectations. "Fitting in" is the goal. "Not making waves" and "conforming to the norm" make it easier on everyone, but what is to happen to the uniqueness of each person if conforming is the ruling value?

I make my point and hope I'm not getting carried away in service to a deep and abiding belief that the responsibility of each of us is to become the authentic, unique Self that we are created to be. I know how hard it is to do that. I know how easy it is to drift into living the stereotype, becoming your role, your image, or your persona, and hiding all kinds of feelings and desires behind a mask that pleases your outer world. I know how easy it is to live a lie, cut off from the Truth that is within you.

Love dies when it is suffocated by hypocrisy and lies.

Love thrives in authenticity and freedom.

(4) *Can you stand to take authority of your own life?*
The mere mention of the word "authority" scares people, and it certainly scares those whose job it is to keep things calm and predictable. It is *really* hard on those whose job it is to keep others in line and following the rules.

Jesus got in trouble with the keepers of the status quo because he dared to act from his authority, which was God, guiding him from within. In fact, that was the question the scribes and Pharisees often asked him: "By whose authority are you doing these things?" So accustomed were they to being "the authorities" that they could not stand to see a mere carpenter from Nazareth acting with such authority.

To take authority of your own life means that you take responsibility for your strengths and your weaknesses, your choices and the times you didn't choose. It means that you don't blame others for

> O, Love, You are the universal soul, crown and jail, all at once.
> — Rumi

your plight or position in life, but you stand up to the challenge of assuming responsibility for every part of your life.

This isn't to say that you aren't affected by others' choices, but the final freedom for all of us is to say, "This is how I reacted to what he did, and I am responsible for my reactions."

To love honestly and freely requires assuming responsibility for how you love and how you respond to the love you are given, with no excuses, no blaming, and no justifications for why you can't or didn't or won't love those who are in your life.

(5) Can you stand to live with integrity?
Can you stand to give up your power trips, your dishonest manipulations, and your need to control others?

Can you stop playing games about the things that matter most and at least work to have integrity from within so that your words and actions match?

Can you take the risks to live the life that has integrity with your strengths, your weaknesses, your desires, and your longings? Does your life represent your True Self, or are you mired in one of Thoreau's "lives of quiet desperation"? Are you trapped in a life that has no meaning for you because it isn't consistent with who you are?

Can you live with rigorous honesty, starting with telling yourself the truth? When you must keep a secret, can you at least tell yourself the truth about why it is you are doing that?

I have heard James Hollis speak about "the holy lie," the lie that is told to serve a higher purpose. For example, people who gave safety and a hiding place for Jews during World War II often told lies to protect the lives of those they were hiding. A holy lie is one that is told because to tell the truth would do unnecessary harm either to the person who hears it or to another. A holy lie is different from "a little white lie" because it carries life-altering potential and must be told sparingly and with great thought, as well as the willingness to be conscious of what it is you are doing and why you are doing it.

Sometimes a holy lie has the most integrity to it and is the most loving thing to do, but a lifestyle of lies will shred relationships and personal character. Being conscious requires deep thoughtfulness and discernment to know the difference.

(6) Can you drink the cup of faithfulness?
Priest, sociologist, and prolific author Andrew Greeley wrote profoundly about love and intimacy within marriage. In his book *Sexual Intimacy*, Greeley said that faithfulness in marriage is not simply about staying out of another's bed, but that it is more faithfulness to the person and the relationship. It was not about avoidance of affairs, but faithfulness is about giving to the relationship, being for the person, protecting that person's back, encouraging that person's True Self, loving that person toward wholeness.

In his wedding ceremonies, my father always counseled a couple to grow to the place where their primary joy was in giving happiness to the other. That's not a bad goal!

Faithfulness is what makes my family gather for our grandchildren's performances and events, cheering them when they do well and propping them up when they fumble or fail. It is what motivates my cancelling something I'd planned so I can attend a staff dinner with my husband. It is what makes me encourage my children and my friends to risk to make their own dreams come true. Faithfulness means that I show up for those who matter most to me and that I tune in to the things that matter most to them.

Faithfulness means that I am interested in others, and where I can, I give support, encouragement, help, or comfort. It means that I don't abandon my loved ones when things get hard, but that I lean in closer, as I can, to give presence in lonely, scary times.

Faithfulness is *fierce love* in action. It is active and not passive. It is love that is involved in a helping, supportive, healing way, and that is different from codependency.

(7) Can you take risks for the sake of love? Can you drink the cup of knowing and being known?
How many times I have heard someone say, "I can't risk being my True Self. If people knew me like I am, they wouldn't like me."

Part of my mission in life is to reeducate people within my sphere about that True Self so that there is an understanding that who you are at your core is *good*. To risk being known, you do have to allow being seen for who you are, but that very vulnerability is what creates intimacy, closeness, and connection.

The model of Jesus is powerful. He took his closest friends into his life in a way that reveals radical vulnerability and risk. His first invitation to his first disciples, "Follow me," was an invitation for them to follow him around and observe who he was, what he did, and how he lived his life. Jesus invited people to get up close and personal with him; he risked loving intimately, and when his friend Lazarus died, he let himself cry in front of Mary and Martha, the sisters.

Jesus told his disciples about his struggles after his baptism, when he wrestled with the Adversary in the wilderness. He put himself out there, exposing himself to the doubt and fury of the religious establishment of his day, making himself known and vulnerable to all.

Jesus allowed his inner circle, Peter, James, and John, to witness the full impact of who he was in that moment on the hike up the Mount of Transfiguration. It is one thing to let people see your suffering, but it is also a risk to let people see you at your best, to witness the fullness of who you are.

Jesus took people into the garden. He reported the extent of his suffering, and then in the most extreme vulnerability, he hung, naked, on a criminal's cross.

What kind of love is that?

What kind of vulnerability and transparency is that?

What does Jesus' risk-taking reveal about God and his love for us?

(8) *Can you drink the cup of mercy, the cup of forgiveness?*
"Please forgive me for being late for that appointment," my friend said to me.

"I need to ask your forgiveness," someone said to an acquaintance. "I've forgotten your name."

Perhaps we need to differentiate between excusing someone for a minor offense and forgiving someone for an actual hurt. Forgiveness is a big concept, a hard reality, a costly experience and should be reserved for those things we do that cause injury to another. Giving mercy and receiving it require deep humility, and in a culture where it is deemed weak to say "I'm sorry" or "I was wrong," forgiveness is often a lost art.

Authentic forgiveness, however, is one of love's greatest manifestations. Mercy is love made visible, and grace is a gift of inestimable worth. We cannot take either the use of the words or drink the cup of forgiveness lightly, for forgiveness is often a bitter cup. At least, it is a hard cup to drink at times, and yet it can be the sweetest cup.

(9) *Can you drink the cup of suffering for the sake of love?*

You do not know, starting out, what is going to be asked of you when you choose to love another person. You don't know, when someone loves you, what will be required of you if you let yourself be loved by that person.

Nor can anyone know upon entering into a deep friendship, a marriage, or parenting a child when circumstances will end that relationship. Conflicts, drifting apart, divorce, and death all are part of the mix in loving and being loved. Ultimately someone leaves, and someone gets left behind. We hurt each other, sometimes intentionally, but mostly out of carelessness, neglect, or ignorance, and we cause sometimes unbearable suffering to each other.

"It's not worth it," a broken, wounded person

> It was about that time that the mother of the Zebedee brothers came with her two sons and knelt before Jesus with a request. "What do you want?" Jesus asked. She said, "Give your word that these two sons of mine will be awarded the highest places of honor in your kingdom, one at your right hand, one at your left hand." Jesus responded, "You have no idea what you're asking." And he said to James and John, "Are you capable of drinking the cup that I'm about to drink?" They said, "Sure, why not?"
>
> Matthew 20:20-22

told me. "I'm done with love," she said, and we both wept because, in the moment, it seemed that, for her, everything was pretty much lost for her in loving and being loved. As much as I hated to admit it, I could understand the despair this person had. It did seem like loving and being loved, for her, was a lost cause.

There is another level of suffering, however, when all the love we give to a person or a relationship is not enough to save that person. There is terrible suffering when you have to stand by and watch a person you love destroy himself in one of the seemingly endless ways people have of injuring themselves beyond repair.

To experience the deterioration of a marriage, to endure the rejection of someone who matters deeply to you, to go through betrayal that forever damages the trust necessary for intimacy, or to walk up to the wall of defense erected by someone who doesn't want to be in relationship with you—all of these are excruciating experiences.

Ultimately, as well, we all face the terrible pain of separation by death. Eventually, someone dies first, and the other is left to learn how to live in a world without the beloved. Whether death comes suddenly or after a long illness, the separation is hard.

"We suffer much because we love much," my friend and spiritual director Bishop Michael Pfeifer told me on the day that my mother died. It did not matter that she was ninety-two and had outlived most of her friends. It did not matter that she died "of natural causes." What mattered to me on that July day was that she was gone. Her body, now unresponsive, unsmiling, unable to talk, was evidence that she had crossed over to a reality I didn't understand, leaving me behind.

I was grief-stricken, and I had to cry it out.

"Tears are the body's way of praying," my friend Keith Hosey told me.

My prayer now, after a lifetime of loving and being loved, is that I can drink ever and ever more deeply of the cup of love for the rest of my life, and that I will have the courage and the stamina and patience to rise to the occasion of love's cost.

I know for sure that love really is what matters most.

Getting Personal

1. When have you said about something in life "This isn't what I expected" or "This is harder than I expected"?
2. When have you run away from your own call to authentic personhood and deep love?
3. When did you stay and bear the burden of pushing through the pain?
4. What do you think it means "to become conscious"?
5. What have you learned about love from losing?
6. What have you learned about staying?
7. How does your faithfulness to the people in your life reflect God's faithful love to you?
8. What have you learned about love from leaving or from being left?
9. What happens when you try to hold on to that which has left you?
10. How do you suppose Jesus felt about leaving his disciples and his family behind?

Growing Edges

I like the idea of "becoming conscious" more in theory than in the process of it all. Sometimes I prefer denial. It sounds so fabulous to be described as "evolved," as if whatever position one holds is more enlightened than the one others hold.

I'll admit it freely that growth is a good thing. Waking up, becoming conscious, becoming whole, authentic, enlightened, and all the rest are some of the hardest and most courageous steps human beings ever take. Life, if you really live it and don't just sleepwalk through your days, is costly. Friendships and all other relationships are costly, and usually you don't know on the front end just how the cost will be exacted.

As a lifelong member within the Christian community, I love to sing "I Have Decided to Follow Jesus." It's a beautiful song, and I have a history with the words and music, built up over a lifetime of revival services, camp meetings, and opportunities for rededication of my life to following Jesus.

When it comes to following him down the path of love, I can get scared when I run into one of those "growth opportunities" in that path.

Carl Jung said that he calls God that *"which flings itself violently across his path, for the good or for the ill."*

The first time I heard that, I cringed. Now, I've come to understand that there really is no better way to live than the way of waking up, and that there is nothing that can awaken you to life and its adventures like loving God, loving others, and loving oneself.

Love really is the refining fire.

Chapter 14

Street-smart Love

It isn't news that now and then, relationships get complicated, problematic and even dangerous, even among people who call themselves Christian.

What is a person supposed to do when she decides to be a serious follower of the teachings of Jesus and immediately runs into someone who seems committed to making her forget her decision to love as Jesus loved?

What happens when people of faith encounter shady business dealings within the workplace? How do you handle dishonesty within the church? Who is qualified to differentiate between an idiosyncrasy and a personality disorder in a family member or church member who continuously creates conflict or worse, is disrupting the safety, security and certainly the peace and harmony of others?

What would Jesus do?

That's a good question, and while there are no simple solutions for complex problems, Jesus gives guidance for handling difficult situation. The parable of what is called "the shrewd manager" often baffles us as we try to reconcile Jesus' words to his disciples with other teachings of his.

Basically, this parable from Luke 16:1-14 is loaded with street-smart wisdom and a manager who had been accused by a rich man of wasting his possessions. The entire parable presents a picture of a manager either trying to save his own skin or a man who is simply trying to make the best of a bad situation.

Read it for yourself and then ponder Eugene Peterson's rendition of Jesus' words from *The Message*:

> Streetwise people are smarter in this regard than law-abiding citizens. They are on constant alert, looking for angles, surviving by their wits. I want you to be smart in the same way—but for what

is right—using every adversity to stimulate you to creative survival, to concentrate your attention on the bare essentials, so you'll live, really live, and not complacently just get by on good behavior.

It seems to me that what Jesus teaches in this parable is that we need to grow up in our understanding of human nature. Whether we are dealing with difficult people, people with disorders (personality or otherwise), or dysfunctional group systems, we must identify problems more quickly and learn how to cope with them productively and redemptively. Christians need to learn how to be street savvy when setting appropriate boundaries in relationships, naming problems honestly, and being proactive in keeping the state of the family, the workplace, and the church as healthy as possible.

Naiveté is charming in a three-year-old, but it is dangerous on an adult. Jesus' ability to see "what was in a man"—beyond the outward appearance and the person of the ego—should be a model for us. Taking people at face value may be easy, but it can also be dangerous when what is lurking below the surface could come out to bite you. How do we balance being "streetwise" with being loving and compassionate? How do we know when to be tender and compassionate toward each other, and when it is time to give tough love? How do we set appropriate boundaries and still keep our hearts open? How do we see and accept the truth about things when the facts are hard to admit?

We do struggle integrating and applying the teachings of Jesus in everyday situations, and often, the naiveté or idealism of young Christians sets them up for disappointment and even ridicule. We want young Christians to learn the depth of God's love for every person, and we also want them to learn that just because they might have had a religious experience that set them on fire for Jesus doesn't mean that others in their sphere will want to go along with that change!

Just because a person says he is a Christian doesn't necessarily mean that he knows the teachings of Jesus or is able to apply them, and just because a business has a symbol of Christianity on its door doesn't mean that the people who work there are going to love you, practice honesty or treat others fairly.

Fervent and sincere Christians may attempt to work in a secular setting with the principles Jesus gave the disciples and assume that others will do the same. Naive Christians may attempt to "set a good example" with a hidden agenda of winning converts to Christianity without regard or respect for others' religious affiliations or desires.

"I don't want to know that about him," the young or immature Christian often says when a character defect, a moral lapse or failure or a destructive act shows up in someone who is supposed to be "a mature Christian." In our naiveté, we expect our mentors or heroes to be perfect specimens of good character and be exempt from the flaws of human beings.

"This can't be true; she is a *Christian!*" a naive person declares upon seeing the truth behind the facade of someone she thought lived "by Christian values."

Jesus did say that we are to love and give and serve. He told us to forgive seventy times seven, but then he castigated the scribes and Pharisees, even describing them as "white-washed tombs," full of filth inside, but polished on the outside. He told us that if we are asked to walk with brother, we should be willing to go the second mile with him, but he also said that there are times when we are to shake the dust from our sandals and move on. Figuring out where the to draw line between going that second mile and shaking the dust from our shoes is Jesus' challenge to us.

Recently, I was involved in a discussion among people who wanted to help someone who has gotten himself in terrible trouble. The discussion evolved painfully into a philosophical discussion about when "help" is truly helping and when "help" enables that person to avoid taking the personal responsibility he needs to take. We struggled to discern the best course of action that would help this person without contributing to his tendencies to repeat the same mistakes. We wanted to be idealistic enough to go the second mile with him . . . but savvy enough to help end the cycle.

With this dual task, we have to ask ourselves some hard questions and we have to accept that often there are no easy answers or quick fixes:

> *We're all precious in the sight of the Lord. He may shake his head a lot, but we're still precious.*
>
> Author unknown
>
> *For the people of this world are more shrewd in dealing with their own kind than are the people of the light.*
>
> Luke 16:8b

- When are we being a friend to someone in need and when are we simply telling the person what she wants to hear, stroking her ego, and helping her avoid the consequences of her own behavior?
- How do we know when we are projecting our reality onto someone else and when we're perceiving the truth about that person?
- How do we deal with a problem so that we both address the short-term crisis and the long-term cause that led up to the crisis?
- Do we dare to speak the truth in a situation when we all know our own failings? Can we speak the truth in love without being or sounding judgmental?

The hard truth is that conflict, dysfunction, and trouble exist among Christians. The call for all of us is twofold: Each of us needs to take responsibility for the particular and specific character defects in our own lives. And we all need to become more savvy and street-smart about discerning the difference between an idiosyncrasy and a real disorder that can disrupt families and churches, organizations, and nations.

Just because you are a follower of Christ doesn't mean you can get away with being naive, guileless or childish. We do not have to become licensed counselors or psychologists to function in the world, but if we learn more about the devastating (and far-reaching) consequences of mental illness, addiction, and other disorders, we will be better able to identify and find assistance for the people who need help the most. If we fail in this, we risk destruction of our congregations and our institutions at the hands of people whose disorders lead them to destroy themselves, their relationships, and the systems that might have helped them.

Love demands that we be wise people, seeking guidance from God and from the helping professionals who are trained to teach us to how to get along with each other and deal with our problems more effectively.

The truth is that sometimes we do have to deal with personality disorders and mental illnesses in the lives of people we love. There are people who are unable to be close or intimate, giving or forgiving in relationships. There are people whose wounds make it nearly impossible for them to connect with another person, and there are, tragically, people who are so damaged and so mean that it is dangerous to try to relate to them.

A good rule for the streets comes from an unlikely source, at least for me. Nevertheless, truth is often found in unlikely places and good, common, street-smart sense often comes from the streets of life I haven't traveled. That rule came from musician Jimi Hendrix: *Don't be reckless with other people's hearts. Don't put up with people who are reckless with yours.*

There are people who will use you and use you up, leaving you in a crumpled heap on the pavement of your best efforts.

There are people who will have an agenda for you, but are so sly and smooth that you don't know it until you are left behind, once you're served your purpose for them.

There are people who get a buzz off making you nervous, fearful or anxious, and there are people who are cruel beyond imagination.

There are people who will lie to get what they want from you, and there are people who will rejoice when you are hurting or when you fail.

"The ways we have of hurting each other in families seems to be infinite," a friend of mine told me, and we cried.

"There are many ways to wound a child," a friend said, lamenting yet another story of a wounded child, floundering in the world, acting out his wound on anyone and everyone.

I am told that one of the first things first-year medical students are taught is that when they are working with symptoms of a patient (hearing the hoof beats), now and then those symptoms indicate something exotic, rare, and interesting (a zebra). However, the young, eager doctors are told, most of the time those symptoms (hoof beats) indicate merely a horse. That is, the diagnosis is usually something commonplace.

Thanks be to God, most of our problems with each other are horses, but when a zebra comes along, it's good to know how to deal with it with love and with wisdom.

Seeking help for knowing how to handle those things that are outside our expertise and experience may be difficult, but it is a loving thing to do. It is loving and smart to not only for the other person, but for yourself.

Knowing how to draw boundaries, protecting yourself from abuse and knowing when it is time to walk away can be extremely difficult to discern and even harder to do. Patterns of behavior can be deeply entrenched and hard to change.

"Why did you do that?" I asked someone about a particular action that was self-defeating.

"I thought I had to!" she told me, but as soon as she said it, she realized that she had done that self-defeating action out of a lifelong pattern of letting herself be used, abused and manipulated. "No," she said, painfully. "I did it because that is what I've always done."

That is not love and, in fact, enabling and harmful patterns kill love.

Indeed, most of our problems with each other are everyday garden-variety problems. The truth is that our ordinary, annoying idiosyncrasies, flaws, and character defects affect others, just as theirs affect us.

Sometimes you can shrug those things away, but sometimes, you'd better pay close attention. It may be simple, but what you are seeing and experiencing may be something serious.

Sometimes you can turn away and ignore it, hoping that by not giving attention to the flaw or the incident, it will go away. It is true that sometimes a little bit of judicious neglect and the tincture of time are just what the doctor orders. Sometimes, things have a way of working themselves out.

"Is this normal adolescent behavior," I asked my husband when our girls were teen-agers. "Or is this something we need to be worried about?"

At least, asking the question is an act of love, and most of the time, our issues are developmental, from infancy to the grave.

Most of the time in everyday life, the issues that muddy the waters of love are fairly simple to address and manage, if we can drum up the compassion to be kind and the resolve to forgive as often as we can.

As Christians, however, we are not asked to tolerate the intolerable. We are not to accept behavior from another that is abusive in any way, nor are we to give it. Violence enacted on another makes the victim hate himself for tolerating it and the perpetrator for doing it, and it makes the perpetrator hate himself for doing it and the victim for taking the abuse, and so the terrible cycle of hate continues, wrapped in the poisonous fumes of shame and guilt.

Tragically, there are those who find exhilaration in causing pain and destruction, and there are those whose moral compass is so broken that they do not care what damage they do to others. There are those who are incapable of any sense of right and wrong and who have no empathy for others.

Thankfully, most of our engagements with others are with ordinary humans like we are who do irritating things.

Perhaps this puzzling parable is not so much about settling accounts as it is in showing the nature of God to us.

Perhaps God, who owns everything, isn't quite as interested in making sure that everything come fair and even as we are.

Perhaps God keeps a different kind of books from ours, and perhaps Jesus wanted his disciples to know that God loves us even as we do not do the best we *know*, but the best we *can*. And maybe Jesus was counseling his disciples about the tendency to be so "heavenly" that we are no earthly good, as my friend Jack Goss used to say. Maybe we love best when we are savvy, informed, and street-smart.

Being street-smart must be tempered with mercy, lest we become cynical and hard-edged, losing our empathy and compassion toward others.

I think that God sees the side of a person we like least and is able to see inside the heart of the person with whom we are locked in battle, the person with whom we cannot work, the person we cannot forgive—and longs for us all to have what we need, to do well.

Could it be that, after all, God doesn't have favorites, but loves all of us the same?

It is a radical thought that God loves the person I love least as much as he does me!

God loves the person who calls him by another name as much as he does me.

God loves the person whose baptism was at infancy as much as he does my people, who insist on believer's baptism, and immersion, at that.

> *Above all else, guard your heart, for it is the wellspring of life.*
>
> Proverbs 4:23

I'm learning, however slowly, that God loves the person whose theology and doctrine and politics don't match mine, and maybe God isn't very concerned about right theology, right doctrine and right politics.

Maybe God is more concerned with our wholeness and the condition of our hearts, even when we fuss and fight over whose religion is right and whose is wrong. Maybe he is most especially concerned about our hearts when we wage our religious wars, destroying each other in his name.

Reading the parable of the shrewd manage and considering all of the renegades with whom Jesus had relationships in his short life on earth wakes me up to the need I have to become more conscious. Indeed, to "become more like Jesus" is not some high-minded goal of living in sinless perfection. Instead, it may be more that we learn to recognize the dark side of life and the shadow side of ourselves in order to know how to work for the good in relationships.

In my innocence and ignorance and certainly in my denial, I am at the mercy of forces that are destructive.

The truth is that in my avoidance of hard truths, I project my values and my way of doing things onto God and assume that God shares my opinions, biases and prejudices. What a small, impotent God I created when I think that I've got him all wrapped up in a box of right-ness, designed and made according to my specifications.

We are all flawed and we all make mistakes, but thanks be to God, we have the opportunity to begin again every day, for his mercies are new every morning.

I love this quote by Plato:

We can easily forgive a child who is afraid of the dark;
the real tragedy of life is when men are afraid of the light.

As someone who has been afraid both of the dark (the actual dark and the darkness that lies deep in me, outside my reach) and of the light (either the light of truth or the responsibility of bearing the burden of my own light), I am pressed to my knees once again, praying, "Lord, have mercy."

Today, a long-time friend and I explored the ways our lives had drifted apart. Both of us lamented the loss of time, the misunderstandings that had nothing to do with either one of us and the regret that each of us had in not recognizing the force that had created the distance between us.

I'm so glad we talked openly and honestly.

I'm so glad we were able to understand the dynamics that neither of us could control, dynamics that had created the separation.

Most of all, I'm so grateful we have another chance at a deep, sweet friendship.

Sometimes, being street-smart means you have to go your own way, but sometimes it means that love's grace makes you wake up to something you hadn't or couldn't see before.

Sometimes, love's mercy restores that which you thought was beyond restoration.

Recently, I facilitated an event at a retreat center where a family of peacocks had taken up residence. In one of the courtyards at that retreat center, two females watched over four baby birds, and we humans clucked and carried on about how cute they were.

Between the main buildings, a male peacock in great distress created drama and a lot of racket over the three days I was there, standing in front of a window and fighting his own reflection.

The beautiful peacock paced back and forth in front of the window, pausing periodically to throw his head back and squawk. Of course, his enemy in the window did the very same thing back to him, which only increased his rage toward his perceived foe.

About every thirty minutes or so, the peacock squawked, as if to warn the other peacock, and then he flew with great fury and fanfare into the window, hoping to defeat the other bird. Sadly, the only thing that happened as a result of these regular assaults was that the peacock became more and more agitated, weakening himself by throwing himself at the glass.

No matter what that real peacock did, however, his reflection would not go away.

It's not much of a leap from the absurd warfare between an actual peacock and his mirrored image to the absurdity of a human being who projects his reality onto another person or group and then fights that reflection of himself in "the other." If fighting our projections and reflections solved our problems, the world would be a nicer place.

How often we humans see in someone else that which we don't like in ourselves. Without self-awareness, we continue to see in "the other" that which we find repugnant or distasteful in ourselves. Perhaps we clash with others because we cannot deal with the disowned, unacknowledged, and shadowy parts of our own lives. Indeed, we allow someone else to carry those parts of us instead of confronting and addressing them directly.

"How do you know if it's projection or perception?" I asked Dr. Jim Hollis in class one night at the Jung Center in Houston. He quickly responded.

"That's the hard part," he said, and the implicit message was, "and you have to be careful and conscious in order to know the difference."

My ego, like others', is highly skilled in deceiving me into thinking that it's all about the other, and if only the other person would straighten up, do right or *go away*, my problem would be resolved and I would feel better. It takes practice to remember that the first line of defense when threatened is denial. It takes a lot of courage to see what you don't want to see, especially in yourself.

It's no small task to discern the difference between perception and projection, so prone are we to self-protection, avoidance of recognizing our own flaws and our love and devotion to the status quo, especially when it comes to seeing ourselves for who we really are!

On the third day I was at this retreat center, someone taped cardboard to the

> Lots of people want to ride with you in the limo, but what you want is someone who will take the bus with you when the limo breaks down.
>
> Oprah Winfrey

window, hoping that the peacock would give up his fight and go play with the mama birds and their chicks.

It was not to be. The peacock simply went around the corner to another window and started another fight with yet another reflection of himself. "Some birds just love to fight," someone commented. "I guess this one needs an enemy," someone else observed.

"Reminds me of one of my neighbors," his friend responded, shaking his head. (And was that projection or perception?)

Often, I hear someone ask, "Is this my problem, or is it his?"

The question reveals a degree of consciousness, doesn't it? At least the one who questions whose problem it is has to be struggling with the issue of responsibility.

Growing Edges

Early on, I made choices not to do some things because I didn't want to hurt my parents. That's what I prefer to think, but there's another voice inside my head that reminds me that the church ladies, who were so quick to tattle on the preacher's kid, scared me to death. Much of the time, I stayed out of trouble to avoid those "ladies."

Growing up, I was much more afraid of those women than I was of God.

Looking back, I did save my parents a lot of grief by my choices, but I don't think they would have wanted me to be as scared of others' disapproval as I was.

Through much of my life, I made certain choices because I believed those particular choices were expected of me. I wanted the approval of certain people, but I also wanted to avoid the disapproval.

While I thought my choices were made out of love for others, the truth is that I was afraid of disapproval and punishment. Honestly, that fear kept me in line, a lot.

When I was very young, I overheard my grandmother telling my mother that I had "good sense," and her approval was really important to me.

My contrived notions of what my grandmother meant about "having good sense" have kept me from doing some really stupid things, I suppose, but those same notions have likely made me a little too cautious.

Perhaps I have saved myself some trouble by "being a good girl," but perhaps some of the pain I have had in my life is connected to the fear I have carried for much of my life.

God, as I understand God now, wouldn't want me to be so scared of others' disapproval or criticism, would not want me to be so naive or gullible. God would want me to live free and bold, love deeply, and laugh much.

However, I think God and my grandmother would agree that being street-smart and having common sense are good things.

Chapter 15

A Higher Love

"I didn't know it was going to be this hard," the new mom confessed. "What if I'm not able to love this child enough?"

I remember that feeling when we brought our newborn home from the hospital. I had no idea that I was holding in that seven-pound bundle one of life's greatest teachers and that being a mother would ask me to reach inside myself for strength I didn't yet have, insight and wisdom I would get in on-the-job training, and courage and patience I would have to develop one day at a time.

"I don't want to get involved with church committees and find out the shadow side of the church," a man told me. "I just want to show up, give my offering, worship God, and go home."

I get that. Sometimes I want to say, "Me too!"

"Friendship takes a lot of time and effort and money," a committed loner announced. "The first time I feel someone pulling on me, expecting something of me I don't want to give, I run and hide!"

The odd thing is that human beings are meant for relationships, yet we seem to have agendas competing internally all the time. We want both independence and relationships. We are pleasure-seeking creatures; at the same time we avoid pain and discomfort. It's hard to get all of our needs—safety and security, belonging and freedom, responsibility and fun—met, and most of the time we are out of balance, to one degree or another.

The truth is that there is nothing that has introduced me to my weaknesses like attempting to maintain a love relationship, whether that relationship is with the Almighty, a family member, a friend, or a group. Nothing exposes my self-centeredness and selfishness like the call and commitment to another person. Nothing reveals my fears like commitment to another human being. Nothing shows me my how much I need love like the pain of not-love.

So it is choosing to love with faithful and fervent love, the *fierce love* of courage and commitment, is a high calling. It is a calling from the highest of sources, God. It is a calling to reach deep within ourselves and access the best that is in us. Indeed, the complexity of love relationships is such that I have concluded that love is, indeed, our assignment while we are on this earthly plane. We are created to give love and receive it, and finding the balance between caring for oneself and caring for others is a lifelong struggle with few days off.

What adult, having chosen to enter into a deep and intimate love relationship, has not come to a point in that relationship when it is too hard to go on, too painful to endure, or the conflicts or differences too complicated to solve? "It's not one thing after another that gets me," my teacher and mentor Madeleine L'Engle said. "It's the same damned thing over and over."

Who hasn't at some point in an ongoing relationship, either with a person or a group of people, despaired at the way the same patterns or problems keep showing up, as if to taunt you with your delusion that you can forever change that pattern or solve that problem forever?

Who hasn't grown weary of forgiving seventy times seven? Our faults and flaws get tedious, don't they?

Is there anyone who doesn't understand the frustration of not being able to resolve an ongoing problem with someone else?

Who hasn't been disappointed in another person when that person isn't who we thought he or she was, based on our expectations or preconceived notions of how that person *should* be?

Is there any human being who has ever not experienced that moment of admitting that someone has not met all your needs?

"I've let them know how it's going to be from now on!" a conflict-weary friend declares, as if a pronouncement from one person in a family is a magic-waving wand that can sprinkle stardust over other people's wills and stubbornness, needs and wishes, opinions and habit.

We would all like for love to be easy and romantic, costing us nothing but the time we choose to invest in the relationship, but the real test of authentic love is lived out in the everyday, mundane, ordinary routines of making a living, running errands, and paying bills.

Even if you have enough money to have someone else take care of the ubiquitous cleanup, maintenance, and repair of your outer world, there's always the inner world of each other—our complexes, unmet needs, expectations, and feelings—bubbling along underneath the words and actions and sometimes roaring to the surface, demanding to be faced, solved, noticed, and dignified by appropriate attention.

"Long-term relationships are complicated," a wise person told me, and in the same breath he said, "If I waited until all of my friends are perfect, I wouldn't have many friends."

Long-term relationship rest on a history of patterns, and with every new person that is added to a group, the more dynamics there are. Unsuccessful problem-solving opportunities and unresolved conflicts build up over time, like mildew, and every unforgiven failure or offense festers somewhere in the people who are involved in the relationship.

The old principle "out of sight, out of mind" may work for clutter you've stuffed in the closet, but it isn't a good or healthy principle for relationships. What is buried alive stays alive, often erupting in a second or third generation or at a most inconvenient time.

> *Bring me a higher love,*
> *Bring me a higher love,*
> *Bring me a higher love,*
> *Where's this higher love,*
> *I've been thinking of?*
>
> Steve Winwood,
> "Higher Love"

Who doesn't understand the poignant words of Steve Winwood in his song, "Higher Love"?

> *Worlds are turning, and we're just hanging on,*
> *facing our fear, standing out there alone. . . .*
> *In this whole world, what's fair?*
> *We walk blind, and we try to see.*

Couldn't you just weep sometimes for the human condition? Don't you wish that life could be easier, simpler, more full of love, joy, and peace?

It's a good thing that God has compassion for us. After all, there is something in each of us that longs for that which is better, higher, nobler, greater, yet we are confined and earth-bound. We are trapped in our weaknesses, flaws, and fears, and they make us hesitant to reach for what seems to be—and perhaps is—an impossible dream. It is in the reaching that we go further than we could have if we hadn't reached, and now and then, we reach something so powerful or beautiful that it seems to be a foretaste of heaven. Thankfully, there is a force that is at work in our lives that graces our efforts and makes bearable our failures, and that force is *forgiveness.*

Jesus' words about forgiveness are clear and easy to understand, but they are hard to put into practice, and his wisdom in tying our forgiveness to others with the forgiveness we receive reveals a powerful truth about the interconnectedness among us and between us. There are inescapable rules of engagement that, if honored, can enhance a relationship. If ignored or violated, love dies.

"I could never do that," a friend told me, referring to an unbelievable act of violation one human being had inflicted on another.

"You could, if you had been in that situation and at that time, with that person's history," I responded, and a lively discussion followed about how being human means that whatever any one of us is capable of doing, all of us have the capacity of doing.

It is a hard truth to face that the capacity for evil is in all of us. We who are within the Christian community, who tend to see ourselves as the "good" people, working for good and free of the sins of unbelievers, can so easily blind ourselves to our own capacities for evil.

In my lifetime I have learned that living under the banner of "Christian" or "church member" does not guarantee either goodness or the absence of evil. Just because I gave my heart to Jesus when I was nine years old does not exempt me from pride or prejudice, hate or anger, jealousy or greed, or the actions that emerge from those emotions. Just because I see myself as a good person doesn't mean I cannot act with selfishness that, once out in the open, stuns me with its scope.

Even if I am blind to my faults, that doesn't mean that they are invisible to others. Even if I pretend to be something other than I really am, that doesn't mean that others won't detect the lack of authenticity, and if I try to pretend that I love someone I don't like, someone will feel the discrepancy between what I say and what I do.

Two of the most important books in my library are *People of the Lie*, by M. Scott Peck, and *Why Good People Do Bad Things: Understanding Our Darker Selves*, by James Hollis. One of the most important practices in my life has been the working of the Twelve Steps of Alcoholics Anonymous, for my codependency, which has included the laborious and painful process of facing my own demons, character defects, failures, and the harm I have done to myself and to others as I have worked the Fourth, Fifth, and Sixth Steps.

Facing my shadow—those parts of myself I have plunged into the cellar of unconsciousness and defended against allowing to come up into the light—has been an excruciating experience for me. To look at myself with as much honesty as I could stand, to call things what they are, to own my fault in a relationship conflict, to admit to myself and to others what I have done that was wrong or harmful as part of that process has been terribly painful—*but not as painful as denying the truth or lying to myself and others about the truth.*

Hardly anything takes more energy than living a lie, covering up the truth, or pretending to be something you aren't. Hardly anything is as liberating or life-giving as telling the truth about yourself, especially in the presence of someone who is not there to pronounce judgment or condemnation, but to listen with a heart of mercy and grace.

My own religious tradition prides itself on having direct access to God, without the need of a mediator. I believe in that doctrine of the priesthood of every believer as well, but we carry it too far and have limited our own experience of peace and joy when we do not avail ourselves of the opportunity to make confession to another, to hear the pronouncement of forgiveness, grace, and mercy, and to make amends to those we have harmed.

There is nothing like being known and accepted for who you are by another human being, and if I were running the world and could wave a wand of grace, I would teach little children, regardless of their ages, the practical processes of admitting your own wrong and that which has separated you from God and from others (the definition of sin), asking for forgiveness, learning how to say "I'm sorry" or "I was wrong," and then making appropriate amends.

I have come to understand that forgiveness is another expression of love, but with this caveat: Forgiveness is the process of working together to change the dynamics that created the problem or the offense in the beginning.

Forgiveness requires the effort of both people. It requires speaking up and listening. It involves give and take, compromise, and repeated starts and stops, most likely, to change habits, speech patterns, and actions.

> *If by some magic you could eliminate the pain you are caused by the pain of someone you love, I for one cannot imagine working such magic because the pain is so much a part of the love that the love would be vastly diminished, unrecognizable, without it.*
> *To suffer in love for another's suffering is to live life not only at its fullest but at its holiest.*
>
> — Frederick Buechner,
> *Listening to Your Life*

In his teaching prayer, which rolls off most tongues with an ease that indicates an unconsciousness about the power of the prayer, Jesus gave one of the most important teachings of his whole teaching ministry, a teaching he repeated in other settings. In using the plural pronouns "us" and "our" when he said "Forgive us our debts (or trespasses) as we forgive our debtors (or those who have trespassed against us), Jesus indicates that forgiveness is a collective need. We do often collude with each others' sins, buttressing each other up in lies and deceptions, denial and avoidance, and thereby keeping "group evil," releasing its toxicity from many directions.

Rarely do we commit sin in isolation or in a vacuum, and rarely is the result of the sin of any one of us confined to one's own personal life.

Forgiveness, as Jesus taught us, can be practiced together and in reciprocity. Jesus' words are a thundering statement about how important forgiveness really is.

How we forgive others, in fact, is both indicative of our own inner state and predictor of whether or not we will be forgiven.

"I don't forgive to change the past," a friend told me. "I forgive to change the present and the future."

One of the most painful experiences in my life occurs when there is an unresolved conflict with someone who is important to me. Sometimes that unresolved conflict occurs when someone will not forgive me, and equally unsettling is the discomfort and pain of having been wronged when the other person wants to act as if nothing has happened and we can go on as usual, ignoring the elephant in the room.

Struggling with one of these experiences in which I could play only the hand of cards I had been dealt, I lamented that I wanted to forgive the person who had hurt me, but I didn't seem to be able to do that.

"Has that person asked for your forgiveness?"

That one question stunned me, and I responded that the person had not asked for my forgiveness and would not likely do so.

"Forgiveness, if it is to be complete, requires two parties, Jeanie. Somebody has to ask for forgiveness, and somebody has to give it. Your suffering isn't caused by your unwillingness to forgive. You are hurting, and you keep on hurting about this because the other person does not or cannot see his/her part or doesn't feel the need of forgiveness."

In that moment, a long-held wound began to heal, and the tyranny of my obsession with my need to forgive began to lose its stranglehold on my heart.

I wish things were different, yes. I wish we could experience confession and forgiveness, given and received, but I have finally accepted that that is not going to happen.

From those experiences of incomplete forgiveness, I came to a new understanding of Jesus' words from the cross, "Father, forgive them, for they don't know what they are doing" (Luke 23:34). Indeed, he had done all he could do in his short time of ministry on earth, and given what his enemies had done, he handed over their plight, their unconsciousness, and their sin against him to God. It was as if he said, "I am entrusting this to you."

Was Jesus saying that we are to excuse the unforgivable? Was he saying that we turn our heads away and ignore or avoid wrong? Was he saying that we allow the same sick and hurtful behaviors, the same violence or abuse to continue?

The answer has to be a resounding "NO!" to all questions. Maybe we get a little closer to the truth of what he was saying if we think about forgiveness as a way of life, and if we realize that it is in the context of the whole Lord's Prayer and the whole gospel.

One fo the most amazing realities I have experienced is filled with irony. The deeper the pain in a relationship, the higher the calling to love. The greater the brokenness, the greater the potential for healing. The commitment to the high calling of fierce love will likely involve trips to the depths of pain and journeys to deepest joy.

Following a bitter separation from his wife, a man left California and drove to Houston, Texas, to see revenge on his wife and four children. The couple had been living in Utah, but she had fled their home because of his violence.

He must have rehearsed all of her offenses mile after hot mile on those long highway stretches, building resentment and rage with every mile, for when he got to Houston, he forced his way into the home of his former wife's sister and murdered her, her husband, and four of their five children. The fifth child, a fifteen-year-old girl, had the presence of mind to play dead after a bullet only grazed her head, and when he left to continue his massacre, she found a phone and called her grandparents. Without her action, her former uncle likely would have murdered the whole family.

How many other people, like this man, are carrying such pent-up fury, just waiting for someone to throw a match of criticism or rejection into the combustible jumble of grudges, lifelong resentments, unresolved conflicts, and unmet needs?

How many people, sitting around you at church, are rehearsing slights and offenses in their minds, even as they repeat the Lord's Prayer and take Communion? How many people get up in the morning with an axe to grind that they take out into their workplaces? How many people take out on some innocent person what someone else did to them?

A refusal to forgive, harbored over time, is one of the most dangerous and insidious evils that wreaks its lethal havoc and destruction on innocent people every day. Forgiveness, practiced as a lifestyle and on a daily basis, could be one of the most powerful antidotes to hate and anger available to human beings.

> *I find that it is better to love badly and faultily than not to try to love at all. God does not have to have perfect instruments, and the Holy One can use our feeble and faltering attempts to love and transform them. My task is to keep on trying to love, to be faithful in my continuing attempt, not necessarily to be successful.*
>
> Morton Kelsey,
> Companions on the Inner Way

Let's go back to Jesus' teaching about prayer from the cross when he handed over the ones who had tried, convicted, and were killing him to God.

Beam the light onto what he said from the cross: *Forgive them, because they don't know what they are doing.*

The cost of love is waking up. It is becoming conscious of how what I do affects other people in the everyday encounters of my life. Becoming conscious means that I examine my motivations and behaviors; it means I take responsibility for those times when I try to get from others either what is not mine to demand or what I instead should be giving. Becoming conscious is about going out into the world knowing my particular weaknesses and faults—my *stuff*. With that knowledge, I build compassion for myself so that I can more easily practice compassion, understanding, and empathy for others.

The gift of taking consciousness seriously, when it comes to how I love, is that the quality and depth of loving and being loved increase exponentially. Higher consciousness, stronger self-awareness, and greater responsibility are a part of the calling to a higher love, a love that is gift-love.

Getting Personal

1. Give thanks for those moments of grace when life and love have been easy for you. Then think about someone who has experienced misfortune or made mistakes in life and love. How do you express your attitude toward others' tribulations?
2. If you could do one thing now to make your life flow more smoothly with love, what would it be?
3. If you could start over, what three things would you do differently?
4. How can you improve the life of someone you've hurt?
5. Who is harder on you about the mistakes you have made, you or someone else? What can you do to change the ongoing punishment?

Growing Edges

During a recent gathering of my grandchildren, we came upon a morning when one of those darlings kept coming to me with the same complaint about one of the others. The pattern had gone on long enough that I thought it was time for a life lesson about blaming.

"Children blame," I told the tattler, "and adults take responsibility."

Without missing a beat, that child looked me in the eye and said, "Well, he blames, and I tattle. That's what we do."

The child said it as if it were an acceptable best practice. Clearly, he felt he needed to enlighten me about the established patterns. The whole scene continues to make me laugh, as much at myself as the situation.

After they all left and things were quiet again, I tuned in to see what had been going on in the world since they had all arrived for "Cousin Camp." Lo and behold, what I heard on the evening news was exactly what I'd heard from these young grandchildren. Some people around the world were blaming, and the rest of them were tattling. Like children, those famous people and supposed leaders would switch roles regularly. All of these adults were proficient at either blaming or tattling, neither of which made anything any better.

So back to my big life lesson: Children blame. Adults take responsibility.

In my life, it makes tons of difference in how I negotiate conflicts, take care of business, and make decisions when I take responsibility for myself, owning my own power but not overpowering others. It makes a big difference if I can be conscious enough to know when I'm sending mixed messages and when I'm being straightforward with my words. It makes a difference as well when my words and my actions are in harmony.

> Love is the first ingredient in the relief of suffering.
> Padre Pio

Things go better and smoother for me in every transaction with others when I am respectful, both in listening to the other people and in speaking up and out about my own needs, wants, desires, and feelings. The art of "give and take" makes the world run more smoothly.

Life is far easier when I avoid manipulating others and when I don't let others manipulate me. Power and control need to be shared, and when power and control rule, peace and love evaporate into thin air.

Growing up is a lifelong process, and all the bumps and hurdles along the way contain within them opportunities to behave in a mature way. The truth is that conflicts arise when one of us of any age is trying to take something that belongs to someone else, dominate the other or gain position, privilege, power, or prestige for all kinds of "reasons" that may sound high and mighty but are actually motivated by the need to be on top of the heap.

Given enough fatigue, hunger, frustration, loneliness, or pain, I am shocked by how quickly I can regress back to a child's state of mind and behavior. With enough stress piled on me and with either too much time on my hands or not enough, I can resort to blaming or tattling, just like my grandchildren. And just like my grandchildren, sometimes I too need a timeout.

All of us need to learn how to back off, get a grip, chill out, take deep breaths, reboot, or simply take a long look at where the road we're on is going to take us. Blaming and tattling take me down a road filled with land mines and dead-ends. Taking responsibility for myself, my fatigue, my state of being, my emotions, and my needs takes me down the road of peace.

When it comes to higher love, we are all children, learning our way through the complexities of our connections, and that includes our connection with God.

Nobody, including Jesus, said it would be easy, did they? If it were, more people would be doing it.

Chapter 16

Trust and Trustworthiness

Toward the end of what is called the Sermon on the Mount, Jesus included a simple statement that, if practiced, would change the world. It is called the Golden Rule: "Do to others what you would have them do to you."

Eugene Peterson renders it this way, suggesting that these words are a simple, rule-of-thumb guide for behavior: "Ask yourself what you want people to do for you, then grab the initiative and do it for them."

I used to think that we Christians were the only ones who had this Golden Rule, but the reality is that as many as two dozen or more religions have what is sometimes called "the law of reciprocity" as a guiding, ethical principle. The principle or rule is often turned upside down with an equally important truth, and that is, "Do not do to others what you would not want them to do to you." Either way, the Golden Rule is perhaps one of Jesus' most important teachings. Practicing it has the potential of radical transformation of relationship between and among all people.

Sometimes I ponder what might happen if all the world could practice that rule, but then I remind myself that what matters is that *I* keep it foremost in my consciousness and behavior. I am responsible for carrying out this simple and profound rule of engagement in my everyday life as a conscious act of kindness and a radical way of love.

"How do I know I can trust you?" I asked.

My question startled me, and I have learned to pay attention to the words that seem to fall out of my mouth without having originated in my head. Those slips of the tongue often come from a deeper place than my conscious mind. Sometimes they come from an old wound or a great fear, but sometimes they come from a well of inner wisdom and stark honesty.

The response to my question was equally startling because it was immediate and spontaneous: "Because I am *trustworthy*."

Looking back on that moment, I remember that the brief silence that followed felt like the awe and reverence I feel when I am standing on holy ground. The moment took my breath away. It revealed and contained *truth*, and has become a kind of gold standard for me in my life. I'd never asked that question of anyone before. My basic orientation toward other people is to start out by trusting them, and sometimes that has worked out better than at other times.

That the person who had declared himself to be *trustworthy* spoke with such conviction woke me up—indeed, startled me awake—to a deep reflection both of my own trustworthiness and my wisdom and discernment in trusting others.

"Are you trustworthy?" is a different question from "Can I trust you?" (which implies the question *Am I able to trust?* in addition to *Do you deserve my trust?*). Both of those questions press me to turn inward and ask, "Can I trust myself?" and "Am I trustworthy?" in ways that keep me humbled before the complexity and mystery of loving and being loved.

I began to question myself. Do others trust me? Am I trustworthy? Am I worthy of the trust that others place in me, in the beginning of the relationship and as that relationship unfolds? And what does that mean?

> I hold this to be the highest task of a bond between two people: that each should stand guard over the solitude of the other.
>
> Rainer Maria Rilke

For starters, being trustworthy means that I will treat you as I want to be treated and that I will not treat you in ways I don't want to be treated.

The words of Rainer Maria Rilke stir something deep within me, for the act of "standing guard over the solitude of another" seems to be one of the primary characteristics of love that heals and love that empowers. "Standing guard over the solitude of another human being" calls for a deep, abiding trust of oneself and the other, and I believe that that is the way of mature gift-love.

"Standing guard over the solitude of each other" is similar to what we mean when we say "I've got your back," but it is more than that. I believe that standing guard over the solitude of another is a way of "loving your neighbor as yourself." It is a way of honoring and respecting and, yes, loving the very True Self/soul of another. Standing guard over the soul/solitude of another is more than saying, "I won't let you down" or "You can count on me" and "I'm here for you."

Guarding the solitude of another seems to me to have the gravitas of guarding the very essence of another. It has to be about watching carefully to make sure that you don't injure a person's sense of security and safety, and to the best of your ability, you behave in such a way that another person feels safe with you.

The level of safety and security within a relationship is complicated because it depends on the ability of each to trust and the ability of each to be trustworthy. Every person in a relationship contributes to the quality and depth of the relationship.

I cannot "make" another person feel safe with me, particularly if that person feels unsafe with others in general and if that person has a problem with trusting other people. All I can do is remain trustworthy and be as authentic as I am able within the relationship.

"I don't trust you, and I don't trust God" are words that still make me catch my breath as I remember hearing them. I had been listening to someone's life story and came to understand that his earliest experiences of fear, abandonment, and abuse with authority figures and caregivers had warped his understanding of God and of other people. His mistrust of me was less about me than it was about him.

What I had to discern, over time, was whether my continuing to be present and responsive to him in spiritual direction was enough to change his mind and heart. Could I help him give up his old image of God for a new, life-giving one? I have learned that to guard the solitude/soul of another means that you don't force your will on another, but you accept and allow the other person a free range of choice-making, thinking, feeling, and doing. Guarding the solitude of another person means that you respect the "otherness" of another person and are unwilling to manipulate the other into being someone that person either cannot or will not be.

When you examine the attitude and behavior of Jesus toward others, what you see is that he never forced his way or his will on anyone. He left others completely free to be who they were and to follow him—or not. In fact, when I read about how he healed and transformed people, it looks to me as if he moved through the outer layers of the person's roles, masks, or defenses and touched the very soul/essence of the other, often liberating that precious part of the person from chains put on the person by society or chains of his own making.

When I think about what it takes for trust to grow between and among people, I am aware that, for many, baggage from the past can really inhibit the growth of trust. Just because it is hard, however, doesn't let us off the hook of giving and receiving trust in our most intimate and valuable relationships. Love is about letting go of things that hamper us, isn't it?

I've pondered what I think it means to guard the solitude of each other. By reflecting deeply on this great mystery of love, I have formulated a statement of my own personal ethics. Sometimes what I attempt falls short of my ability, but I remember that I am in a lifelong school of learning. I try to be as patient with myself as God is and still hold myself to a high standard.

- To the best of my ability, I will tell you the truth.
- When I am wrong, I will tell you I was wrong. I will apologize, ask forgiveness, and then, if necessary, I will make amends appropriately.

- When I have forgiven you, I will not hold the wrong over your head. I will encourage you to become the person you are created to do, and I will negotiate ways for both of us (or all of us) to fulfill the God-given potential that is within each of us.
- I will not attempt to control or manipulate you, and I will not overpower you, either verbally or physically, and I will not let you do those things to me. If I do any of those, I want you to tell me, and I will tell you.
- I will speak respectfully to you, both in private and in public.
- I will work for the good for you and for myself so that we can, as much as possible, live in a win/win relationship.
- I will respect your relationship with God and never ridicule that relationship, attempt to sabotage your private or public worship, and will honor your religious life.
- I will work diligently to do my part to resolve our differences and our problems. I can count on you to be straightforward with me about your limitations and not tell me you will do something if you have no intentions of doing it.
- I will listen to your thoughts, your feelings, and your desires, as I want you to listen to mine.
- I will protect your personhood and will act in such a way that you feel safe, secure, and at ease with me.
- I will not collude with others against you.
- I will not use my wounds as weapons on you, and if I do, please let me know.
- I will, as much as I can, lay down my defenses around you so that you don't have to tiptoe on eggshells around me.
- I will not embarrass or ridicule you in public, and I will not demean you or take advantage of your particular vulnerabilities either in private or in public.
- To the best of my ability, I will not abuse you verbally, physically, emotionally, sexually, or spiritually.
- I will not allow you to abuse me, for to do that makes me a part of your self-abuse.

All of these statements could come under the heading "I will be faithful to you, working for your good." I'd be curious to see what others would add to my list.

When my father performed a wedding ceremony, he always included a challenge that continues to inspire me: "May you grow to the place with each other that you receive primary joy from contributing to the happiness of each other."

I suppose that none of us can fully transcend filaments of "need-love" that linger in our motivations, and the truth is that all of us have valid needs that we want to have met in our relationships, but there really is no greater joy than loving another person in a way that contributes to that person's happiness.

Is there anything more beautiful than seeing someone's eyes light up with pleasure when you give them something they really want or do something that really does make life easier or more pleasant? Is there anything more beautiful than the joy that emanates from a group of friends who have spent a lifetime contributing to the well-being of each other?

"I have been loved well," a woman told me, following the death of her spouse, and the effects of that love sustained her through the hard process of grief.

Take that idea to another level and imagine being able to say, "I have loved well."

Not perfectly.

Not at all times and in all circumstances, and not all people.

Not without mistakes or failures.

Not without regrets, and not without struggle and sorrow, but to have loved well is a worthy goal.

Getting Personal

1. Are you trustworthy?
2. What is the difference between being trustworthy and being dependable?

3. How easily do you trust others?
4. Can others trust you to keep the Golden Rule in relationships with you?
5. Is your word to others good? Do you keep your promises?
6. How easily do you trust God's love for you?
7. How well do you love others?
8. How well do you love God?
9. How well do you love yourself?

Growing Edges

When I was fourteen, a family friend in Roswell, New Mexico, gave me a gift when we moved from Roswell to Dallas, Texas, and on the card that accompanied the gift, she wrote, "Hitch your wagon to a star," a quotation by Ralph Waldo Emerson.

I took that guidance seriously.

When I was an English major at Baylor University, I took the Browning course. Baylor has the largest collection of Robert and Elizabeth Barrett Browning memorabilia in the world, housed in the Browning Building, and for me, there was an unspoken expectation among my friends and family that "of course you take the Browning course."

> *Let us keep in step with the Spirit.*
> Galatians 5:25b

I still recall the day Dr. Jack Herring lectured on Robert Browning's poem "Andrea del Sarto" when one line jumped off the page of my textbook and landed in my heart, alongside Emerson's quotation: "Ah, but a man's reach should exceed his grasp, or what's a heaven for."

Later, I read these words in a magazine at the beauty shop: "Reach for the moon, and even if you miss it, you'll land among the stars."

Recently, my husband and I attended a performance of *Man of La Mancha* at the Hobby Center in Houston. It had been years since I had been captivated by the story of Don Quixote and his daring quest, but quickly I was *all in* as the story unfolded on the stage.

By the time the words and music of "The Impossible Dream" began filling the room, tears were rolling down my face, and once again I connected to my youthful idealism and, yes, romanticism about how the world could be and what is possible in life that is shaped and formed and motivated by the power of love.

Love may be an impossible dream, and it may require people brave or foolish enough to walk into hell for that heavenly cause. Certainly, my life has been changed by those who have been *willing to bear the unbearable sorrow and run where the brave dare not go*, pushing past the limits of fear or hate to make the world better.

Love flourishes and grows, transforming and redeeming life and people when there is someone who is willing to keep on holding out love's potential and love's reality as a way of being in the world. Love heals and empowers people and restores and recreates life when some brave person will not give up on the impossible dream of what could be, what can be, what is yet to be.

It was said about Don Quixote that "he was either the wisest fool I've ever known, or the most foolish wise man I've ever known." The people who have changed history had a vision that defied the facts of their present circumstances. They were able to articulate a vision of hope and possibility, freedom and love that drew people to them, and they were able to hold that vision, no matter what the personal consequences were. And, yes, some believed those game-changers were either wise fools or foolish wise men, but their names are written large in history.

Love is controversial, and isn't that strange? Love threatens the status quo, over and over, and yet love keeps on keeping on, showing up in places I'd never imagined and through people like Don Quixote and Gandhi and Martin Luther King and countless others whose names will never be in the headlines who speak up and show up, for the cause of freedom, to keep hope alive and to give us a picture of what it means to be a lover in the world.

The words to "The Impossible Dream" still make chills run up and down my spine: "And the world will be better for this, that one man, scorned and covered with scars, still strove with his last ounce of courage to reach the unreachable star."

Jesus' message of love tore up his world and landed him on a criminal's cross, but his message lives on, and his resurrection is a loud proclamation, cascading down through the centuries, that no one can destroy the power of God, whose very name is Love.

"Trust in God; trust also in me," Jesus told the disciples at the end of his time on earth with them.

It's a bold request, isn't it?

Or is it one of Jesus' commands to us?

It's bold, and so is his other big one, the great commandment:

Love the Lord your God with all your heart and with all your soul and with all your mind . . . and love your neighbor as yourself.

It's a challenge big enough for a lifetime.

Chapter 17

How We Love

If you look at the way Jesus related to the outcast, the broken, and the marginalized in the Gospels, you see his love in action. Over and over, Jesus looked beyond whatever was on the outside to the true person. He saw all the way through the personage to the person and connected not with the failures, reputations, or illnesses of those people but with their very souls.

Repeatedly, Jesus widened the circle of his love and compassion to embrace and include those who did not fit the mold of the religious world of his day. He lifted up the downtrodden, gave respect and dignity to those who were shamed, and healed the sick. He especially moved with power and tenderness to elevate the women he encountered in his brief ministry on earth.

Jesus didn't give only second chances, which often turn out to be simply another way to repeat the past or embed a faulty pattern or habit in the relationship. Jesus changed people's lives.

On a quest for a specific quotation about second chances, I stumbled onto this: *Sometimes giving a person another chance is handing a person an extra bullet for their gun because they missed you the first time.*

I include the quotation with regret because it contains within it a caution and because, in some instances, it is true.

Giving another chance and forgiveness both require a change in the behavior of the people involved.

Sometimes love demands a careful and thorough analysis of a problem within a relationship, and that process can be excruciating, depending on the complexity of the problem or the depth or length of the relationships. Usually, the most painful part is the realization that no matter how patient, loving, compassionate, and forgiving you have been, either the problem continues or worsens.

It is so painful for me to accept that sometimes my love for another person isn't enough to solve his problem, and it is painful for me to accept that perhaps what I have considered to be "love" toward another person has actually contributed to the other's dysfunction. When I sing "Love, It Changes Everything," I have to admit that sometimes what is changed is my approach to another person.

"I know you want to be compassionate toward this person," a wise friend told me as I described my repeated attempts to get beyond that particular person's wounds of a lifetime.

> Simon, son of John, do you love me?
> John 21:17

Indeed, I had felt such sorrow and compassion for her that I had overlooked her repeated insults, slights, and outright attempts to drive a wedge between others and me. Over the years, the hurtful comments and behavior had become more blatant, and my efforts to overlook them because of her early wounding were not, to say the least, helping her or shielding me. This was a classic case of "hurt people hurt people" and using one's wounds for weapons.

This wise friend helped me see that my efforts to be compassionate could be directed toward the person's original wound, but that I needed another approach to her behavior and her caustic words. Since I could not stop her, I had to stop putting myself in the position of being the recipient of her verbal and emotional abuse.

"You are enabling her to keep on hurting you," my friend told me, "and not only is your behavior not solving her inner hurt, but you are enabling her bad behavior."

I had been hurting for a long time and avoiding this painful truth. This truth, spoken gently but forcefully, opened my eyes to my part in the crazy dance the two of us were doing.

Indeed, it takes two to dance a crazy dance.

"Love calls for discernment," my friend continued, and I listened because I was sick and tired of the dynamics I had not been able to change or, seemingly, avoid.

"If I'm going to die on a cross, it isn't going to be on that one," a friend told me about a similar relationship. "If I die on the cross of that person's abuse of me, it won't help anyone and will only give her permission to keep on acting out her racket on someone else."

Those are tough words, calling for tough action, but they moved me out of unhealthy love to a *fierce love* for myself and a sense of clarity in what it means to have compassion and faithful, *fierce love* in a healthy relationship.

It may appear that what Jesus did was give people another chance, but there was much more involved in Jesus' transformative work. He didn't focus only on the outer behavior; instead, he healed at an internal level as well as at a physical level. He transformed lives so that people like the woman caught in adultery, the Samaritan woman at the well, the woman of ill repute who anointed his feet with precious perfume, and Mary Magdalene were forgiven, accepted, healed, liberated, and empowered to be more than their former lives would allow them to be. Jesus' behavior and actions toward women represents a radical change for then and in his culture.

We see through our own lenses, and those lenses are often clouded with our biases and prejudices. We relate only to the role a person fulfills or plays in his life. We label ourselves and other people, stereotype them, and when we see someone who is having a bad day, we often hold them to their worst moments.

Jesus had a clear eye about people. He "knew what was in" a man or a woman, and he challenged that which held them in bondage, but with deep discernment he worked to change the outer, defeating conditions from the inside out.

The woman with the alabaster jar gave her gift to Jesus in the presence of those who condemned her, but she gave it with a seeming lack of self-consciousness. Whoever she was and whatever her purpose was for anointing him, Jesus received her gift with dignity and respect.

Jesus saw something about the woman at the well that apparently fascinated him. If you read about their conversation in John 4, you will see that he engaged her intellect and connected with her deep sense of spirituality, which may have been unconscious to her at first.

Notice that he wasn't concerned at all about the racial or cultural or religious prejudices that said he shouldn't even talk to her.

The story of the Samaritan woman contains more lines than almost any other encounter Jesus had, as recorded in the Gospels. Note as well that this woman culture deemed as shameful was so influential that she brought her neighbors back to Jesus. "Many Samaritans believed" because of her, according to John. Some have called her "the first evangelist."

Imagine that.

The story of Mary Magdalene is one of my favorites. I love what happened to this woman "from whom Jesus cast out seven demons," but I also love what has happened to her story in the last thirty years as she has been liberated from her label as "prostitute" and restored as one of Jesus' best students. She has been called "his first apostle," and apparently he respected and loved her enough to appear first to her after his resurrection. It was to Mary Magdalene that Jesus gave the assignment of announcing his resurrection to the other disciples.

> *In spite of our mistakes, chances come again*
> *If we lose or if we win*
> *All that matters in the end is how we love*
>
> Beth Nielson Chapman

There is some reason that three of the Gospel writers listed her first in their lists of women (Matt 28:1; Mark 16:1; Luke 24:10). I can speculate and imagine what those reasons might be, but I hope someday to know the reasons *for sure*.

Check out this incident that is recorded in the Gospels Matthew Mark, and Luke and then wonder with me about the story of Mary Magdalene's transformation because of her encounters with Jesus. Wonder with me, as well, about the transformation in our understanding of why the label "prostitute" stuck on her for thirteen centuries, why that label has been disproven, and more curious still, why some people refuse to give up that label of "prostitute."

Jesus exhibited extravagant love and love that was deeply redemptive. His love changed lives in radical ways, but the key to that change was the person's willingness to change. The key to his effectiveness was in him, of course, but it also was in the hearts and wills of those who were willing to cooperate with him in his transforming love.

"Say *yes* sooner!" my friend Keith Hosey tells me when I am struggling to surrender yet another layer of self-will to the living Christ, and it is that "saying *yes*" that sets the love of Christ free to work deep and wide in our lives.

I know that it is possible to have a vital, personal, dynamic love relationship with the living Christ, and I believe that that mysterious presence wants to transform us in the same way his actual presence as the human Jesus transformed the people with whom he met and talked, lived, and loved.

In the rational world in which we live (which seems pretty irrational most of the time!), the rule is "I'll believe it when I see it." The rule in the spiritual world is "I see it when I believe it."

Getting Personal

1. What part of your life would you like for the living Christ to transform?
2. What part of your life would you like for the living Christ to empower? heal? liberate?
3. Do you believe that it is possible to have a relationship with the living Christ?
4. What might happen if you surrender your capacity to love to the living Christ?
5. What might happen if you surrender your limitations to the living Christ?
6. In a class at the Jung Center in Houston, analyst Pittman McGehee said that "the more you love, the more you can love. Like any talent, it can be developed." Do you believe that? Are you willing to try?

There's no story that better illustrates the attitude toward change and transformation than the actions of Jesus toward his disciples after the crucifixion and the resurrection when they had abandoned him, fleeing for their own safety in a locked room away from the center of the action. Jesus' behavior toward them, and especially toward Peter, who had lied about knowing him, betraying him in one of the most hideous ways possible, is so radical that it makes me think about how the experience of resurrection is about behaving in new ways that affirm life in ways that have not been possible before.

I can only imagine how Peter must have felt when he looked into the face of Jesus, the one he had betrayed, at that cookout on the beach after the resurrection. If I had been Peter, I might have run for cover. I know that my heart would have been pounding out of my chest when Jesus looked me straight in the eye and asked me if I loved him, not once but three times.

On the other hand, perhaps something had died and then been resurrected in Peter as well in those terrible three days after the crucifixion. Maybe his ignorance and his small-mindedness, his fear and his shame died. If not during those three days, it must have surely died when Jesus went to him and asked him if he loved him.

Jesus' words evoked something powerful and courageous in Peter, and I'm guessing that his affirmation, "Lord, you know I love you," set in motion the ongoing

> *So, chosen by God for this new life of love, dress in the wardrobe God picked out for you: compassion, kindness, humility, quiet strength, discipline. Be even-tempered, content with second place, quick to forgive an offense. Forgive as quickly and completely as the Master forgave you. And regardless of what else you put on, wear love. It's your basic, all-purpose garment. Never be without it.*
>
> Colossians 3:12-14, (*The Message*)

transformation of Peter the fisherman into Peter the great leader of the disciples in the early church.

It is easy to sit back at a safe distance from history and declare that I could never have betrayed Jesus, but the truth is that in a variety of ways, some of which are conscious to me and some of which are not, I have the same capacity to betray the living Christ within me as Peter did when he betrayed the human Jesus.

However, when I can come out of my failures and imagine Jesus' question coming to me, "Do you love me?" I am on my way back toward the path I have chosen to walk, the path of love and the path of following the teachings of Jesus.

I think that must be why Bishop Mike instructed me to sit in the silence and love God, for declaring and extending love toward God gives God access to our innermost lives and to our depths, where his presence and action work most powerfully.

Saying "I love you" to God activates something powerful in my soul.

Perhaps the story of the reinstatement of Peter shows us how the living Christ, the Holy Spirit at work in us, is all about being given not only another chance, but a transplant of the heart. Perhaps in this story we see that the love of Christ for each of us can extend out to all of us, helping us love each other and to love God and to be instruments of God's redeeming love in the world.

We aren't here just to gratify each other's egos, but to love each other in the name of Christ, to love each other toward wholeness, and to keep on working at it and keep on forgiving each other until somehow we get it.

Country singer Trisha Yearwood covered an old song whose words come to me often: "I'll just keep on falling in love until I get it right." I think that that is good news, made clear in the words of a song.

Sometimes loving each other is about giving a second chance, but it may be that loving each other is about saying "I can't let you do that to me again."

Sometimes loving each other is about giving a cup of cold water or a cup of hot coffee to someone in need.

Sometimes loving each other begins with telling the hard truth to each other.

Loving may mean that you take down the walls you have built between yourselves and reconstructing good boundaries that guard the soul and solitude of each other. Loving each other may mean that you let the work of forgiveness work itself out in your life and another's in its own time, being patient while the hurt is managed and then released. Loving another means that you delight in the other, and that sometimes you look beyond a slight, a mistake, a misstep, an idiosyncrasy and focus on the person's strengths.

Sometimes we have to allow love to turn our temples, the ones we have made and the ones we are, upside down and inside out for a good, thorough cleansing.

We may always have someone who is hard to love in our lives, and we may have our enemies. My friend Sylvia Drake says that "I can forgive my enemies, but I don't have to go to lunch with the people who have hurt me or who are damaging or dangerous to me." Even with those whose actions toward us are toxic, we can still maintain a posture of love or wanting to love.

> Let us keep in step with the Spirit.
> Galatians 5:25b

Sometimes love means "I'm not going to let you hurt me."

Keeping the great commandment is hard. Of course it is hard, and sometimes it seems like an impossible dream.

Love is going to mean loss, and it's going to involve pain. Sometimes you may get your heart broken. You will get discouraged, about your own ability to love and the behavior of others, but the call to love is a mission worth our finest efforts.

Getting Personal

1. In what ways do you betray the life of Christ within you?
2. Is betraying your True Self also a betrayal of the living Christ within you?
3. What do you feel when you imagine Jesus looking into your eyes and asking, "Do you love me?"

4. Do you spend more time wondering about whether or not God loves you or whether or not you love God?

Growing Edges

Now and then, it helps me to get down to the basics. I learned that from my friends in Twelve Step recovery groups. When tossed about or "building up to drink," as they call it, they use anchors such as their slogans, meeting with a sponsor, returning to Step One, and other similar and simple methods to get themselves out of a bad place and into serenity.

One of the things that tosses me about is getting caught up in what I've learned to call "not-love," situations or thought patterns, self-talk, dynamics, or conversations that are negative, hurtful, or even harmful.

One of the slogans that has helped me come out of a fog or a spin is *keep it simple.*

I've spent a lot of time learning about human psychology, the dynamics of relationships and how people grow spiritually. I've had incredible teachers and wise guides.

I've also studied the Bible for a long time.

God's love has reached me through my reading and through my efforts to learn. Love works in intellectual pursuits, and I think God must approve of our developing our minds.

Sometimes, though, I get stuck in my head, paralyzed in analysis.

In my study—in the midst of my many books, my computer, and my elaborate set-up for writing—I often return in my memory to the moment I stood in the home of English novelist Jane Austen in a tiny village in Chawton, Hampshire. There, in a simply furnished room, was a small writing table on which Jane Austen wrote by hand six of the most famous novels in the world. Born in 1775, Austen's books are still being published and read around the world.

> *So, friends, every day do something that won't compute. Love the Lord. Love the world.*
>
> Wendell Berry

People still take entire courses on her work and make pilgrimages to her house in England.

If I could leave tomorrow and enroll in a Jane Austen course at Oxford, I would do it.

It was her tiny writing table, scarcely larger than a platter, that brought me to tears. The simplicity of it all, the well-used surface, her quill, and yet the scope of her work rendered me speechless.

Standing there, the words *keep it simple* came to me, and as I complete this book, those words return.

Love one another as I have loved you were the words Jesus left with us.

The simplicity of the words belies their significance.

Make a choice. Take a stand. Shower your people with love.

Do it again, and then again.

Love, it changes everything.

Within a week after delivering the eulogy at the funeral of my brother-in-law, I was slated to lead the Women's Retreat at Laity Lodge.

Walking over to the Great Hall in this place I have loved for my entire adult life, I was still raw with grief. Nevertheless, I had to step over myself and my own intense feelings and do my job. After all, the women who gathered in that place for those days had expectations for what they heard and experienced on that retreat. They deserved my best efforts, and I wanted to give that to them.

The character and life of my brother-in-law were summed up by my sister, who said that the love chapter of Paul, recorded in 1 Corinthians 13, described

> *I know that I have life only insofar as I have love.*
>
> *I have not love except it comes from Thee.*
>
> *Help me, please, to carry this candle against the Wind.*
>
> — Wendell Berry, *Leavings*

John Williams, to whom she had been married for almost sixty years. My memory of John included his incredible courage and calm grace—through Vietnam, illnesses related to Agent Orange, severe lymphoma, and then Alzheimer's.

So it was that I pulled myself together to rise to the occasion of the Women's Retreat. It was by God's grace that I was able to stand up in front of the retreat participants at Laity Lodge and give my offering, being transparent about what had just happened in my life, but moving past that to focus on the content for the week. It wasn't easy.

I drew on John's courage and his love in every session. If he could have such courage and come out of such difficulties with such love and gratitude, I could surely do my assignment.

After one of the lectures I gave, I sat down, trembling.

The silence in the room was deep, and I'll never forget the moment when singer Cynthia Clawson, my long-time friend, moved quietly to the piano and began singing the perfect words for the moment from the song "How We Love," written by singer Beth Nielson Chapman.

In that holy moment, Cynthia opened her heart and mind to the wind of the Spirit, becoming a conduit of love for those of us gathered in that sacred space. It was the perfect song, and Cynthia was the perfect instrument of love for that specific moment in time:

Life has taught me this: Every day is new, and if anything is true, all that matters when we're through is how we love.

The music and the moment were beautiful, a holiness that was almost palpable. Love, emanating through the room via music, graced us with healing balm. Gathering together, affirming God's love, all of us were strengthened and empowered to begin again, loving one another.

It's all so simple: *God is love. Love one another.*

Amen and amen.

Lessons for Group Discussion and Personal Reflection

What follows in this section are the study questions prepared for a twenty-one-week Bible study I wrote and taught for the women of the Thursday Morning Bible Study at River Oaks Baptist Church. While the questions reflect what I have written in the rest of the book, the twenty-one lessons and the seventeen chapters are not intended to track with each other, but to support each other.

The questions in these lessons begin with Scripture readings and Bible study questions. There are also questions titled "For Your Eyes Only" because they are personal and intended for your own private reflection.

Any of these questions, whether in the chapters of the book or within these lessons, can be used for small group discussions or for private journaling and prayer. However you use them, my intent is for the questions to deepen your awareness of God's love for you and the power of love that is within you.

Lesson 1

1. Read Matthew 22:37-40. What is the context? To whom is Jesus speaking? What precedes his words?
2. Mark 12:28-33. How is this like Matthew's account? How is it different?
3. Why do you think Jesus chose this as "the greatest commandment"?
4. Read Deuteronomy 6:4-9. This is called the Shema, the creed that an observant Jew recites every morning upon awakening. What does Jesus add to the Shema in his commandment?
5. Read John 13:34. What is the context? What had happened, as recorded in the first part of John 13?

6. What does Jesus say is the "test" by which others will be able to identify them as his disciples? What do you think that means, practically?
7. Read 1 Corinthians 13. Which parts of this chapter are the most meaningful to you? Why do you think Paul, shaped by the Jewish law, was able to write these words?

For Your Eyes Only
8. What is the difference between "need-love" and "gift-love"?
9. Do you think that some people are born with a natural capacity to love and be loved, or do you think that everyone has that basic need?
10. What do you think blocks people in their love relationships?

Lesson 2
1. Read Genesis 1 and Genesis 2:1-7. From the beginning, God's nature, which is love, manifested itself in creative activity. Describe God's creative activity with adjectives.
2. From these verses, what attitude toward his creation best describes God?
3. Genesis 1:27 and 28 reveal the first biblical statement about the original relationship between God and humans. Describe that relationship.
4. Read Genesis 2:7. Thinking symbolically, what is the meaning of this verse? (Read John 20:22. Why do you think Jesus did this?)
5. Remember the old hymn "Holy Spirit, Breathe on Me"? When we sing/pray that, what are we wanting, needing, asking for?
6. Read Genesis 2:15-25. What evidence in these passages do you see of God investing in humans the capacities of *intimacy* with each other, *the power to choose,* and *the ability to communicate with God and with each other?*
7. In Genesis 2:25, primary characteristics of love are revealed. What are they?

8. Genesis 3:21 reveals a God of love, providing for his children by making coverings for them. What do the coverings represent/symbolize?
9. Read Genesis 12:1-3. This is the event that marked the beginning of God's *covenant* relationship with the children of Israel. In your own words, describe what a covenant relationship is. How is a covenant relationship different from a business deal or a contract? What does love have to do with a covenant relationship?
10. Read the rest of Genesis. Repeatedly in the rest of Genesis, you read "And God said," revealing a primary characteristic of God's nature and God's love, and it is *communication.* How is communication an instrument of love?
11. Now read all of Exodus. Read Exodus 33:14 How is *presence* a manifestation of love?
12. Read Exodus 33:6-7. What does God say about his love in these verses?
13. Read Deuteronomy 6:4-5. God had given the children of Israel the Ten Commandments (see Exod 20:1-17), which were intended to be the "rules" by which they would participate in the covenant relationship. In this verse, however, God takes the relationship to a higher level—that of love. Why is loving God good for people?

For Your Eyes Only
14. Who was the person who first taught you about God's love?
15. What is your first *experience* of God's love?
16. How has your religious life enhanced and supported your sense of God's love for you and nurtured your spirituality?
17. In your relationship with God, do you feel as free and "naked" (vulnerable, transparent, open, innocent) as Adam and Eve did in the garden of Eden?
18. What "fig leaves" (defense mechanisms, masks, "coverings") do you wear to hide yourself from God? from yourself? from others?
19. For you, personally and practically, what does it mean for you to *love* God? In what ways do you love God?

20. What barriers exist between you and God? What can you do about those barriers? fear? guilt or shame? hate or anger? unbelief? skepticism, cynicism? insecurity? confusion?
21. Do you believe, really, that loving God could remove the barriers?
22. What's the one thing you wish God would do in you/for you/through you?
23. What winds blow against the candle of love in your life (see lines by Wendell Berry at the beginning of this section)?

Lesson 3

1. Read Exodus 1–6:8. What actions did God initiate on behalf of the children of Israel?
2. Why would God do this, given that the children of Israel had gotten themselves in bondage in the first place?
3. What promises did God make to Moses for this project of liberating the children of Israel (see Exod 3–4)?
4. What provoked God's anger toward Moses (see Exod 4:1-17)?
5. What promises did God make to Moses, as recorded in Exodus 6:1-8?
6. In Exodus 14:1-29, what is the evidence of God's provision? God's protection? God's guidance? God's presence?
7. How did the children of Israel make it hard for God to liberate them?
8. Read Exodus 15:13. What does this tell you about the nature of God?
9. Read Exodus 16. What did God provide for the children of Israel? How did they make it hard for him to provide for them?
10. Read Exodus 20:1-17. How are these commandments evidence of God's love for the children of Israel?
11. Scan the book of Leviticus. How did the restrictions and guidance of God concerning everyday, ordinary life reveal God's love? Why is there such specificity?
12. Read Numbers 6:24-26. What does this reveal about God's attitude toward his children?

13. Read Numbers 11–14. What do these passages reveal about the intimacy of God with the children of Israel?
14. Read Deuteronomy 1:29-33. Does the tension between God and his children reveal distance in their relationship or intimacy?
15. Once again, God sets the terms of the relationship and the liberation process. What are the terms? See Deuteronomy 6:13-25. Why did God have to keep repeating himself?
16. Read Joshua 1:9. What is our attitude to be when God is attempting to guide us, liberate us, provide for us, and protect us?

For Your Eyes Only
17. Make a list of the ways God has provided for you in your lifetime. Do you see those ways as God's everlasting love for you?
18. Make a list of the ways God has protected you. Who represented God's protective love for you?
19. Make a list of the ways you have felt guided by God. What was that like?
20. From what might God be trying to liberate you?
21. How are you cooperating with God?
22. How are you making it hard for God?
23. Sometimes we are afraid to be free, and sometimes our fears keep us from going after what we want. At some point, though, we can choose to "feel the fear and do it anyway" or we can allow our desire for something to grow larger than our fear.

    Suppose the thing you want is freedom from an afflictive emotion, such as fear, guilt, shame, inadequacy, resentment, hate, anger, or envy. Why would you be afraid to give that up? Suppose you want freedom from an addiction. How has God tried to help you with that in the past? How have you made it hard for yourself and for God? Suppose what you want is freedom from negativism, pessimism, cynicism, or skepticism. What lies do you tell yourself about how those attitudes "protect" you? How do those attitudes mesh with the truth of God's love for you?
24. Ponder the words in Joshua 1:9. What feelings do those words evoke in you?

Lesson 4

As background reading for the lesson's emphasis in the Psalms, you may want to read about the life of David. The story of David begins in 1 Samuel 16 and continues through 1 Kings 2:12. The notorious relationship between David and Bathsheba can be found in 2 Samuel 11–12, which is thought to be the event that precipitated the writing of the beautiful prayer of confession in Psalm 51. (Please note that scholars believe people other than David contributed to the 150 prayers we know as "the Psalms.")

I. Read as many of these psalms as you can, and underline the verses that speak of the love, compassion, mercy, and grace of God. As you have time, especially read these: 1, 2, 5, 7, 8, 18, 19, 23, 25, 26, 27, 30, 31, 32, 33, 36, 46, 51, 56, 63, 67, 68, 78, 86, 91, 94, 95, 107, 116, 118, 121, 122, 131*, 139*, 144, 145*, 146*.

1. Which of these psalms is most meaningful to you?
2. What parts of God's nature do the psalmists reveal that appeal to you most?
3. What evidence of God's work that is consistent with his nature described in these psalms do you see in your everyday life?

II. Read Psalm 136 every day for a week. Linger over the phrase "His love endures forever" (to linger over: sit with it, mull it over in your mind, journal about it, question it, affirm it).

4. Why was it so important for the children of Israel to repeat that phrase over and over?
5. Look back over your life. Imagine that you were going to make statements about God's enduring love out of your own life. What events might you include that, when written, you could also say, "His love endures forever"? Do you dare write your own psalm, using this pattern of Psalm 136?

For Your Eyes Only

6. How hard is it for you to believe in the enduring love of God in *your* life?
7. What makes you question or doubt the enduring love of God in your life?
8. Writer Diane Ackerman says, "It begins in mystery and it will end in mystery, but what a rare and beautiful country lies in between." How does a God-concept of God as love help you see the mystery and the beautiful and rare country of life?

Lesson 5

Read the Song of Solomon.
1. Why do you think this book was included in the canon?
2. What kinds of conversations/debates/dialogues were held pertaining to the inclusion of this book in the canon?
3. What does this book say about God?
4. What does this book say about human sexuality, beauty, the love between a man and a woman?
5. Is this book to be interpreted as being about the relationship between God and an individual? Or is it about what it says it is about?
6. Why do you think it is that there is so little preached or taught from this book?
7. Have you read *Life of the Beloved*, by Henri Nouwen? If not, how quickly can you remedy that?

For Your Eyes Only

8. Read Song of Solomon 6:3. Are you willing to take that verse and internalize it for yourself as a description of your relationship with God?
9. Thomas Merton says this about love: "Love affects more than our thinking and our behavior toward those we love. It transforms our entire life. Genuine love is a personal revolution. Love takes your ideas, your desires, and your actions and welds them together in one experience and one living reality which is a new you." What

part of that quotation resonates most with you? How does it challenge you? Is Merton speaking of any love or primarily of the love of God?

Lesson 6

1. How does Jesus define "eternal life"?
2. What does it mean "to know God"?
3. Describe how a person might be who is "one with God," as Jesus prayed for his disciples to be?
4. What does love have to do with being one with God?
5. Whose love creates the unity with God—ours or God's?

Read Song of Solomon 1–2:7.

6. If you interpret this book as analogy and attempt to understand "intimacy with God" as the underlying theme, what verses support the idea of "yearning for God"?
7. How would you apply 1:6 to one's life? What is the meaning of this for us?
8. What could the phrase "his banner over me is love" possibly mean to us symbolically?

Read Song of Solomon 2:8–3:5.

9. What do you think is meant by the invitation in 2:10-13, if you interpret this passage as an analogy?
10. The section from 2:16–3:5 seems to indicate a faltering in the relationship. Why does "faltering" happen in our relationship with God?

Read Song of Solomon 3:6–5:1.

11. In these verses, it could be said that there is a growing intimacy between the lover and the beloved. In what ways do you see that love can grow between God and an individual? In other words, what signs would indicate growth in intimacy? And what can one do to facilitate that growth of intimacy?

Read Song of Solomon 5:2–7:13.
12. What feeling do the words in 6:3 evoke in you? Is there anything to fear in this kind of intimacy with God?
13. What are the components that nurture a love relationship with God?
14. What does it mean to "belong" to the lover (see 7:10)? What is scary about this? Why would anyone want it?

Read Song of Solomon 8:1-14.
15. What does it mean to "place a seal over your heart" (v. 6)?
16. Verses 8:6b-7a are some of the most well-known verses of the book. What do they mean?

For Your Eyes Only
Seventeenth-century French mathematician, physicist, and philosopher Blaise Pascal said this: "There is a God shaped vacuum in the heart of every man which cannot be filled by any created thing, but only by God, the Creator, made known through Jesus."

17. With what kinds of things do you think you try to fill that "God-shaped vacuum"? How is that working?
18. What spiritual practices seem to help fill that vacuum?
19. How do you think it was that a mathematician and physicist came to this belief?

In the fourth century, Augustine of Hippo struggled mightily in his life. Before he "found God," he had a series of desperate searches in excessive pleasure, false religions, philosophy, dissipation, and distractions. Finally, desperate and exhausted from these futile efforts, he cried out, "How long, Lord, how long?"

From that time, he was almost immediately led to the Scriptures and an intense search for God and an intense search to know himself, which led to his writing the famous *Confessions*. The following quote is attributed to Augustine: "Almighty God, you have made us for yourself, and our hearts are restless till they find their rest in you."

20. How is it that a fourth-century seeker and a seventeenth-century philosopher could come to the same idea about intimacy with God?
21. How do you assuage your "restlessness" of spirit and heart? How well does that work for you?
22. Could it be that we could interpret the God-shaped vacuum and the restless heart as evidence that God is calling to us and that it is God's love that is yearning for us?

In the twentieth century Henri Nouwen wrote in his classic book *Life of the Beloved* these words: "The greatest gift my friendship can give to you is the gift of your Belovedness. I can give that gift only insofar as I have claimed it for myself. Isn't that what friendship is all about: giving to each other the gift of our Belovedness?" (p. 26).

23. How generous are you giving the gift of that kind of friendship to another?
24. From whom do you withhold it? What does that do to you?
25. Have you read Nouwen's book yet? If not, why not?

Lesson 7

Read Isaiah 53:6.
1. What does this say about our tendency as human beings?
2. What does this say about God?

Read Romans 1:18-32.
3. What does this say about sin?
4. What does it say about the nature of God?

Read Romans 5:6-8, 7:18-19, 8:1-2, 3:23.
5. What does this say about human beings?
6. What does it say about God?

LESSONS FOR GROUP DISCUSSION AND PERSONAL REFLECTION

Read 1 John 1:8-10.
7. What does this say about human beings?
8. What does it say about God?

Read Genesis 4.
9. What was the problem between Cain and Abel?
10. What is the "sin" God is talking about in verses 6-7?
11. Why does God say that the "sin is crouching at your door"? What does that mean?

Read Genesis 5.
12. Why do you think Genesis 5:1 is written here?
13. What does it mean in this chapter that people "walked with God"?

Read Genesis 6.
14. What was the essential problem God had with the men and women of this time?
15. What do you think the violence and corruption mention in verse 11 was?

Read 2 Samuel 11. (Background of David's life, leading up to this point, begins in 1 Samuel 16.)
16. What were the feelings and factors behind David's behavior?

Read 2 Samuel 12.
17. How did God use Nathan as a redemptive agent in David's life?
18. What might have happened to David if Nathan hadn't done this intervention?
19. What does it say about David that he admitted his sin?
20. Why did David say that his sin was against the Lord (see v. 13)?

Read Psalm 51.
21. What does this psalm reveal to us about the nature of a love relationship between an individual and God?
22. Why is this psalm so powerful?
23. What is so powerful about confession?

Some Things to Think About

24. How would you differentiate among these words/terms?

sin	breaking a civil law	a mistake
breaking God's law	hurting someone or yourself	an error in judgment
a wrong	a crime	self-destructive behavior

25. What is the difference between the act of sin and the motivation behind the sin?
26. In dealing with a crime, jurors are asked to determine motivation. What difference does it make to determine if the crime committed was done out of ignorance, neglect, or willful intention? Isn't it still a crime?
27. Why is it that human beings have a tendency to project their own "stuff" onto someone else? What's the point of doing that? Does it solve anything?

For Your Eyes Only

28. What is the one thing that separates you from God's love?
29. What is the thing you truly hate in other people?
30. Is there something you just cannot bring yourself to forgive, either in yourself or in someone else?
31. What is the difference between judgment and discernment in your mind?
32. Do you think God's forgiveness includes the worst thing you have ever done, the worst thing that has been done to you, or the worst thing you have ever heard about?
33. If sin is "missing the mark," what does that mean for you personally?

Lesson 8

1. Read Isaiah 26:3. Why is this practice essential in keeping your focus and your footing? In what ways do we "keep our minds steadfast"?

LESSONS FOR GROUP DISCUSSION AND PERSONAL REFLECTION   235

2. Read Isaiah 5. How does the prophet visualize the relationship of God with the children of Israel? Where have the people gone wrong? What have they done that has brought on "the woes"? What is the reason for the problem given in verse 13? What do you make of verses 25b-26?
3. What do you make of Isaiah 7:9b?
4. Where is the hope? See Isaiah 7:14, 9:1-7, 11:1-3a, 12, 40:1-5.
5. Read Isaiah 40:25-31, 41:10-20, and 42:1-9, 14-17. What is the most important thought/idea in these verses?
6. Read Isaiah 43:1-19 and 45:2-7. What do these verses reveal about the nature of God?
7. Read Isaiah 45:9-10. What is the warning?
8. What is the counsel in Isaiah 48:17-19?
9. Read Isaiah 49:8-16. What does this say about God and his attitude and action toward people?
10. Read Isaiah 53:1-6. What does this mean to contemporary people?
11. What invitations do you find in Isaiah 55? To whom are they written?
12. Read Jeremiah 6:16. What does this mean for contemporary people?
13. Read Jeremiah 17 and 18. What counsel in those passages still works today?
14. Read Jeremiah 29:4-14; 31:3-4, 31-34. What is the reason for hope?
15. What is hopeful about Jeremiah 33:3? 33:6?
16. Read Lamentations 3:22-27. How is this "good news"?
17. Read Micah 7:18-19. What kind of God is like this?
18. Read Habakkuk 3:17-19. In what circumstances might this Scripture give you the strength to keep on keeping on in the journey of faith? What does it say about persistence? about endurance? about hope?
19. Read Zephaniah 3:17. In what circumstances might you "need" this image of God?
20. Read Haggai 2:4-5. Does this counsel apply to us today?

21. Read Malachi 3:6-12. What is the most important teaching of these verses? Why does God ask the people to test him in the way it is described here?

For Your Eyes Only
22. In what area of your life are you being called to surrender something to God?
23. In what area of your life are you being asked to be strong?
24. What people encourage your ability to stay strong?
25. Is your hope in God? in your abilities? resources? ingenuity? in an outcome? in other people?
26. Is there anything you think God may have asked of you that you have not been willing to do? How has that refusal affected your life?

Lesson 9

Read Hosea 1.
1. Who was Hosea?
2. What did God tell him to do?
3. Why on earth would God tell someone to do what it says God told Hosea to do?
4. Who was Gomer?
5. What happened after they married?
6. Was this a setup for poor old Hosea?

Read Hosea 2.
7. Is this book about Hosea and his dysfunctional family, or is it about Israel and its dysfunctional relationship with God?
8. What is God talking about in verses 16-23?
9. Specifically, what does God mean by verses 19-20?

Read Hosea 3.
10. What are the specific charges against Israel?
11. How do you see the idea of sin as "separation from God" at work in this passage?

LESSONS FOR GROUP DISCUSSION AND PERSONAL REFLECTION

12. Which of the seven deadly sins do you see in the account of Israel's state of being?
13. What is the difference between individual sin and collective sin?

Read Hosea 4.
14. What are the specific judgments against Israel? What are the consequences of their behavior?
15. What does it mean that Israel is "adulterous"?
16. If adulterating yourself can be defined as letting yourself be used for the wrong purpose, how has the nation of Israel done this?

Read Hosea 5.
17. What is going to happen to Israel because of their sins?
18. Are we punished more *for* our sins or *by* them?

Read Hosea 6–10.
19. In Hosea 6:1-4, there is a glimmer of hope. How would you define the hope? For what is this a call?

For Your Eyes Only
20. Read 1 John 1:5–2:11. Based on this passage, what is the biblical "attitude" toward our sin?
21. What does this passage say about *denial*?
22. Based on the reality of God's unfailing love for us, what is our attitude toward our own sin to be?
23. My belief system is based on the idea that the "little s sins" are the behaviors that separate us from others and are the symptoms of the Big S Sins, which are fear and guilt and shame, hate and anger and insecurity. The Big S Sins are at the root of our problems; they are afflictive emotions that are internal to us. Based on those ideas, how would you complete these sentences?

Today I am more aware of _____
regarding my own Big "S" Sins.

I am most prone to experience separation from God when
_____.

The sin in others that bothers me the most is
_____.

Of the four Big S Sins, the one that gives me the most trouble is _____, and the way it manifests itself is _____.

The mask I wear to hide my Big S Sins is
_____.

24. Thomas Keating says that if we hold on to guilt for more than two minutes after we have made confession, we are praying to the wrong God. Is there any guilt you are unwilling to surrender?
25. Cecil Osborne says guilt will find a way to be punished or forgiven. What do you think that means?

Lesson 10
Read Hosea 11–12.
1. These chapters reveal a great deal about the nature of God. What adjectives would you use to describe God, based on this chapter?

Read Hosea 13.
2. Describe God's anger toward Israel. What is his chief complaint against the children of Israel? Why is he so angry?
3. How would you describe "redemptive wrath"?
4. In the face of what they have done, what is God's attitude and intention toward the children of Israel?
5. Are the consequences of Israel's unfaithfulness, as stated in verse 3, God's punishment or the results the people brought on themselves?

Read Hosea 14.
6. So what is God's "final word" toward his wayward people?

7. What is the necessary response of the children of Israel?

Read Amos 6 (and all the book of Amos, if you can bear it!).
8. What are God's complaints against the children of Israel?
9. What are the results of their actions?
10. Why are the religious acts of the people hated by God (see vv. 21-23)?
11. Why are justice and righteousness (v. 24) "the way back" (see also Jer 22:2-3)?

Read Micah 6:8.
12. Why is this counsel so crucial to spiritual health?

Read Obadiah.
13. What is this prophet's message to the children of Israel?

Read Jonah, especially Jonah 2:8-9.
14. What hope/help does this prophet hold out for the children of Israel?

For Your Eyes Only
15. If *faithfulness* is more than simply *not* being intimate with another person (as in marriage) or *not* worshiping or serving another god, what *is* it?
16. What do you think about the first four commandments? Are they "useful" or relevant now?

Lesson 11
1. What have you learned about the love of God? How have you put what you have learned into action?
2. What has been most difficult for you to accept in this study? What has been most liberating?
3. What are your own personal barriers to experiencing the love of God for you? What in you separates you from God?

4. What spiritual practices actually enhance the experience of God's love for you?
5. In what one area of your life do you most need to experience the love of God? the forgiveness of God? the mercy of God? the grace of God?
6. What do you do to repair the breach (or separation) between yourself and God?
7. Who in your life is a resource for you, helping you experience the love of God?
8. For whom are you a resource or an instrument of God's love?

Lesson 12

Read 1 Corinthians 12–13.
1. Read 1 Corinthians 12 before you read 1 Corinthians 13. Why do you think Paul positioned the counsel in these two chapters together?
2. Why do you think the "swing sentence" between the two chapters refers to "a more excellent way"? What is the more excellent way?
3. How does Paul put the "showy gifts" in the larger context of what matters most?
4. Why are tongues, prophecy, faith, and generosity rendered weak or even impotent without love?
5. How can one know if one has love?
6. What might be the danger of majoring on tongues, prophecy, faith, and altruism and forgetting love?
7. How does love humble us?
8. Paul sets a high standard of love in verses 4-8a. In what ways can a person ever know if she is manifesting this kind of love?
9. What is the difference between love as Paul describes it and codependency?
10. What is the difference between love as Paul describes it and caretaking?
11. What is the difference between caretaking and caregiving?
12. What important truth is Paul telling us in verses 8b-12?
13. Why is love the greatest of spiritual virtues?

14. How does love help us be more discerning?

For Your Eyes Only

15. How would you describe your love relationship with God?
16. When do you most deeply experience God's great love for you?
17. What person in your life has truly loved you for who you are?
18. What effect does being loved have on you?
19. What is the opposite of love—hate, indifference, power, control, or fear?
20. What decision could you make about giving love that would improve your life?

Lesson 13

Read John 13:1-17.

1. What do you think the Gospel writer meant when he began the recounting of this event by writing about Jesus "having loved his own who were in the world" (v. 1b)?
2. What did John mean when he wrote that Jesus "now showed them the full extent of his love" (v. 1b)?
3. What evidence do you see in this passage that Jesus was following the guidance of the Father?
4. What do you think the disciples thought and felt when Jesus began to wash their feet?
5. How did what Jesus did "show the full extent of his love"? What qualities of love did that action reveal?
6. Why do you think Peter resisted Jesus' initiative?
7. What does Peter's response to Jesus' explanation—"wash my hands and my head as well"—reveal about Peter and about human nature?
8. Why did Jesus ask the disciples if they understood what he had done?
9. Move beyond the literal interpretation of this event and see it symbolically. How can people love each other in ways that reflect the spirit of what Jesus did?
10. What qualities of love and loving was Jesus teaching his disciples by this action?

11. What qualities does a human being need in order to receive love?
12. What qualities does a human being need in order to give love?

Read John 13:34-35.
13. What is different about Jesus' "new commandment"?
14. What is the evidence that proves discipleship? Was that true just for Jesus' actual disciples or for all of us who call ourselves "followers of Christ"?

For Your Eyes Only
15. The human Jesus isn't available to wash your feet today, except through the action of another human being. What similar action would communicate God's love for you in a way that you would experience healing and transforming love for you?
16. Who is hardest for you to love? What's the problem? What's the solution?

Lesson 14
1. What do you think are the five prevailing "rules" of relationships in your particular culture? your family? your church? In other words, what "norms of behavior," either conscious or unconscious, govern the interactions of people with whom you live and work?

Read the Beatitudes in Matthew 5:1-12.
2. What do each of these principles (beatitudes) have to do with human relationships?
3. Why do you think human relationships are so hard?

For Your Eyes Only
4. What is your most difficult relationship right now? What would it take to change it?
5. In what ways do you express love to your loved ones? How does that work for you? for them?
6. In what ways do others express love to you? How good are you at receiving what others give to you?

7. Which one of the beatitudes do you most need as an active principle, working in your life?

Lesson 15

Read 1 John 1:8-10 and 1 John 2:9-11.
1. How does the problem of self-deception taint our relationship with God?
2. How does the problem of self-deception taint our relationships with other people?
3. What do these verses say about the problem of denial, self-justification, and rationalization in relationships?
4. How are those behaviors a problem in our relationship with God?
5. How are those behaviors a problem in our relationships with other people?
6. What do you think it means to "confess" our sins? How are we to do that?

Read Matthew 6:9-13.
7. List your three most significant relationships. What would it be like if, within those relationships, you could honestly pray "on earth as it is in heaven" for those relationships? What would it be like if you prayed "Thy will be done" for each of the people who are most important to you?
8. What is the most important organization to which you belong? Where are there "knots" in that organization? What is the cause of them? Are the knots caused in any way by the principle that "where love is lacking, power and control rush in"?
9. Using the definition of the word *trespasses* in verse 12, list the ways you trespass in other people's lives. How do others trespass in yours? In contemporary language, this verse can be interpreted to be about having good boundaries. Why is that important?
10. Why is forgiveness so important in human relationships? What happens when forgiveness is withheld?

For Your Eyes Only

11. What is your *reflexive* pattern of behavior in dealing with conflict? How well does that work for you? What would you like to be different in your behavior?

Lesson 16

Read Matthew 18:15-35.
1. What is Jesus teaching the disciples about lifestyle forgiveness in this passage?
2. How is "lifestyle forgiveness" possible?
3. How is "lifestyle forgiveness" a form of love?
4. What is Jesus *not* saying about forgiveness?
5. Why didn't the servant who had been granted mercy give what he had been given?
6. Why is forgiveness so hard?
7. What is the difference between forgiveness and excusing?
8. What is the difference between tolerance and forgiveness?
9. Why are human beings so prone to want justice for others but mercy for themselves?
10. What does it mean that "guilt will find a way to be punished"?

For Your Eyes Only

11. A wise person once said, "I am more afraid of non-forgiveness than almost anything." What is your experience with the damage that comes from non-forgiveness?
12. It has been said that "Resentment is like taking poison and waiting for the other person to die." In what ways is this statement accurate?

Read John 12:1-11 (also recorded in Matthew 26:6-13, Mark 14:3-9, Luke 7:37-39).
13. How are these accounts of this event alike? How are they different?
14. Why was this event was so important that all four Gospel writers included it in their accounts of Jesus' life?
15. What does this event tell you about Jesus?

16. Why was the woman so determined to do this act?
17. Why did she know where Jesus was?
18. Why was she willing to risk what other people would say in order to do this act?
19. Can you say that this act was an act of love? If so, explain.
20. What is the "central truth" taken from this event?
21. How are forgiveness and love connected?

<u>For Your Eyes Only</u>
22. In what places or relationships are you free and able to express love and forgiveness without fear or self-consciousness?
23. In what places do you hold back, or is "holding back" the way you live in most relationships?
24. What is your "alabaster jar of precious ointment" (your gift) that is uniquely yours?
25. In what ways do you "pour it out"?
26. How do you hold back?
27. Is there anyone who ever ridicules your gift? or says that it isn't worthy? or makes you feel embarrassed for giving it?
28. Can you accept that giving your unique gift that flows from your unique mix of talents, abilities, affections, passions—your bliss—is your alabaster jar of precious ointment?
29. How would you define "spontaneous and free" when it comes to love?
30. How does fear keep you from loving others? from receiving love?
31. How does guilt keep you from expressing love freely? from receiving it?
32. How does shame hamper your ability to love and be loved?
33. How do hate and anger, prejudices and biases, judgment and negativism trash up the well of your life?
34. How does your insecurity or inadequacy prevent you from giving and receiving love?
35. When confronted with your own inner barriers to love, remember these steps as a way out of the trap:

Awareness: I become aware of what it is in me that is causing a separation from God, from myself, or from others.

Acceptance: I accept full responsibility for this barrier (sin). It is mine. No one is making me hold on to it. I chose it, and I choose it.

Abandonment: I abandon this inner barrier (sin) into the hands and heart of God, who longs to take it from me, heal me, and free me from this bondage of sin. Remember that nature abhors a vacuum, and so it is here that we are to pray that God will fill the vacuum created by the abandonment of sin with his love.

Practice: I practice new behaviors and attitudes that are consistent with my decision to live in love rather than fear, guilt, etc.

Patience: I am as patient with myself as God is with me.

Persistence: I keep on doing what is of love and what is healthy, one day at a time.

Lesson 17
For Your Eyes Only
1. What is the one way you get in your own way in having the kind of loving relationships you say you want?
2. What is the *reason* you give yourself (the rationalization or excuse) that you keep on doing the same thing, expecting a different response?
3. If you were honest with yourself (crazy thought, right?), is there someone in your life that you have decided is "the problem," keeping you from peace and happiness? How did this person get that position?
4. Are there relationships in your life where you keep trying to have a close friendship or relationship with someone who really cannot reciprocate or does not want to or does not want that kind of

relationship *with you* for any number of reasons? What is your response?
5. How do you determine if "the problem" between yourself and someone else is your problem or theirs?
6. If "the problem" has been created by both you and the other person, how do you go about working on your part of the problem? How do you engage the other person in the solution? What do you do if the other person won't do his/her part?
7. What is your biggest pet peeve in relationships? Be honest: Are you seeing in someone else what is in you?
8. What about your relationship with God? Is there a problem there? Is it satisfying or not?
9. Is there something in your life you need to change—an attitude or a habit that is producing behaviors that hurt you or others?
10. Is there something for which you need to make confession or make amends?
11. If you could wake up on Easter morning with a "clean mind and a pure heart," what would that mean for you?
12. What are you willing to do to experience the forgiveness, grace, and mercy of God in a way that you know you are being transformed?
13. Do you try to get God to do your bidding? How is that working for you?
14. How do you decide what is God's business and what is yours?
15. When you are truly experiencing the fruit of the Spirit—love, joy, peace, patience, kindness, gentleness, faithfulness, and self-control—what is that like?
16. What prohibits you from experiencing the fruit of the Spirit more often?
17. Thomas Keating says that if we continue to feel guilty two minutes after we have made confession, we are confessing to the wrong God. Is that relevant to you?
18. What keeps you from giving love freely, spontaneously, and without strings?
19. What keeps you from letting the love of God—sometimes mediated through others and sometimes given in mysterious,

intangible ways—fill your mind, heart, and soul with joy and peace?

Lesson 18

Read Luke 16:1-17.
1. If the rich man is symbolic of God in this parable, what does this parable tell us about the nature of God?
2. Who accused the manager of wasting the rich man's possessions?
3. How did the manager get in the predicament he was in? Was it negligence? laziness? stupidity? revenge? age or infirmity? fear? ignorance? carelessness? or something else?
4. Was his "solution," described in verses 5-7, an act of desperation? an act of heroism? a last-resort moment of brilliance? an act of amends toward the rich man? self-serving? making the best of his failure?
5. Why does the master commend him? What does that say about God?
6. What is the central truth of this parable?
7. What is it about this parable that makes you uncomfortable?
8. What about this parable irritates you?
9. Is there anything about this parable that makes sense to you? If so, what?
10. How can we apply the central truth of this parable to our lives today?
11. Exactly what does Jesus mean by the words in verse 13?
12. What does he *not* mean?
13. Why is Jesus' teaching about serving two masters hard to follow?
14. How would following that teaching make life easier?
15. Is verse 15 pertinent or applicable to us today?
16. Is being shrewd a good thing or a bad thing?

For Your Eyes Only
17. Why is it hard to live in the world and, at the same time, live kingdom values?

18. What does it mean to be street-smart? Why is it important to be street-smart?

Lesson 19
Read John 4:1-26.
10. How did Jesus change this woman's life?
11. How did he show respect for her?
12. How did he liberate her? From what did he free her?
13. How did he empower this woman?
14. How is love *transformative*?
15. What did this woman get that the disciples did not get?

Read John 20:1-18.
16. What was it that drew Mary Magdalene to the tomb of Jesus?
17. What risk do you suppose this was to her?
18. What does this scene tell you about *fierce love*?
19. What did it do for Mary Magdalene for Jesus to appear first to her and also to give her the message to take to the disciples?

For Your Eyes Only
20. Who in your life has honored your intelligence?
21. Who has challenged your mind and your thoughts?
22. Who has seen past your mistakes and failures to the real you?
23. When was a time in your life when you felt a breakthrough of God's grace/love?
24. From what have you been set free?
25. For what have you been set free?
26. What are you willing to risk in order to be who you were meant to be?
27. How do you know that God really loves you—you, yourself?
28. In what ways has someone empowered you to be who you really are?
29. In what ways do you hold back your uniqueness?
30. How did Mary Magdalene's love for Jesus change her?

Lesson 20

Read John 6:1-15 (also found in Matthew 14:13-21, Mark 6:32-44, and Luke 9:10-17).

1. How might Jesus have felt about the crowds who followed him because they were looking for miraculous signs?
2. What do you make of Jesus' question to Philip, asking where "we" should buy bread for the crowd? What was he hoping to do, testing Philip like this?
3. If he already knew what he was going to do, why did Jesus ask Philip this question? What does that tell you about Jesus?
4. Wasn't Philip's response a realistic response? Why should Jesus and/or the disciples be concerned about what this crowd had to eat anyway? Couldn't they have brought their own lunch—or stopped by the local deli?
5. Was Andrew's response (v. 8) sarcastic?
6. What do you make of Jesus taking the loaves from the small boy? What do you think the boy thought about that?
7. Why is there such a point made about Jesus "giving thanks" before he distributed the bounty of loaves and fish?
8. How do you think these words relate to each other—genius, generous, generativity, genuine?
9. Jesus' nature was to give lavishly, generously, authentically—to meet people's needs. What do you think he was trying to teach the disciples in this lived parable?
10. What do you think this story teaches about giving the gift(s) one has?
11. What does this parable teach about love?

For Your Eyes Only

12. To what degree are you a giver when it comes to life and love? To what degree are you a taker?
13. To what extent do you withhold affection, encouragement, affirmation, love? Why? What is the result?
14. How does it feel to give love to someone when they won't accept it?
15. How do you suppose it affects God when we block his love for us?

16. How does it affect you when you defend yourself against loving or being loved?
17. What is the one afflictive emotion that blocks your experiencing love from others?
18. What is the one afflictive emotion that prevents you from giving love to others?

Lesson 21

Read Matthew 25:14-28.
1. If you were hearing Jesus teach this parable, what truth do you think you would hear?
2. What is the most interesting part of this parable?
3. What is the most disturbing part of this parable?
4. What does this parable have to do with love—if anything?

Read John 21:15-23.
5. Why did Jesus gave Peter a second chance?
6. Why did Jesus asked Peter if he loved him?
7. How might Peter have felt, hearing that question?
8. Why did Jesus ask the question three times?
9. What does this incident have to do with love?
10. From reading this passage and from our study this year, what does it mean to "follow Jesus"?

Read Matthew 5:13-16.
11. What does "being salt and light in the world" have to do with love?
12. How does "letting your light shine" contradict teachings about humility?
13. What is humility anyway?
14. How is "hiding your light under a bowl" arrogance?
15. How is "letting your light shine" humility?

Read Matthew 5:38-49.
16. Do Jesus' teachings make good sense, or is he just an idealist?

17. It's hard enough sometimes to love one's neighbor, but how can one really love an enemy? What does Jesus mean?

Read Matthew 22:37-40.

18. So what do you think about Jesus' greatest commandment now?

Other available titles from SMYTH & HELWYS

#Connect
Reaching Youth Across the Digital Divide
Brian Foreman

Reaching our youth across the digital divide is a struggle for parents, ministers, and other adults who work with Generation Z—today's teenagers. *#Connect* leads readers into the technological landscape, encourages conversations with teenagers, and reminds us all to be the presence of Christ in every facet of our lives. 978-1-57312-693-9 120 pages/pb **$13.00**

Beginnings
A Reverend and a Rabbi Talk About the Stories of Genesis
Michael Smith and Rami Shapiro

Editor Aaron Herschel Shapiro describes storytelling as an "infinite game" because stories "must be retold—not just repeated, but reinvented, reimagined, and reexperienced" to remain vital in the world. Mike and Rami continue their conversations from the *Mount and Mountain* books, exploring the places where their traditions intersect and diverge, listening to each other as they respond to the stories of creation, of Adam and Eve, Cain and Abel, Noah, Jacob, and Joseph. 978-1-57312-772-1 202 pages/pb **$18.00**

Choosing Gratitude
Learning to Love the Life You Have
James A. Autry

Autry reminds us that gratitude is a choice, a spiritual—not social—process. He suggests that if we cultivate gratitude as a way of being, we may not change the world and its ills, but we can change our response to the world. If we fill our lives with moments of gratitude, we will indeed love the life we have. 978-1-57312-614-4 144 pages/pb **$15.00**

Choosing Gratitude 365 Days a Year
Your Daily Guide to Grateful Living
James A. Autry and Sally J. Pederson

Filled with quotes, poems, and the inspired voices of both Pederson and Autry, in a society consumed by fears of not having "enough"—money, possessions, security, and so on—this book suggests that if we cultivate gratitude as a way of being, we may not change the world and its ills, but we can change our response to the world. 978-1-57312-689-2 210 pages/pb **$18.00**

To order call **1-800-747-3016** or visit **www.helwys.com**

Contextualizing the Gospel
A Homiletic Commentary on 1 Corinthians
Brian L. Harbour

Harbour examines every part of Paul's letter, providing a rich resource for those who want to struggle with the difficult texts as well as the simple texts, who want to know how God's word—all of it—intersects with their lives today.   978-1-57312-589-5 240 pages/pb **$19.00**

Crossroads in Christian Growth
W. Loyd Allen

Authentic Christian life presents spiritual crises and we struggle to find a hero walking with God at a crossroads. With wisdom and sincerity, W. Loyd Allen presents Jesus as our example and these crises as stages in the journey of growth we each take toward maturity in Christ.   978-1-57312-753-0 164 pages/pb **$15.00**

A Divine Duet
Ministry and Motherhood
Alicia Davis Porterfield, ed.

Each essay in this inspiring collection is as different as the mother-minister who wrote it, from theologians to chaplains, inner-city ministers to rural-poverty ministers, youth pastors to preachers, mothers who have adopted, birthed, and done both.   978-1-57312-676-2 146 pages/pb **$16.00**

Ethics as if Jesus Mattered
Essays in Honor of Glen H. Stassen
Rick Axtell, Michelle Tooley, Michael L. Westmoreland-White, eds.

Ethics as if Jesus Mattered will introduce Stassen's work to a new generation, advance dialogue and debate in Christian ethics, and inspire more faithful discipleship just as it honors one whom the contributors consider a mentor.   978-1-57312-695-3 234 pages/pb **$18.00**

Ezekiel (Smyth & Helwys Annual Bible Study series)
God's Presence in Performance
William D. Shiell

Through a four-session Bible study for individuals and groups, Shiell interprets the book of Ezekiel as a four-act drama to be told to adult, children, and youth groups living out their faith in a strange, new place. The book encourages congregations to listen to God's call, accept where God has planted them, surrender the shame of their past, receive a new heart from God, and allow God to breathe new life into them.

Teaching Guide 978-1-57312-755-4 192 pages/pb **$14.00**
Study Guide 978-1-57312-756-1 126 pages/pb **$6.00**

To order call 1-800-747-3016 or visit www.helwys.com

Marriage Ministry: A Guidebook
Bo Prosser and Charles Qualls

This book is equally helpful for ministers, for nearly/newlywed couples, and for thousands of couples across our land looking for fresh air in their marriages. 1-57312-432-X 160 pages/pb **$16.00**

A Hungry Soul Desperate to Taste God's Grace
Honest Prayers for Life
Charles Qualls

Part of how we *see* God is determined by how we *listen* to God. There is so much noise and movement in the world that competes with images of God. This noise would drown out God's beckoning voice and distract us. Charles Qualls's newest book offers readers prayers for that journey toward the meaning and mystery of God. 978-1-57312-648-9 152 pages/pb **$14.00**

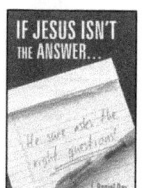
If Jesus Isn't the Answer . . . He Sure Asks the Right Questions!
J. Daniel Day

Taking eleven of Jesus' questions as its core, Day invites readers into their own conversation with Jesus. Equal parts testimony, theological instruction, pastoral counseling, and autobiography, the book is ultimately an invitation to honest Christian discipleship.

978-1-57312-797-4 148 pages/pb **$16.00**

I'm Trying to Lead . . . Is Anybody Following?
The Challenge of Congregational Leadership in the Postmodern World
Charles B. Bugg

Bugg provides us with a view of leadership that has theological integrity, honors the diversity of church members, and reinforces the brave hearts of church leaders who offer vision and take risks in the service of Christ and the church. 978-1-57312-731-8 136 pages/pb **$13.00**

James M. Dunn and Soul Freedom
Aaron Douglas Weaver

James Milton Dunn, over the last fifty years, has been the most aggressive Baptist proponent for religious liberty in the United States. Soul freedom—voluntary, uncoerced faith and an unfettered individual conscience before God—is the basis of his understanding of church-state separation and the historic Baptist basis of religious liberty. 978-1-57312-590-1 224 pages/pb **$18.00**

To order call **1-800-747-3016** or visit **www.helwys.com**

The Jesus Tribe
Following Christ in the Land of the Empire
Ronnie McBrayer

The Jesus Tribe fleshes out the implications, possibilities, contradictions, and complexities of what it means to live within the Jesus Tribe and in the shadow of the American Empire.

978-1-57312-592-5 208 pages/pb **$17.00**

Judaism
A Brief Guide to Faith and Practice
Sharon Pace

Sharon Pace's newest book is a sensitive and comprehensive introduction to Judaism. What is it like to be born into the Jewish community? How does belief in the One God and a universal morality shape the way in which Jews see the world? How does one find meaning in life and the courage to endure suffering? How does one mark joy and forge community ties?

978-1-57312-644-1 144 pages/pb **$16.00**

Living Call
An Old Church and a Young Minister Find Life Together
Tony Lankford

This light look at church and ministry highlights the dire need for fidelity to the vocation of church leadership. It also illustrates Lankford's conviction that the historic, local congregation has a beautiful, vibrant, and hopeful future.

978-1-57312-702-8 112 pages/pb **$12.00**

Looking Around for God
The Strangely Reverent Observations of an Unconventional Christian
James A. Autry

Looking Around for God, Autry's tenth book, is in many ways his most personal. In it he considers his unique life of faith and belief in God. Autry is a former Fortune 500 executive, author, poet, and consultant whose work has had a significant influence on leadership thinking.

978-157312-484-3 144 pages/pb **$16.00**

Meeting Jesus Today
For the Cautious, the Curious, and the Committed
Jeanie Miley

Meeting Jesus Today, ideal for both individual study and small groups, is intended to be used as a workbook. It is designed to move readers from studying the Scriptures and ideas within the chapters to recording their journey with the Living Christ.

978-1-57312-677-9 320 pages/pb **$19.00**

To order call **1-800-747-3016** or visit **www.helwys.com**

The Ministry Life
101 Tips for Ministers' Spouses
John and Anne Killinger

While no pastor does his or her work alone, roles for a spouse or partner are much more flexible and fluid in the twenty-first century than they once were. Spouses who want to support their minister-mates' vocation may wonder where to begin. The Killingers' suggestions are notable for their range of interests; whatever your talents may be, the Killingers have identified a way to put those gifts to work in tasks both large and small.

978-1-57312-769-1   252 pages/pb   **$19.00**

The Ministry Life
101 Tips for New Ministers
John Killinger

Sharing years of wisdom from more than fifty years in ministry and teaching, *The Ministry Life: 101 Tips for New Ministers* by John Killinger is filled with practical advice and wisdom for a minister's day-to-day tasks as well as advice on intellectual and spiritual habits to keep ministers of any age healthy and fulfilled.

978-1-57312-662-5   244 pages/pb   **$19.00**

Mount and Mountain
Vol. 1: A Reverend and a Rabbi Talk About the Ten Commandments
Rami Shapiro and Michael Smith

Mount and Mountain represents the first half of an interfaith dialogue—a dialogue that neither preaches nor placates but challenges its participants to work both singly and together in the task of reinterpreting sacred texts. Mike and Rami discuss the nature of divinity, the power of faith, the beauty of myth and story, the necessity of doubt, the achievements, failings, and future of religion, and, above all, the struggle to live ethically and in harmony with the way of God.

978-1-57312-612-0   144 pages/pb   **$15.00**

Mount and Mountain
Vol. 2: A Reverend and a Rabbi Talk About the Sermon on the Mount
Rami Shapiro and Michael Smith

This book, focused on the Sermon on the Mount, represents the second half of Mike and Rami's dialogue. In it, Mike and Rami explore the text of Jesus' sermon cooperatively, contributing perspectives drawn from their lives and religious traditions and seeking moments of illumination.

978-1-57312-654-0   254 pages/pb   **$19.00**

To order call 1-800-747-3016 or visit www.helwys.com

Of Mice and Ministers
Musings and Conversations About Life, Death, Grace, and Everything

Bert Montgomery

With stories about pains, joys, and everyday life, *Of Mice and Ministers* finds Jesus in some unlikely places and challenges us to do the same. From tattooed women ministers to saying the "N"-word to the brotherly kiss, Bert Montgomery takes seriously the lesson from Psalm 139—where can one go that God is not already there?

978-1-57312-733-2 154 pages/pb **$14.00**

Overcoming Adolescence
Growing Beyond Childhood into Maturity

Marion D. Aldridge

In *Overcoming Adolescence*, Marion D. Aldridge poses questions for adults of all ages to consider. His challenge to readers is one he has personally worked to confront: to grow up *all the way*—mentally, physically, academically, socially, emotionally, and spiritually. The key involves not only knowing how to work through the process but also how to recognize what may be contributing to our perpetual adolescence.

978-1-57312-577-2 156 pages/pb **$17.00**

Preacher Breath
Sermon & Essays

Kyndall Rae Rothaus

"The task of preaching is such an oddly wonderful, strangely beautiful experience. . . . Kyndall Rothaus's *Preacher Breath* is a worthy guide, leading the reader room by room with wisdom, depth, and a spiritual maturity far beyond her years, so that the preaching house becomes a holy, joyful home. . . . This book is soul kindle for a preacher's heart."

—Danielle Shroyer
Pastor and Author of *The Boundary-Breaking God*

978-1-57312-734-9 208 pages/pb **$16.00**

Quiet Faith
An Introvert's Guide to Spiritual Survival

Judson Edwards

In eight finely crafted chapters, Edwards looks at key issues like evangelism, interpreting the Bible, dealing with doubt, and surviving the church from the perspective of a confirmed, but sometimes reluctant, introvert. In the process, he offers some provocative insights that introverts will find helpful and reassuring.

978-1-57312-681-6 144 pages/pb **$15.00**

To order call **1-800-747-3016** or visit **www.helwys.com**

Reading Deuteronomy
(Reading the Old Testament series)
A Literary and Theological Commentary
Stephen L. Cook

A lost treasure for large segments of the modern world, the book of Deuteronomy powerfully repays contemporary readers' attention. God's presence and Word in Deuteronomy stir deep longing for God and move readers to a place of intimacy with divine otherness, holism, and will for person-centered community. The consistently theological interpretation reveals the centrality of Deuteronomy for faith and counters critical accusations about violence, intolerance, and polytheism in the book. 978-1-57312-757-8 286 pages/pb **$22.00**

Reading Hosea–Micah
(Reading the Old Testament series)
A Literary and Theological Commentary
Terence E. Fretheim

Terence E. Fretheim explores themes of indictment, judgment, and salvation in Hosea–Micah. The indictment against the people of God especially involves issues of idolatry, as well as abuse of the poor and needy. The effects of such behaviors are often horrendous in their severity. While God is often the subject of such judgments, the consequences, like fruit, grow out of the deed itself. 978-1-57312-687-8 224 pages/pb **$22.00**

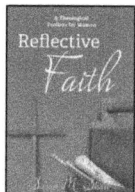

Reflective Faith
A Theological Toolbox for Women
Tony W. Cartledge

In *Reflective Faith*, Susan Shaw offers a set of tools to explore difficult issues of biblical interpretation, theology, church history, and ethics—especially as they relate to women. Reflective faith invites intellectual struggle and embraces the unknown; it is a way of discipleship, a way to love God with your mind, as well as your heart, your soul, and your strength.
978-1-57312-719-6 292 pages/pb **$24.00**
Workbook 978-1-57312-754-7 164 pages/pb **$12.00**

Sessions with Psalms (Session Bible Studies series)
Prayers for All Seasons
Eric and Alicia D. Porterfield

Sessions with Psalms is a ten-session study unit designed to explore what it looks like for the words of the psalms to become the words of our prayers. Each session is followed by a thought-provoking page of questions that allow for a deeper experience of the scriptural passages. These resource pages can be used by seminar leaders during preparation and group discussion, as well as in individual Bible study. 978-1-57312-768-4 136 pages/pb **$14.00**

To order call 1-800-747-3016 or visit www.helwys.com

Sessions with Revelation (Session Bible Studies series)
The Final Days of Evil
David Sapp

David Sapp's careful guide through Revelation demonstrates that it is a letter of hope for believers; it is less about the last days of history than it is about the last days of evil. Without eliminating its mystery, Sapp unlocks Revelation's central truths so that its relevance becomes clear. 978-1-57312-706-6 166 pages/pb **$14.00**

Spacious
Exploring Faith and Place
Holly Sprink

Exploring where we are and why that matters to God is an ongoing process. If we are present and attentive, God creatively and continuously widens our view of the world. 978-1-57312-649-6 156 pages/pb **$16.00**

The Teaching Church
Congregation as Mentor
Christopher M. Hamlin / Sarah Jackson Shelton

Collected in *The Teaching Church: Congregation as Mentor* are the stories of the pastors who shared how congregations have shaped, nurtured, and, sometimes, broken their resolve to be faithful servants of God. 978-1-57312-682-3 112 pages/pb **$13.00**

Time for Supper
Invitations to Christ's Table
Brett Younger

Some scholars suggest that every meal in literature is a communion scene. Could every meal in the Bible be a communion text? Could every passage be an invitation to God's grace? At the Lord's Table we experience sorrow, hope, friendship, and forgiveness. These meditations on the Lord's Supper help us listen to the myriad of ways God invites us to gratefully, reverently, and joyfully share the cup of Christ. 978-1-57312-720-2 246 pages/pb **$18.00**

To order call 1-800-747-3016 or visit www.helwys.com

A Time to Laugh
Humor in the Bible

Mark E. Biddle

An extension of his well-loved seminary course on humor in the Bible, *A Time to Laugh* draws on Mark E. Biddle's command of Hebrew language and cultural subtleties to explore the ways humor was intentionally incorporated into Scripture. With characteristic liveliness, Biddle guides the reader through the stories of six biblical characters who did rather unexpected things.

978-1-57312-683-0 164 pages/pb **$14.00**

The World Is Waiting for You
Celebrating the 50th Ordination Anniversary of Addie Davis

Pamela R. Durso & LeAnn Gunter Johns, eds.

Hope for the church and the world is alive and well in the words of these gifted women. Keen insight, delightful observations, profound courage, and a gift for communicating the good news are woven throughout these sermons. The Spirit so evident in Addie's calling clearly continues in her legacy.

978-1-57312-732-5 224 pages/pb **$18.00**

William J. Reynolds
Church Musician

David W. Music

William J. Reynolds is renowned among Baptist musicians, music ministers, song leaders, and hymnody students. In eminently readable style, David W. Music's comprehensive biography describes Reynolds's family and educational background, his career as a minister of music, denominational leader, and seminary professor.

978-1-57312-690-8 358 pages/pb **$23.00**

With Us in the Wilderness
Finding God's Story in Our Lives

Laura A. Barclay

What stories compose your spiritual biography? In *With Us in the Wilderness*, Laura Barclay shares her own stories of the intersection of the divine and the everyday, guiding readers toward identifying and embracing God's presence in their own narratives.

978-1-57312-721-9 120 pages/pb **$13.00**

To order call 1-800-747-3016 or visit www.helwys.com

Clarence Jordan's
Cotton Patch Gospel

The Complete Collection

Hardback • 448 pages
Retail 50.00 • Your Price 25.00

Paperback • 448 pages
Retail 40.00 • Your Price 20.00

The Cotton Patch Gospel, by Koinonia Farm founder Clarence Jordan, recasts the stories of Jesus and the letters of the New Testament into the language and culture of the mid-twentieth-century South. Born out of the civil rights struggle, these now-classic translations of much of the New Testament bring the far-away places of Scripture closer to home: Gainesville, Selma, Birmingham, Atlanta, Washington D.C.

More than a translation, *The Cotton Patch Gospel* continues to make clear the startling relevance of Scripture for today. Now for the first time collected in a single, hardcover volume, this edition comes complete with a new Introduction by President Jimmy Carter, a Foreword by Will D. Campbell, and an Afterword by Tony Campolo. Smyth & Helwys Publishing is proud to help reintroduce these seminal works of Clarence Jordan to a new generation of believers, in an edition that can be passed down to generations still to come.

 To order call **1-800-747-3016**
or visit **www.helwys.com**

www.ingramcontent.com/pod-product-compliance
Lightning Source LLC
Chambersburg PA
CBHW062048080426
42734CB00012B/2582